Talking Leaves

Narratives of Otherness

Critical Education and Ethics

Editors

Barry Kanpol, Indiana University—Purdue University Fort Wayne
Fred Yeo, Southeast Missouri State University

Talking Leaves

Narratives of Otherness

Suzanne SooHoo
Chapman University

HAMPTON PRESS, INC.
CRESSKILL, NEW JERSEY

Printed in the United States of America

Library of Congress Cataloging-in-Publication Data

SooHoo, Suzanne.
    Talking leaves : narratives of otherness / Suzanne SooHoo.
      p. cm.
    Includes bibliographic references and index.
    ISBN 1-57273-646-1 (cloth) -- ISBN 1-57273-647-X (pbk.)
      1. Education--biographical methods. 2. Educational Sociology--United States. 3. Multicultural education--United States. 4. Critical pedagogy--United States. 5. Marginality, Social--United States. I. Title.

LB1029.B55S665 2006
370.11'5--dc22

                          2005058902

Hampton Press, Inc.
23 Broadway
Cresskill, NJ 07626

May these leaves fall upon your pathway
and guide you towards liberation.

Contents

Foreword

Christine Sleeter
California State University Monterey Bay

Often I am asked what prompted me to commit myself to social justice work, why I care. Although academic discourse helps to analyze and communicate many things, it is not the discourse I turn to when asked these kinds of questions. Instead, I tell stories. Through stories, I can bring readers or listeners into the world of emotion and imagery that gets lost in theory and data. I can tell stories about pain I experienced as a child when well-meaning adults and not-so-well-meaning peers felt sorry for me for growing up in a single-parent household after my father died. Or, pain I experienced during adolescence when I realized that I was born smart, which was entirely the wrong characteristic for a girl. Through stories, I can tell how it felt to be an outsider in a Japanese community, and later in an African-American community. I can also tell stories of delight when my Japanese sister and I discovered shared interests and insights, despite a language and cultural barrier; and stories of warmth laced with pain after cross-cultural groups of educators had struggled through conflicts. Someone else might put my stories into psychological theory, postmodern theory, or sociolinguistic theory. As an academician, I often put other people's stories into theory.

But I cannot tell my life without story.

Suzanne SooHoo recognizes the power of story to mine and to convey personal experience, emotion, and identity. As an author, she weaves stories of her own life into her analysis of the struggles of teacher education students as they grapple with difference and oppression. As a teacher, she uses potential of story to create bridges of insight, communication, reciprocity, and solidarity. As an activist, she brings the reader as well as her students along the path of her own transformative work. *Talking Leaves* not only tells stories, it also conveys truth and moves action. And it offers windows into storytelling as a way of learning across differences in teacher education.

ix

It provides a resource to help students look at themselves, and to help teacher educators along the dangerous and difficult work of getting students to examine oppression in order to challenge it.

Today, educators are being told to decide how to teach on the basis of "scientifically based research." Without dismissing value of empirical research, we simply cannot reduce teaching, or life, to it. Narrative as an art form gets at truth in a different way from empiricism. In her book *Philosophy in a New Key*, Langer (1976) distinguished between discursive and non-discursive ways of knowing. Discursive knowledge uses the verbal symbolism of language to abstract ideas from concrete experience and construct propositions that are logical, linear, intellectual, and decontextualized. Nondiscursive knowledge, which resides in the arts, makes meaning of "the flux of sensations" that we experience daily (p. 93). Nondiscursive symbols, such as colors, rhythms, and poetry, encode experience, meaning, and emotion in ways that discursive language cannot. Ultimately, art has the power to move people and to communicate some forms of truth that cannot be rendered discursively. As Casey (1995) said in a discussion of narrative research, in an increasingly alienating world, "story telling is the way to put shards of experience together, to (re)construct identity, community, and tradition" (p. 216). *Talking Leaves* offers the art of storytelling as a way of teaching, engaging, knowing.

Schools historically have strongly privileged discursive forms of knowledge and ways of knowing. Students who come from communities with rich narrative traditions often find traditional forms of school knowledge to be alienating. And teacher educators who try to teach social justice through traditional discursive ways of knowing find the experience frustrating. I remember, for example, in my early days as a multicultural teacher educator, giving a lecture about how schools historically were organized along race and class lines, in order to build a conceptual framework for analyzing dynamics of oppression today. The lecture was probably sound academically, as was the analysis I would be doing for students. But I remember painfully the blank stares of my students, the insipid notes they took, and the complete lack of engagement they displayed. They knew the ritual well: The professor delivers knowledge, and the students write it down, give it back on an exam, then go back to their actual lives. As I looked at them, I realized that putting them through this ritual had little, if anything, to do with transforming schools. I finished the lecture, then went home to rethink what I was doing. Ironically, as I later found out, many of the students in the class had deep and painful experiences with oppression in their lives. To them, a lecture about oppression that did not open spaces for them to talk, trivialized their struggles.

Talking Leaves honors the struggles of a wide range of students, and offers space for students engage with social justice from the very diverse vantage points of their lives. *Talking Leaves* brings storytelling into the teacher education classroom, and illustrates how it serves as a tool for students to learn about themselves, hear others, and act based on having heard at a deeper level. Artists emerge in the pages that follow. Students who might otherwise sit passively become gifted poets and wordsmiths. In the students' stories, we hear pain and laughter, vision and hope. We also see a mode of expression that released the creativity that many of our students bring.

In one of my classes recently, teachers struggled with what to include in a multicultural curriculum. Having analyzed textbooks, they could see whose voices are generally absent. Through readings and discussion, stories emerged in the spaces textbooks leave silence. A white teacher confessed that some of the stories were painful and hard to digest. A Filipino teacher countered that students of color find it painful when their stories and realities are excluded from the curriculum. Another white teacher was becoming more confused about what to teach because the possibilities seem so broad. How do you include literally everyone in the curriculum? What is appropriate for fifth graders, and how do you handle feelings of guilt? I replied, "Let's leave the questions open for a while, as we talk and listen. There is no one answer, but there are many ways of thinking about what to do."

Suzanne SooHoo invites us to sit with the questions as we listen. When you finish this splendid volume, you may find yourself a bit more connected to the complexity of humanity, and more inspired with the possibilities for action.

Introduction

This book represents a 6-year collection of student narratives on otherness. More than 500 narratives were collected from a preservice course in Chapman University's teacher preparation program, "Voice, Diversity, Equity and Social Justice." The composition of students over this period of time was approximately 80% Euro-American female, 15% Latina, 5% Asian/Black/Middle Eastern. The research question that prompted this self-study and the collection of these narrative data was, "What themes will students write about, when given the prompt, 'Describe a time in your life in which you were *othered*.'" *Other* was defined as socially marginalized or alienated.

The narratives selected for this book represent (a) the common themes produced by students each semester, (b) a range of themes that were written within the 6-year study, and (c) those works of which consent was given to publish. Work that did not meet these criteria was left out.

The purpose of the study was to determine from adult accounts, what forms of otherness were experienced by school-age children and young adults in schools. Upon review of the collection, using the constant comparison method, otherness narratives fell into categories named colorism, gender, physical attributes, language, immigration, religion, intellectual differences, and family.

The narratives were shared orally and analyzed by class participants. In these debriefings, in what Freire (1995) called naming and codifying, students identified common threads and differences. Furthermore, the discussions critically interrogated and systematically analyzed the conditions in which the dominant culture has excluded others. Students also deconstructed those conditions that have disabled them to speak about these experiences heretofore.

Later in the course, these discussions were revisited and served as the impetus for social justice projects. These projects involved collaborative, community-based inquiry at school sites on topics like bullying, homelessness, linguistic differences, and so on. The projects culminated in multicultural lessons that equipped aspiring teachers with knowledge and skills to address conditions of prejudice, social alienation, and inequities. The purpose of this book was to illuminate the curriculum of otherness experienced by young people in our schools and to offer conceptual and instructional strategies to teachers to address othering and otherness.

From Otherness, students discover a social consciousness and moral responsibility to confront dominance as they take their places as social justice educators. And finally, this book is a composite of how a teacher learns with her students about each other and ourselves within the storytelling circle. The first time I taught the class "Voice, Diversity, Equity and Social Justice," I asked myself, "What could I bring to my students that would make an unique contribution to the field of critical multiculturalism? What particular perspective or experiences might I offer? In what ways can the multiple facets of my cultural identity be a window for my students? And in our commitment to co-explore 'Otherness', what will I find out about myself as I learn about them?"

> To engage with our students as persons is to affirm our own incompleteness, our consciousness of spaces still to be explored, desires till to be tapped, possibilities still to be opened and pursued. (Walsh, 1989 p. 139)

The author's reflection after each section of the book was to seduce the reader to do the same; to bring his or her own life into introspective inquiry and from that, letting one's moral conscience guide him or her. I am constantly redefined as the student narratives influence me. These stories are disturbing soundbites, and at the very least, should prompt a personal inventory which may unlock our own identity and positionality. Confident of its capacity to transform one's understanding about social identity and marginalization, *Talking Leaves* invites readers to identify instances when they were treated as outsiders. It invites readers to share these stories in read aloud fashion to their students, friends or family members; to interpret the stories against their own lived experiences and respond politically and socially to social forces that perpetuate domination and marginalization. The book is one way of "getting the conversation going" about social justice among friends and family, thereby not leaving to chance, a social agenda that requires thoughtful action. "Getting along should not be left to chance, but developed deliberately and systematically" (Gay, 1995, p. 30).

Acknowledgments

To my students, I offer dragon boats filled with tea, silk, and jade to thank them for the opportunity to learn about Otherness with them. As co-authors of this book, I am most grateful for their heartfelt participation and the communion of trust that represent the dragon's head of this pedagogy. A special thank you to research assistants Esmeralda Perez and Lori Bristol. Follow-up surveys and student letters revealed that the power of our mutual experience with Otherness continues to inform the graduates' work. This evidence represents the dragon's tail of this experiential research. And anyone who has ever believed in dragons, know the dragon's tail has enormous power to clear a path for social change.

Both People of Color such as Sonia Nieto, Paulo Freire, Peter Park, Antonia Darder, Dolores Gaunty-Porter and white allies; Pat Teft-Cousin, Barry Kanpol, Christine Sleeter, Paul Heckman, Neil Schmidt, Jeannie Oakes, Lee Bell, Mara Sapon Shevin, Kathryn Herr and Gary Anderson have profoundly influence my work as a critical multicultural educator. They have helped me affirm my differences and transcend some of my historically inscribed barriers. They have worked with me as the Eastern winds of reflection; fatalism and self-control sweep against my Western spirit of independence, change and self-expression. I use these points of reference to develop what W.E.B. Dubois (1903) called a "double consciousness;" an expansion of multiple cultural insights that facilitates meaning and deepen awareness.

White Allies are define by me as folks who are biologically white and colored in their ideology. By "colored" I mean they are socially conscious of all forms of inequality and oppression; racism, sexism, classism, ageism, linguicism, abelism, and so on. They are people who see themselves "mutually co-responsible" (Howard, 1999, p. 72) with those who have been othered to create social alternatives to social alienation and marginalization. They have unlearned their own privilege and challenge white supremacy. Because they have some social and economic leverage, they use this privilege to effect change in a wider social context in the name of equity, fairness, and justice. They join People of Color in the reweaving of social narratives as a way to resist the reproduction of systems of domination.

My mentors were white, mostly male, a few female. These mentors saw the long-range potential in working with someone like me so that I could make valuable contributions to both people of color and people of non-color.

They were both my advocates and my teachers of advocacy. I did not know how to be my own advocate. I am still learning. They have shown me how to profile my strengths to let my presence be known.

A metaphor of leaves blowing in the wind captures my relationship with allies. I am the wind, felt but not seen. However, you can see me when leaves grace my path. Together, leaves and the wind, we are visibly a force that changes the landscape.

Personal Narrative

The learning tree
the cathedral of learning,
the grantor of wisdom,
the mother of knowledge.

The tree's branches,
expanding and reaching dendrites

The leaves,
start as buds then flower

If the leaves could talk,
what would they say?

This book, *Talking Leaves* brings voice to the fallen leaves. It is a book about otherness, the leaves that are no longer nourished but those that have been dropped and left to destiny's wind. Run your finger through the leaves of this book and listen to their voices.

I include my personal narrative as the opening story as a way showing you the markers from which this book has received life. It also serves as the lens that has graced the poetry and prose. And finally, this narrative illuminates the subjectivities of this self-study research.

I am Who I am Because of a White Man

I write this narrative to illuminate the parts of my life that have been pushed
to darkness—my place within a white man's world.
My inner whiteness

I am who I am because of a white man.

Mother divorces my father and marries a white man.
We move from a house above the tunnel near Chinatown to a brick and
 wrought iron house in San Francisco's posh Marina district.
The other two Chinese families that live in this area are also part white.
This was the only way Chinese could live in this part of town.

My formative adolescent years are newly rooted in the white part of town,
 away from Chinatown's little dark alleys, smells of roast duck and
 garbage, clicking Cantonese tongues.

Mother has new friends—white friends.
She quickly forgets the language she spoke to her parents with.
She only speaks Cantonese when she swears at the cooks in her restaurants.
Although I am a Chinese-American, I don't speak Chinese.
I understand only a little.
The word behind the hyphen was emphasized in my household
Even as she prepares for her death, mother told her daughters
she didn't want to be buried on the side of the cemetery with all those
 "Chinamen."
Not until I am an adult do I mourn the lost of my Chinese identity.

I am who I am because of a white man.

When I grow up, I'll be just like him.
He was the best fifth-grade teacher in the world.
We stayed in almost every recess just to hear his stories.
He loved our round faces and almond shaped eyes.
At the school carnival, we cheered him on as he used chopsticks to pick up
 marbles from a bowl of soapy water.
Later he transferred to a school of mostly African-American children.
He said they needed him more.
I will never forget him.

I am who I am because of a white man.

I am 9 years old when I go to church for the very first time.
The walls are tall and cold.
Frozen marble faces stare at me.
A shiver runs down my arms.
An altar boy lights the candles with formal deliberateness.
I look at the flickering flames, which are the only signs of movement, and
 like me,

they struggle for meaning in this cold, holy place.
Everything is white: the pillars, the pews, the altar, the people,
and Jesus.

I am who I am because of a white man.

My first boyfriend is the basketball captain, class president, and member
　　of the honor society.
He teases me and always wants a kiss.
We are "going steady."
Everyone in school thinks we're a cute couple,
except his white parents.
They say we're too young to go steady.
We ignore them until his mother cries.
She says, "It's nothing personal but he should date 'white girls.'"
This is the first time my skin feels dirty, my eyes too small, my hair too
　　black.
I lighten my hair to brown, color my eyes to make them bigger, and cover
　　my arms,
but I am still not white enough.

I am who I am because of a white man.

I am a teacher.
My principal is a white male.
He chooses me over others because I am a UCLA graduate
I know how to write behavioral objectives.
He laughs when my bulletin boards are crooked.
He says it must be because of my slanted eyes.
He buys us instructional materials, takes us to visit schools and teaches us
　　"the ropes."
Two years later, the teachers and he have a power struggle.
He is angry and feels betrayed.
We are irreverent because we challenged him
I realize by joining my colleagues, I have challenged an elder.
My ancestral gods will be angry.

I am who I am because of a white male.

I am a school principal.
My supervisor is a white male.
He thinks I'm intelligent, a team player, a change agent.
He flirts with me reminding me I am female.

He tells me I may not order "pink princess" telephones for my office.
I've stuffed myself into a three-piece suit and also have to remind myself
   I am female.
The suit flattens my chest and binds my hips.
I walk and talk differently in these clothes.

The women principals work hard.
We organize meetings, create initiatives, and follow meticulously district
   directives.
The male administrators humor us, pat us on our backs, and tell us we're
   doing a good job,
then leave for their 2-hour lunch meetings.
We rebel but not pouring coffee or taking minutes at the next meeting.

I am who I am because of a white man.

Can he lead me through this world of academia?
Does he know how very scared I am;
   how I second guess each step of my worthiness?
He is my doctoral advisor.
I don't tell him I have come from a home with no books.
I am embarrassed about my "bookless" pedigree.
It's a secret locked in my heart.
My father was a simple man who shared his wisdom with me by telling me
   stories and writing me letters.

How does an Asian woman exist in this omnipotent world of scholarship?
My voice seems so small.
I read works by other women and people of color.
I come to realize my personal and acquired knowledge may have a place in
   this world.
I find out new things; things my advisor doesn't know.

How does an Asian woman teach a white man?

I am who I am because of a white man.

We drink lots of coffee.
With each cup, a new theory.
Feminism, patriarchy, critical theory, spirituality.
He pushes my thinking.
I get lost in his.
He makes me read and write, read and write, read and write.

Then we talk.
I'm starting to find my place in academe.
I am no longer "less than" white.
He is my mentor.

I am who I am because of a white man.

It's my pre-tenure year at the university.
Will I make it or am I merely ethnic window dressing?
I have traversed many boundaries to get here.
While I know it is me who I must not disappoint,
I also respect what the community thinks of me.
I want to be a part of shaping this institution's future
not be a temporary house guest.
My destiny primarily lies in the hands of white men.

I am who I am because of a white man and so are you.

❖ ❖ ❖

I am who I am because I am an Asian woman.

Grandmother took care of me the first 5 years of my life before she died.
I remember her gray streaked hair, her broad smile, and her frail walk;
the crippling results of early foot binding.
She would soak them in a large tin pan each night.
I would help towel-dry her broken feet.
What kind of life did she want for me?

I am who I am because I am an Asian woman.

Thick, hand knitted, itchy sweater-vests worn under dresses were the stan-
    dard school uniform imposed on young Chinese girls by their mothers.
Sometimes we would also wear tiger balm on our chests, wrists, and
    temples.
These two practices were aimed at keeping out the mysterious "bad wind"
    that Chinese aunties said would give us rheumatism in our old age.

If we had a cold, salted plums and lemon peel were stuffed into our pock-
    ets with instructions to suck but not eat them.
We did as we were told.
This was better than swallowing the one hundred, bitter, black bee bee tea;
a proven Chinese remedy.

When my wisdom teeth were removed, my father went to the herbalist
and brought home a bag of dirt, nested with twigs which he carefully
boiled in a large pot.
As the silt sank to the bottom, Dad ladled up the bubbling juices from the
top into a bowl.
I was made to drink this curious, culinary mud puddle in the interest of
fast healing and unquestioned obedience.

For 30 days after giving birth to each of my children, I was restricted from
leaving my house, my mother-in-law standing guard by the door to
ensure this rule was not violated.
Ginger chicken and stewed pigs feet were my daily diet.
Both of these dishes promised quick recovery, shrinking of the uterus, and
preventing "bad winds" from entering my vulnerable body.
The headaches I now suffer occasionally, 20 years later, are the result of my
stepping outside of my house and not obeying this old Chinese super-
stition.

I am who I am because I am an Asian woman.

My white wedding dress is adorned with nine, heavy, 24-carat gold neck-
laces.
I wear eight gold and jade bracelets; four on each arm.
Three gold rings have been added to my fingers.
My husband's pockets are stuffed with little red "lay see" envelopes filled
with money.
Our Chinese families have been very generous in wishing us a good future.
Twenty eight years later the money is long gone, but the jewelry sits in a
safety deposit box, awaiting the weddings of our children.

One month after our children are born, they too are laden with gold
jewelry.
At the customary red egg and ginger party, Chinese aunties and uncles
tuck lay see under the pillows of the bassinets.
In return we give each guest a red egg to ensure their future fertility.
Our children's baby-sized jewelry sits with our wedding jewelry in the
bank security box, awaiting the births of their children.
I will need to hock the jewelry to pay for the wedding of my son.
My daughter will be "bought" by her future husband's family and we will
not be responsible for paying for the wedding.
That is—if she marries a Chinese.
If she doesn't, who will pay?

The customs and celebrations which have survived three generations have
   lost their original meaning through their migration from China causing
   confusion and ad hoc Chinese practices.
The quasi-Chinese customs continue and escape scrutiny because of the
   "don't-ask-questions,-it-just-is" discourse between youngers and elders.

I am who I am because I am an Asian woman.

Contemporary Chinese wives must cook, or at least find a book to learn to
   cook, Chinese food.
Black bean paste, oyster sauce, and dried mushrooms are among the staples
   found in their pantries.
A wok, a butcher knife, and an electric rice cooker are among the kitchen
   appliances.
Chinese children become proficient with chopsticks by age three and can
   even catch slippery scallops served in porcelain bowls.
My Chinese mother-in-law shows me in her quiet, undemonstrative way
   how to put Chinese dishes together, never talking; a silent role model to
   me.
The contrasts between her and me are sharply defined;
I work hard at "becoming," she works quietly at "being."

I am who I am because I am an Asian woman.

"If you don't speak Chinese, you are not Chinese," jeered my Chinese
   cousins.
You are what you speak.
You become what you hear.
I am now only "white noise" to them; a translated woman.
I hide my face when someone asks me to speak.

The language I do share with my Chinese cousins is the language of
   silence.
Walk into any of our relatives' homes and you can hear the loud quiet.
While the vocabulary is speechless, the meaning is profound.
So much is said in our wordless world; our silent way of knowing.

I am who I am because I am an Asian woman.

My public life is western.
My private life is eastern.
Sometimes east clashes with west like mah jong tiles.
Sometimes east and west converge in a satisfying stir fry.
I am a cultural hermaphrodite, always crossing identity borders.

❖ ❖ ❖

I am who I am because I am the white man.

I am an able bodied, heterosexual, wife and mother,
An English speaking, middle class professor.
I am both privileged and "othered."
I am both the mentor and the mentee.
I am both the oppressor and the oppressed.
I am a part of "their" oppression and my own.

I am the model minority
"Making it" on the backs of others.
Top of the diversity totem
Pretending to be white
Colonizing "them;" othering "them."

I am who I am because I am both the white man and the Asian Woman

the strong, silent woman warrior
Who stretches her unbound feet and boldly crosses borders
Whose influence like burning incense perfumes the air
to stir social consciousness.

1

The Culture of Marginalization

Everyone is othered and everyone others Others.
—Frederickson (1997)

As I sit down to write this book, I find myself surrounded by old newspaper clippings about the two high school shootings that occurred here in southern California just 2 weeks apart—March 7 andMarch 23, 2001. The first shooter claimed the lives of 2 students and wounded 13 in what the community self-described as a "suburban paradise." Six miles down the road, in urban San Diego County, a shooter wounded 5 students before taking his own life. All of this just 2 years after Columbine.

Both newspaper reports and letters from readers to the editor, in ensuing days following the shootings, described schools as unsafe places with a social culture that marginalizes and alienates students. They described high school shooters, across the nation, as students who have been bullied, persecuted, and "incredibly disenfranchised" (Reza, 2001), who either took their own lives because they couldn't take it any longer or who took the lives of others as way of fighting back. One headline read, "Often Ridiculed, the Suspect Said, I'll Show You One Day" (*Los Angeles Times*, 3/7/01).

The student shooters were reported to be loners "who live on the margins of their culture, noses pressed up against the glass of the hated mainstream society" (Wolcott, 2001) who were characteristically powerless to respond to repeated patterns of physical or psychological intimidation aka bullying. Media accounts on the bullying phenomenon include a study by the U.S. Secret Service and Department of Education of 37 school shootings. It showed that two thirds of the perpetrators believed they had been bullied or persecuted (Ellingwood, 2001). Henry J. Kaiser Family Foundation, a philanthropic health organization released a study indicating that teasing and bullying has become a primary concern among teens. Nationwide survey of more than 1,200 parents and kids conducted in December 2000 and January 2001 showed that 56% of children, ages 8 to 11 years old and 60% of children, ages 12 to15 years old, believe bullying and teasing is a "big problem." A 1991 study conducted by the National Association of School Psychologists. found that one in seven children (male and female) is either a bully or victim of bullying. "Victims of bullying are likely to bear lasting scars in the form of poor self-esteem and depression." Seven percent of America's eighth graders stay home at least 1 day a month because they're afraid of other children, according to a 1992 study from the University of Michigan.

Despite these alarming statistics, it is clear in the writings of reporters and readers who wrote editorials that there is a pervasive social acceptance of ridicule and degradation as part of a normal high school experience. A reporter writes "teasing and taunting are normal and human nature" (Dawson, 3/7/01). A feature article, "High School Hasn't Changed" captured a popularly held understanding about the social order of high schools. "Social order is based on group identity and peer acceptance in a caste system of allies and cliques. People decide someone's a loser and. He is fair game for teasing and assault" (Reza, 2001). "Society has put up with schoolyard bullying for generations . . . because we figured it's just part of adolescent behavior" (Brownfield, 2001). "There's been bullying ever since there's been schools," maintains a criminal justice professor (Ellingwood, 2001).

These data suggest that bullying is an acceptable norm and that schoolyard harassment is part of a rite of passage to adulthood. Schools are places that prepare individuals for the world and submitting to the ritual of personal degradation is a necessary evil, like getting vaccinated from a virus, because it prepares one to face a harsher, crueler adult life. Schools socialize society's members for a social hierarchy of domination and a bully-tolerant social order. Schools are essentially the first places that young people come to understand the concept of social positioning. It is not the social studies unit on India that teach children the caste system of who counts and who doesn't, who's in and who's out, but rather it is their own and witnessed experiences of domination on school playgrounds, hallways, locker rooms, and bathrooms that teaches them of social hierarchy. They learned implicitly the notion of oppression and can name the oppressors and oppressed as bullies, losers, tormentors, and victims. Moreover, these categories are not restricted to fellow students but include adult school personnel who either explicitly assert social power wrongly as adult bullies or do nothing to prevent or change these phenomena and therefore are complicit with the hidden curriculum of domination.

A study conducted by the National Crime Prevention Council (NCPC) in 2002 showed students fear being bullied at school more than they fear terrorist attacks on their school. More than half of the 512 polled teens, ages 12 to 17 years old, said they could identify a student at school who they feel could cause harm to another student. James E. Copple, vice president of public policy for NCPC reported that bullies, victims, and bystanders suffer well-documented, long-lasting damage from bullying (NCPC, January 15, 2003),

Virtually every adult in my class on multiculturalism, when prompted, has a story of being othered or marginalized in school. Some bear lasting scars that, when touched, can provoke the same deep emotional response of pain and fear that inflicted the initial wound. They have suffered a lifetime of mental bondage. Some have buried their stories in the mental memory category of trivial and accepted the hegemony as part of life's passages. All have wounded psyches. All agreed they felt powerless in this period of their lives as they recall the vivid details of the assaults. They remember the visceral body tightness, the silent scream of terror, the salt of their tears. Year after year, new victims as storytellers take their places. The omnipresent of socially sanctioned domination in schools can be characterized as the eternal opiate of degradation; the ceaseless genocide of human dignity and spirit.

The question becomes, what can one do to change the culture of domination at schools? How can we reacculturate schools so that they can be psychologically and socially safe places to pursue learning and knowledge? What can we do to stop the unnecessary human suffering?

This book proposes that the courageous survivors of othering must reveal this concealed Holocaust,[1] aimed at disenfranchising people who are socially vulnerable or different by race, class, culture, language, sexual orientation, religion, ability, or body type. Through their stories, we can name the conditions and identify the social forces that maintain the tolerance for domination. A communal dialogue of "otherness" can stir a collective social consciousness to evoke alternative ways of existing. Silence is death.

---

[1]The use of this word was not meant to trivialize the horrific fissure of the Holocaust but was used to illustrate the parellel assault on the defenseless.

TALKING LEAVES

This book is a collection of pages, of "talking leaves" representing our (Chapman students and instructor) social and cultural identities and our stories of marginality; both as rooted in our pasts, as well as dynamically shifting in our current realities. Our narratives of "otherness" provide graphic details of schoolyard assaults. They have the power to uncover and confront hegemonic forces while birthing personal and public emancipatory life projects. As in feminist pedagogy, the book fuses the personal and the political. It brings together the visceral revulsion of oppression and the deconstruction of ideological dominance.

The narratives are both liberating and confessional testimonial. They are "counter stories" because they rupture the metanarrative that schools in society are the big social equalizing agent (Smith, 1999). Much of the nation's reform efforts have concentrated on student learning in classrooms or on schools' relationships with the community. What has been missed is attention to the space between the classroom and the home; that never, never land that one must walk through to get from home to school; the school playground, the lunch quads, the bathrooms and locker rooms where a curriculum of social hierarchy plays itself out. It is within that unsupervised space that a culture of othering is strongly embedded. Schoolyard social hierarchies are unforgiving as these stories of human suffering and marginalization will show. The stories in this book will look at the human phenomena that occurs in these margins to define future action. "Like a river and its tributaries, it is at the edges, where the water cuts the shoreline, that the river is defined" (SooHoo, 2003).

The book was a means for the victims to name the norms of marginalization and to talk back to the individuals and the social forces that assaulted them. Making "othering" visible and "speaking out" generated empowerment and healing. We forced otherness out of the shadows and silence by publishing the "stories of otherness" on behalf of those who have been "othered." These now legitimized voices are evidence that bullies cannot silence their victims; they will not have the last word. The moment we are able to identify the source of pain, we are free of its power over us (Harjo & Bird, 1997). Writing our stories allowed us to escape the tyranny of the bully.

The stories of Otherness had been silenced for far too long for fear of retaliation, retribution, or that no one would listen. Student authors who contributed to this book were no longer ashamed to tell the world. These stories were thorns in their flesh. By keeping these narratives invisible, there is no critique of the dominant narrative that marginalizes "other" forms of being. The bully is not a group of discernible individuals but rather the imperceptible social forces of dominance that permeate school cultures. Because it is hard to believe that social dominance played outside on the playground may have a far greater impact on shaping the social conscious of our children than the official curriculum inside the classroom, the stories of otherness were the lens from which we uncovered visible evidence of social dominance and marginalization. The collection monumentalizes everyday othering practices, which have gone virtually unnoticed, as some of us had become jaded to this cultural norm. "I feel like I'm a fish who just discovered water. I've been swimming so long in dominance that I wasn't aware of it" (Howard, 1999, p. 30).

These memories of injustice became a powerful text for our course, "Voice, Diversity, Equity and Social Justice" in Chapman University's teacher preparation program and helped prospective teachers to view schooling through the eyes of the marginalized and to know the effects of othering and dominance more intimately.

STORIES OF OTHERNESS GIVE LIFE TO CRITICAL CONSCIOUSNESS

The narratives in this book are the result of deep self-excavation and painfully honest inventories of marginalizing experiences. The process of writing these narratives can be described as the cumulative act of giving of one's self, of sacrificing one's vulnerability for the welfare of others, and of having trust that there was a larger understanding to be had. Although the topic of otherness itself was initially uncomfortable to many students, story as a form of expression and meaning-making was not. Story appealed to their "basic need for organizing their experiences into tales of important happenings" (Dyson & Genishi, 1994, p. 2).

The narratives were graphic and moving as well as intellectual and psychological. They reached deep inside our souls and clenched at our humanity as vivid schoolyard memories of harassment came sharply into focus. Too many of us identified with the victimization of the bully on the playgrounds, the stinging details of daily harassment, avoidance by those who counted, the haunting memories of powerlessness, or the fear of becoming the next victim. Several storytellers took deep breaths before they softly sobbed through their stories. It was all too clear that the scars of marginalization had not healed in these adult hearts. The stories elicited deep emotions, heart-felt empathy, and incredulous disbelief of the degree of casualty of the socially wounded in our schools.

The public sharing of the stories from aspiring teachers becomes the collective remembering of what they may have decided unconsciously or consciously to forget (Smith, 1999, p. 146). To share one's story publicly is to be released from the mental bondage of stereotypes of otherness (Kanpol, 1998). The stories demonstrate the power of victims to change their own teaching practices and set new directions as acts of resistance to social hier-archies, dominance, and othering within school arenas.

To evoke the necessary courage to write these stories, student authors were invited to use diverse writing genres; poetry, letters, narrative biogra-phies as tools for self-discovery. The act of writing provided some students with an opportunity to be reflective as they penetrated those cold places in their hearts to unearth repressed memories of otherness. For others, the act of writing felt detached, one step removed, desensitized from the original human experience. Writing could not capture the visceral punctuation of orally narrated stories, tight bodies, words caught in one's throat, eyes anx-ious and apprehensive. Writing is mediation. Thoughts and feelings must travel through pen, paper, or keyboard before touching another soul.

Oralists avoid the printed word because they feel strongly that a print-ed record cannot capture the success of a speech event (Doetkott, 2000). They recognized the familiar tyranny of print that chokes the subjectivities from the text. This discomfort is historically inscribed as written text has traditionally been the means to colonize others (Villenas, 1996). For those with colonized histories, writing is not a tool of liberation but a club that legitimates views that are hostile to certain groups of people (Villenas, 1996). "The master's tools will never dismantle the master's house" (Lorde, 1979, p. 98). Therefore, it is an act of resistance to opt for unmediated oral narra-tives in their purest authentic delivery, which often cannot be captured by even the author's own pen. Indigenous peoples consider these stories "work of the heart," which might change the world by the words and the telling (Hogan, 1997, p. 331).

And finally, there were those students who spoke a language of silence, where silence was not the inevitable consequence of oppression but a lan-guage of choice. Neither writing nor public sharing communicated their sto-ries; rather it was nonverbal reflection and physical action that told their sto-ries. Similar to the deaf communities in Martha's Vineyard in the 1800s (Groce, 1985), silence was not a disability but a preferred language that refused the reification of sound. In silence, their voices were present.

Speech in its oral and written forms is privileged by Western societies, whereas Zen Buddhist, East Indian, and some other indigenous peoples' tra-ditions embrace silence and other visual signals that override speech in com-municative behavior (Li, 2001). Some of us can see voice better than we can hear voice. Therefore, to silence silence is to disempower those who use the language of silence.

As listeners of the spoken, written, and silent stories, we hear different-ly what we've known before. The transformative power of story cannot be underestimated. We experienced a critical moment in every story; a place where each listener finds one's self within someone else's story. With mag-netic force, the listener becomes inextricably entwined with the spin master.

There was a moment of reciprocal knowing about Otherness; a conjoined Otherness, where the storyteller and the listener became one. Anzaldua (1988) captured the power and potential of story when she described, "The ability of story to transform the storyteller and the listener into something or someone else is shamanistic" (p. 30).

As a participant-observer, I witnessed students surrendering to the moment of the story and simultaneously vowing to protect future victims from suffering the same fate. This vow, upon hindsight, launched a lifelong commitment to students of otherness. "Whenever I hear a student call another student 'faggot,' I will think of you, my fellow friend and classmate, and remember how these stinging words cut deeply into your soul." Collectively, they promised, "never again, not in my classroom, not in my school, not on my watch."

In ensuing class discussions, these dark playground stories helped us recognize the tyranny of Otherness and fueled our desire to dismantle the conditions of othering. We posed problems and asked questions. Is being victimized by fellow school mates every students' fate? What conditions perpetuate playground harassment generation after generation? Are these recurring rituals with such cruel consequences evidence of social sadism in our schools? How do we account for our typical matter-of-fact response to dismiss school children's marginalization? Is there just a large genetic pool of schoolyard bullies who have been left unchecked? Or have we failed in our responsibility to prepare students and society to tolerate human differences? Who benefits from the social construction of exclusion? Who maintains the hegemony of social differentiation? How long will we tolerate this? What will we do to stop this?

In the debriefing of stories, we not only find out about others but we find out about ourselves. As members of the learning community we are being translated as we translate the stories. But it is not only our interpretations that are important; it is what we do with what we've heard that is significant. These narratives are human offerings to awaken and stir visceral responses toward social action. "Narratives represent our struggling to make sense of our own world while also attempting to transform what counts as important in the world" (Smith, 1999, p. 39). Herein lies the important work of reconstituting ourselves as we reorder the world.

OTHERNESS HEARD DIFFERENTLY

In this book, the word *othering* refers to the process of marginalizing individuals for a particular social characteristic that is embedded within the political infrastructure of inequality. *Otherness* is a dynamic social construction imposed on individuals or groups by those who have more power and authority. It is also a condition that is experienced by people who have been oppressed, stigmatized, alienated, subordinated, or victimized.

Student narratives revealed that White Students and Students of Color experienced Otherness differently. This became evident in the patterns of story topics within the respective submissions. Students of Color primarily wrote stories about color, race, culture, language, and immigration. Forms of white otherness included gender, sexual orientation, body image, religion, class, family, intellectual difference, and geographic mobility. There was some crossover by students of color in the areas of language and family. There was also a healthy collection of narratives about whites as minorities in different countries and contexts.

Students differentiated transitory otherness (i.e., "I found myself in a country where English was not spoken") from permanent inscriptions of otherness ("My mother says no matter what I do, I can never hide my black butt"). They also discussed how one is often an outsider in one place and simultaneously an insider in another place (i.e., "I never understood my insider status in the United States, until I became an outsider in Japan"). These data affirmed Lather's (1989) postulate that "Self-identity is constituted and reconstituted relationally, its boundaries repeatedly remapped and renegotiated" (p. 7).

They also uncovered the dynamic construction of Otherness as they probed the meta relationships of superiority and inferiority, of domination and subordination. Otherness is conferred by those who are in power on those who have little control. Students considered the arguments made by critical theorists that suggested that Otherness was determined by the dominant society's interpretation of the degree of social and economic threat posed by certain groups (Kanpol, 1994). By examining history, we found these interpretations changed over time. I used myself as an example once of the "yellow peril" as defined by U.S. immigration officers, now a "model minority" according to university campuses' officials. Tomorrow, I may be othered again because of fragile relationships between the United States and China. My fate lies in the hands of the white man's changing values, that activate my different statuses.

UNDERSTANDING OTHERNESS

How far I am from the center has everything to do with the way I see the world.
—Villenas (1998)

Like the multiple rings of water rippling from the center, the degree of disenfranchisement suffered by "Others" is dependent on how deviant they are from mainstream values. The dominant, ideological center is characterized as white, male, middle class, English-speaking, heterosexual, and Christian. Any departure from this core is off target and nonstandard.

One can have multiple designations of otherness (e.g., Asian, non-English-speaking, woman). However, one can also maintain both insider and outsider status simultaneously (e.g., Asian, non-English-speaking, woman, high social economic standing, heterosexual, and Christian). It is the sociopolitical context that defines which identity becomes significant.

The status designators are those in power: in media, economics, and public policy, who determine the degree of deviancy from the center and the extent of marginalization of "others." Media constructs and promotes images of race and gender that lead to exclusion, discrimination, hierarchy, and domination. There is a common adage that says that those who control the media, control the thinking of all men.

Student narratives revealed that there are some rules that apply across contexts with regard to the hierarchy of otherness experienced by a victim. Generally, the identity, which has suffered the greatest degree of discrimination, is the one with, which individuals will first identify. For example, African-American women identify first as being Black and second as being women (Ropers-Huilman, 1997). The hierarchy of oppression is influenced both by history and contemporary contextuality as construed by media. For instance, according to the *Los Angeles Times* (Moore, 1999), the representation of homosexuals was up in situational comedy in 1998–1999 but Asians, African Americans, and Native Americans were virtually invisible in the lineup for prime-time network shows that year.

Gaining entry to insider status most often is a multigenerational journey. The trip can be poxed by hurdles and insurmountable barriers. Lawrence-Lightfoot (1994) captures the realistic gains that People of Color can hope to make toward insider status:

> We strive to arrive at a secure place only to discover the quicksand of subtle exclusion. We work hard to amass the credentials and signs of status even as we recognize that our status will never assure a sense of belonging, or full membership in the white world. We feel ourselves moving toward the center of power even as we feel inextricably tied to the periphery; our outsider status becomes clearer as we work to claim an insider's place. (p. 10)

OTHERNESS INFORMS DEMOCRACY

Despite our country's rich immigration, we are collectively socialized to believe that a democracy builds consensus through the lens of an undifferentiated human nature. For the purpose of the common good, we have chosen to assimilate and surrender our histories (Dewey, 1980). Cultural self-negation is a necessary prerequisite to acquiring the good life in America. This fundamental universalism not only informed our recent English-only and anti-immigrant policies but is also the metanarrative that informs the hidden curriculum of homogeneity and sameness in schools.

Critical multiculturalists critique this hegemony as one that muffles any sound of human dissimilarity and promotes social inequalities.

> Central to the creation of a democracy is the understanding that all people have a fundamental right of equality. That is, all persons, regardless of race, culture, language, gender, class or religion, are stakeholders in a democracy. "Being different" does not diminish one's access to the full rights and privileges of living in a democracy. (Duarte, 1998, p. 4)

We acknowledge difference, the particular, the multiple, the heterogeneous. We must respect cultural dissimilarity and ensure that nondominant lifestyles are recognized equally, fairly, and justly. We must protect these lifestyle differences in the same way we have traditionally protected the right to dissent or protest (Mouffee, 1988) because this is, in part, our tradition as Americans.

The challenge for critical educators is to use a pedagogy informed by difference as a means toward a pluralistic democracy. This means inviting difference to the center of the curriculum as a way of knowing and emphasizing the transformative power of difference in the rethinking of social structures. These opportunities on center stage encourage those who have been othered to freely raise their voices and to creatively pose alternatives (Guiterrez, 1994, p. 44). Foucault (1977) proposed a similar process when he encouraged prisoners to speak for themselves in prison reform so that changes could be made based on their analysis of their experiences. These voices make us aware of the social forces in schools that award or withhold economic and social privilege reflect the social codes that distinguish between "the haves" and "have-nots" in society at large.

CRITICAL MULTICULTURALISM

Students did not expect to study themselves when they first entered this course. Their intention was to study "those" people; to unconsciously objectify "others." In preparation of their study of others, they had to first learn about themselves. "Learning begins with taking the self as the first object of knowledge" (Aronowitz, 1998, p. 12). It was necessary for students to bring their lives forward in order to locate themselves on a grid of social coordinates.

The accomplishment of critical consciousness consists in the first place in the learner's capacity to situate herself in her own historicity, for example, to grasp the class, race, and sexual aspects of education and social formation and to understand the complexity of the relations that have produced this situation. (Aronowitz, 1998, p. 14)

The narrative pedagogy promoted in this book responded to Giroux's (1993) call for

Critical educators need to provide the conditions for students to speak differently so that their narratives can be affirmed and engaged critically along with the consistencies and contradictions. . . . They must not only hear the voices of those students who have been traditionally silences, they must take seriously what all students say by engaging the implications of their discourse in broader historical and relational terms . . . students must be encouraged to cross ideological and political borders as a way of furthering the limits of their own understanding in a setting that is pedagogically safe and socially nurturing. (pp. 32–33)

It is within this context that the possibility arises for students to see their joint culpability in systems of domination as well as their common experiences of otherness. These border crossings created a dialogical space where we can rethink how the centers and the margins of power structures relate to our individual and collective lives (Kanpol & McLaren, 1995, p. 178) so that ultimately we can discover ways in which power can be "remapped, reterritorialized and decentered" (Giroux, 1993, p. 30).

THE "OTHER" AS SOCIAL JUSTICE EDUCATOR

I bring to this book my multiple social identities as a window to the multifaceted relationships between othering and otherness. My bicultural lens helped me see my students' "otherness" and alternately their positions of privilege. It is limited by what was "seeable" within the context of our classroom, our worldviews, and our experience together. It is therefore only a small screen viewing of the profundity of otherness and othering. "We are what we know." Our narratives represent what we know. We are however, also what we do not know. What we know about ourselves is always distorted by denials and incompleteness (Pinar, 1993).

I borrow from Gloria Ladson-Billings' (1994) genre of scholarship and story by presenting a combination of narrative research laced with my sociocultural interpretation. Like *Dreamkeepers*, this book is meant to be both reflective and empirical, coupling the personal with the academic; reflection and critique; a research base and the culturally founded. Using a bicultural lens to understand "the otherness" of my students, I offer my personal reflections (in *italics*) in chapter 3 to demonstrate the reflective dialogue (as viewed by an Asian woman) that takes place mentally as one listens to the stories. This engagement is a manifestation border crossing into the "borderlands"; a space where disparate cultures meet and find common ground (Anzaldua, 1988). It is here that the promise of the pluralistic, multicultural imaginary is born.

The self-interrogation of one's social cultural legacy requires courage and commitment; courage to conduct an honest personal excavation and commitment to address the findings, pimples, warts, and all. For many of us, this critical sense-making turned out to be a lifetime liberatory project, regularly revisited, fueled by a deep "need-to-know" intensity and a promise of a more humane society.

The following are two stepstones from my journey of self-interrogation.

Asian Woman

I write to erase the pain of otherness and to combat stereotypes. I wrestle with the various social constructions of Asian women as conceived by the dominant society (Chang Bloch, 1997) to free my voice of self-determination and locate myself somewhere between the "lost and found" spaces of culture identity. In so doing, I riddle myself with questions:

Am I the quiet, subservient, dutiful daughter who never speaks or makes waves? The one with a tofu worldview, bland and tasteless? Questioning an elder, for her, is a death sentence. Historically, she was the perfect mail order bride, who obediently served her husband's mother. Asian men, as husbands and fathers have enjoyed the benefits from these domesticated females.

Or am I the industrious, androgynous worker. Conceived in the Mao era, she is the hardworking, conscientious, and dispassionate worker. Her efficiency, loyalty, and unquestionable obedience make her a good foot soldier for any government position. In today's world, she is a good candidate as an objective, emotionally neutral, reliable accountant.

Business reinforces this image: "Businesses want docile, subservient workers who will not complain, file grievances, or organize unions. Many businesses purposely seek immigrant workers with limited English skills. Asians thought to be loyal, diligent and attentive to detail. They, like other minorities, consistently earn less than whites" (Lai, 1992).

Both the dutiful daughter and industrious worker speak the language of silence. It is the unspoken dialect, which communicates more poignantly than words. It is the language of subtle overtures and fortissimo messages, of imperceptible amplification but indisputable clarity.

This language, pregnant with meaning, is preferred over what elders describe as pompous, boisterous, clamorous "noise." Silence in this familial context is a language of choice. Out of respect for others, it is understood that one does not speak unless one can improve upon the silence.

Could I be Suzy Wong, the seductress, who uses her porcelain skin and silken hair to charm those around her? She is exotic, provocative, and mysterious. Both men and women are seduced by her alluring, feminine grace. Hollywood capitalized on this image, as evidenced by shows like, *Madame Butterfly, South Pacific*, and *Miss Saigon*.

Or am I the Dragon Lady, the most powerful and cunning of all. She rules her world with an iron fist in a silk glove. This bold, grand matriarch makes decisions for the entire village. Sharp-tongued and strategic, the Dragon Lady is most often a successful businesswoman.

Popularized by Maxine Hong Kingston, the "Woman Warrior" enters the contemporary scene. She is both a skillful swordswoman and a crusader for social justice who combats oppressive power structures in order to liberate the oppressed. With unbound feet and social consciousness, she carves a path for a new social order that gives voice to the common people.

I am and *have been* all of these women as daughter, wife, mother, teacher, school principal, and professor. Every facet of Asian womanhood is represented in my genetic tapestry. Much of what I have learned about being an Asian woman has come from my ancestors. Most of what I become as an Asian-American woman was dependent on white permission. (See my narrative). "Who I am colors the way I see the world . . ." (Matsuda, 1996, p.16).

(SooHoo, 2003, pp. 259-260)

Asian Woman Social Justice Educator

I am physically different
My face is conspicuous in the halls of academe.
I am "the Other"; misunderstood, omitted, trivialized, less-than.
I am the "model minority"; scholarly, obedient, deferring, industrious
I am a woman warrior dedicated to social and political inclusion.
I am an Asian woman social justice educator.

In an act of faith, I make the personal public as a way of demonstrating the deep engagement that can occur within one's mind as they mentally engage in the narratives. This act is a particularly courageous for me because of my socialized political passivity. I have been culturally socialized to hide my cultural ethnicity, to devalue and disconnect my ethnic heritage from my professional work. I had learned to bury rather than mine my cultural experiences. And I am aware that these cultural proclivities have blinded me from understanding the full complexities of social and cultural identity.

My ancestors had spent hundreds of years of socialization to ensure Chinese people were politically apathetic. The first woman immigrants to the United States were either prostitutes or picture brides with bound feet. Political activity among Chinese Americans has been a function of class, language, gender, and being American-born. One only has to canvass the national political scene to recognize the absence of Chinese players. We are still learning how to enter into the arena and what to do once we are there. The cultural legacy that cripples my political consciousness also culturally inscribes blindness to social injustice. Both Eastern and Western winds act as my cultural informants.

Taken separately, there is an ongoing East/West tension within me. Natural tendencies of submission fight urges to be assertive: obedience versus. independence, fatalism versus. change, self-control versus. self-expression (Chow, 1989). Traditional expectations of Chinese women are barriers as large as the Great Wall to my emerging sense of being and political activism. My Chinese mother-in-law constantly complains, "Why do you ask so many questions? Why do you bother yourself with these ideas?" (SooHoo, 2002).

2

The Transformative Power
of Story

The world is not held together by molecules but by stories.
—Author Unknown

"Multiculturalism is a lived experience" (Fu & Stremmel, 1999 p. vii), there-fore, a critical source of knowledge is the lived stories of diverse human beings in relationships "with" and "to" each other. Stories of Otherness are a way of knowing and of being known. They assist us in locating ourselves on the grid of social/cultural coordinates.

Stories in the form of personal narratives challenge the reification of textbooks as the primary source of knowledge. And rightfully so, for those designated as Other have suffered stereotypes and false histories at the hands of well-intentioned textbook publishers. Furthermore, by scanning who is absent from textbooks, one might almost suspect a conspiracy to keep Others and Otherness invisible.

This book portrays the multiple forms of "otherness" to include stories about color, gender, physical attributes, language, culture, intellectual differ-ences, religion, immigration, family, and sexual orientation. Otherness expe-rienced by some was a permanent condition, for others it was transitory. Each story revealed the dark side of schools and childhood; exposing psychological or physical assault and suffering from schoolyard victimization. Although these stories were emotionally trying to hear, they helped us see the tyranny of otherness that has terrorized young people for generations.

Personal narratives are valuable resources in multiculturalism because we hear stories "by" the person(s) who are members of specific social groups rather than reading stories "about" individuals by detached authors. There is no mediator that "speaks for" or "on the behalf of" an individual. The storyteller holds the position of expert of his or her own social and political location. "By avoiding the indignity of speaking for the oppressed we show respect for the integrity of those who are oppressed" (Walsh, 1991, p. 44). "We will have an authentic theology of liberation only when the oppressed themselves can freely raise their voice and express themselves directly and creatively in society" (Guiterrez, 1994, p. 44).

STORIES AS SELF–LIBERATING

> The longing to tell one's story and the process of telling is symbolically a gesture of longing to recover the past in such a way that one experiences both a sense of reunion and a sense of release.
> —hooks (1999, p. 84)

Stories untold are secrets. Stories-made-public free the storytellers from the mental burden of carrying secrets. Human beings make sense of their lives by knitting the past, present, and future together through story. Narrative organizes our experience and our memory of human happenings (Bruner, 1994).

Storytelling is both a way of knowing and an art form. Cognitive insights are derived from the conceptualization via reflection and self-study and from the often nonlinear presentation of a story. In this volume, students were invited to use oral history, poems, dreams, letters, or drawings to tell their stories. They were encouraged to give themselves permission to use any genre that liberated their storytelling voices. Several students used speech patterns and cultural forms indigenous to their communities (e.g., regional dialects, idioms, etc.). The opportunity to dismiss academic conventions and express one's authentic voice allowed many narrators to deliver a story that was representative of the creators' soul and spirit. What narrators write is bound in complex ways to their own positions or locations in society (Frederickson, 1996, pp. 12-15). Our stories reflect our sociocultural landscapes (Bakhtin, 1981).

The prompt for the story was, "Write about an experience you in which you were 'othered;' that is, a time in your life when you were marginalized by others". Otherness was characterized as a state of being as a result of exclusion or dehumanization. The assignment triggered an unexpected ava-lanche of stories and surfaced a plethora of buried emotions about otherness. "The act of making it present, bringing it into the open . . . was liberating" (hooks, 1999, p. 86).

Narrative is an important mode of thinking that helps us order our experiences and construct reality (Bruner, 1986). "Writing one's story can help one make sense of the information that assaults you every day" (Miller, 1999, p. 1). Story is a fundamental structure of human experience (Connelly & Clandinin, 1990) because "everybody is a story" (Remen, 1996, p. xxv). We are "storytelling organisms who, individually and socially, lead storied lives" (Connelly & Clandinin, 1990, p. 2)

Personal testimony is deep and committed reflective work. Many authors needed to first emerge from their self-negating assimilative practices to discover their own indigenous voices. They needed to reconnect them-selves with their previously denied repressed selves. By doing so, they also got in touch with their critique of social and political inequities. This con-sciousness is consistent with liberation theology, described by Welch (1985, p. 47):

> Liberation theology is based on dangerous memories; it recounts the history of human suffering. These accounts of specific histories of oppression are both descriptions and critiques. They serve as critiques of existing institutions and social structures. (p. 37) . . . The primary source for liberation theology is not the intellectual or scholarly theo-logical tradition, but the experience of those who have been excluded from the structures of power within society and within the church. (p. 33)

STORIES BUILD COMMUNITY

A cultural forum (Bruner, 1986) for dangerous memories can be found in critical multicultural or critical pedagogical classrooms. It is here that one can reveal rather than conceal his or her social/cultural differences. It is "a place where mute birds sing" (Kingsolver, 2000, p. xii). It is here where col-onized folks can decolonize their minds and actions (hooks, 1990) and recover absent voices. It is here that those on the margins are made central in the discussion of the politics of identity. Here we learn the history of oppressor/oppressed relationships. According to Hanson (1989) "the U.S. story has been dominated by 'losers and loners, exiles, women, blacks'— writers who for one reason or another have not been part of the ruling 'nar-rative' or epistemological/experiential framework of their society" (p. 2). Through studying our own otherness and positions of privilege, we better understand the students we teach and inversely, the better we come to know our students, the more we learn about ourselves.

The process of writing about otherness was like an offering to the multicultural gods; it was the cumulative act of giving of one's self, of sacrificing one's vulnerability for the welfare of others and of having a trust that there would be a larger understanding to be gotten. We used our stories to test what others felt and thought, and how we stood in contrast with others. Within a community, we found the collective strength to seek a critical understanding of our relationship to the broader society and a willingness to investigate together the transformative possibilities embedded in our voices and stories (Walsh, 1991).

TRANSFORMING POWER OF STORIES

> Voices from the heart, once heard, can change other hearts.
> —Cai and Sims Bishop (1994, p. 68)

There was a critical moment in each story where every listener hears themselves in the story. With magnetic force, the listener becomes inextricably entwined in the story. The listener figuratively embraces the spin master. That moment of reciprocal knowing about Otherness is the orgasmic DNA exchange of conjoined Otherness, when the storyteller and listener becomes one. For many, this powerful intersection causes the listener to not only surrender to the story but also to commit to the emotional, psychological, cultural, and social well-being of the teller of otherness. From this conjugal moment, empathy is born and its fraternal twin; possibility.

Storytelling forms community and group solidarity. It is the social glue that connects the vast web of humanity. An empathetic and caring community rescued each victim tortured by othering. Rescuers found that within their differences, there was similarity (Kanpol, 1994); the stories used different lyrics, but the music was the same. The stories of dehumanization had pierced our consciousness and bonded our souls. Personal testimony became unified with collective testimony. The universality of social dominance and exclusion became clear in a seemingly epiphanic moment: Although all forms of oppression are not the same, the predictability of exclusion is strikingly clear; we all have been othered and we have all othered others.

Within our classroom, we had created Vygotsky's (1978) zone of proximal development; a hospitable and accommodating space for learning (Moll, 1990). Through mutual trust and vulnerability, storytellers cast a spell that prepared us "to struggle with the strange and unfamiliar so that we can know again what is already known in new ways" (hooks, 1999, p. 152). "By listening to others' stories and how they tell them, we are able to understand our own experiences differently, in contrast, and offer alternative interpretations" (Fu, 1999, p. 21).

Anzaldua (1988) tells us that the assumption behind sharing personal narratives is that stories have the potential to transform the lives of both the listener and the teller. "The ability of story to transform the storyteller and the listener into something or someone else is shamanistic" (p. 30).

Lived stories (narratives) are the catalysts for dialogue, and conversations act as the catalysts for change (Fu, 1999, p. 5). Storytelling allows people to simultaneously live and relive their stories as well as grow toward a new imaginary (Elbow, 1986). We found ourselves thinking through social agendas that commit to the protection of the young, weak, and the vulnerable. This is what Kanpol (2000) described as part of the process of common democratic struggle, when fusion with "the other" occurs in an "intercommunicative dialogue of emancipatory struggle and possibility" (p. 11).

Narratives can be used metaphorically as tools in the struggle against marginalization (Swindler Boutte, 2002). They served as the foundation for critical consciousness in that they counteracted stereotypes, provided insight into marginalization and prejudice, and uncovered social structures that perpetuate "othering." The examination of everyday marginality, laced with suffering and rage, elicited a counterhegemonic awareness and mobilized the necessity for emancipation and radical change. Within critique, there was hope for some degree of liberation from the devaluation of human life. We had faith that the world would co-evolve as we critically examined and interacted with it. Informed by the yin and yang of the universe, we are confident that from chaos and disorder comes new creative order (Wheatley, 1999).

STORY IN TEACHER EDUCATION

My continuing passion is to part a curtain,
That invisible shadow that falls between people,
The veil of indifference to each other's presence,
Each other's wonder,
Each other's human plight.
—Eudora Welt (cited in Wheatley, 1999)

It is with hope that teacher education embraces narrative pedagogy as a way to raise consciousness and political awareness. Fundamental to multiculturalism and democracy is the respect for other people's experiences and their interpretations of those experiences (Kimball & Garrison, 1999). We have faith that the conscious recovery of absent voices ensures the necessary pluralism on which democratic communities are built. Greene (1988) reminds us that democracy is a public space of dialogue and possibility in which there is a continuing effort to attend to many voices, many languages, often ones submerged in cultures of silence.

Kanpol (2000) wrote that "teacher education lacks using personal testimony as a form of pedagogical reflection and interrogation" (p. 17). Instead, it relies heavily on methodological practices that distance the prospective teacher from the self. He called for narrative pedagogy in the facilitation of liberatory theories of self and identity as a way for teachers to disrupt hegemony and listen to the "voices, histories and shifting identities of the students they teach" (p. 4).

The experience of storytelling is not only compelling because of its promising transformative potential but also because of the aesthetics in the experience alone. The actual commitment of pen to paper, capturing feelings and ideas, watching them unfold like a dance, sequencing of paragraphs as movement, pulsating with emotional rhythm—all are dimensions of aesthetics. Stories can stand alone as fully pleasurable experience. They need not serve a moral purpose. They can be an experience and not a message. Keeley (1978) argued that satisfaction in participation is the only common denominator that reflects diverse interests of participants. The experience storytelling held a noncognitive quality; an intrinsic meaning that contributed to what Dewey (1934) called a consummatory aesthetic experience. Stories feed our senses and our spirits.

Herein lies the power of the pedagogy of storytelling as its aesthetic form interrupts traditional didactic teaching practices. Just as the act of writing transforms the writer and stories transform the listeners, so does storytelling transform the teaching–learning experience. Eisner (2002) maintained that education has much to learn from the arts. One can be more "qualitatively intelligent" (p. 9) by integrating feeling and thinking in ways that make them inseparable, as artists have done. By cultivating one's sensibilities, students learn "to act and to judge in the absence of rule, to rely on feel . . ." (p. 9), thus expanding our ways of knowing. Moreover, stories place a greater emphasis on exploration and discovery and less on prediction and control. They mark a designated place in the curriculum for uncertainty; a conceptual space that Eisner argued is a critical requirement in all learning environments.

Although the course had a significant impact on some of the participants, it was different for each one. Students who had come from cultural traditions strong in oral history bonded quickly to storytelling pedagogy because of its familiar calling. Those new to the experience behaved in various ways, everything from enthusiastic participation because they were totally enamored by the experience to entering the storytelling circle cautiously, one toe at a time in uncharted waters. Stories forged memorable bonds across individuals, particularly with those hungry to express their sense of isolation in the world, reliving each other's experiences vicariously, respecting the transformative possibilities of the stories.

The call for stories in education and teacher education, and the arguments for their value are not new. However, the assault on narrative seems especially intense at the beginning of the 21st century. From state-mandated accountability measures to the pervasive framing of education within a narrow economic perspective, we find a constriction of vision in seeing the world of teaching and learning. Dismissed is significance of construction and reconstruction of personal and social stories as part of the circle of human literacy.

This book argues for story as central in classrooms of transformative teachers. Stories of Otherness reflect the pluralism in our selves and our lives. They are the language, which can bring dissimilar people together on common ground (Shapiro & Purpel, 1993). Their interpretations have the power to direct and change our lives. Personal narratives are the language of difference and are essential in classrooms dedicated to ongoing conversations of social justice.

> We want them [our classrooms] to pulsate with a plurality of conceptions of what it is to be human. . . . We want them to be full of the sounds of articulate young people, with ongoing dialogues involving as many as possible. . . . And we want them to care for one another . . . and to stir wide-awakeness; a renewed consciousness of possibility. (Greene, 1994, p. 25)

3

Who is an Other?

If you are an Other, who am I?
If I am an Other, who are you?
Are you my other?

Everyone has been "othered" some time in one's life. There are many different forms of otherness. Some of us have been othered temporarily. Some hide their otherness, others cannot. For some, Otherness was the result of institutional discrimination; for others, Otherness was the result of an esoteric situation. In every instance, the person who had been "othered" has virtually no control over his or her condition or status of which he or she is being "othered." Otherness is a social construction imposed by those who have power over "others." It means that others are "less than" or inferior.

The word *other* is used both as a noun and a verb in this book to describe the state of *otherness*—the position of marginalization from mainstream society and the action of marginalizing others, of pushing people to the fringes. Not only has everyone been "othered," but everyone has "othered" someone else. We all have prejudices. Whether consciously or unconsciously, we have excluded or discriminated a person or group of people who were different from us, for something over which they have virtually no control. These differences have caused conflict and inflicted death in the most extreme cases and death of a psychological, social, or political nature in other cases.

As an Other, one is routinely denied social and economic rights and privileges of a democratic society because of differences in gender, skin color, language, religion, social class, ableness, or sexual orientation. These differences and subsequent exclusion as a result of these differences are invisible to mainstream society that espouses sameness—we are all human beings.

The *Other* is defined in both critical and multicultural literature as involuntary minorities who are oppressed, alienated, and subordinated by the structures of society. They are those marginalized peoples who are underprivileged and minorities. These groups do not have static membership, rather Otherness is a dynamic construct that is always changing, depending on the dominant society's interpretation of the degree of social and economic threat posed by the groups (Kanpol, 1994). Admission into the order of otherness is contigent on social, political, or economical victimization.

Can one understand otherness without having personally known domination and exclusion? If one has never been marginalized, can one know otherness? Do we have to have been victimized before taking an anti-othering stance in schools and society? How might someone else's story pierce our consciousness and help us become more vigilant about countering structures of social hierarchy and domination?

PEOPLE OF COLOR

For most students of color, this assignment was a rare opportunity to define themselves in ways they had never before experienced. It was a chance to use their own social rubric and language to describe what counts and what doesn't. "For students who often find it impossible to define their identities through the cultural and political codes that characterize the dominant culture" (Giroux, 1993, p. 32), the assignment would be liberating and challenging because they have typically come from classrooms informed by dominant ideology that have historically obscured the development of minorities. Some students of color found it hard to know who they were socially and politically because they had learned that doing well in school meant "acting white" (Ladson-Billings, 1994, p. 11). Colonization had alienated them from the spirit of their own culture so that their indigenous voices were buried within their white voice (Darder, 1991). The intent of the narratives was not only to bring awareness to the hidden curriculum of othering but also to make space for the Others to tell their stories so that we all may rethink our positions in society.

Conversely, there were also students of color who were well versed and politically conscious of their socioeconomic and political positions within the dominant power structure. Their writings revealed a learned coping response to oppression; a double consciousness (DuBois, 1989); of looking at themselves through the eyes of both the Other and the white man. They were familiar with the contested construction of both the oppressed and the oppressor (Freire, 1995). It was evident in their narratives that they were proficient in mediating both mainstream culture and ethnic culture (Valentine, 1971).

PEOPLE OF NON-COLOR

Most white students were initially baffled by the writing prompt. They did not see themselves as victims of othering. "We're just plain white bread," they explained. "We have nothing to write about." The assignment perplexed them and caused them to ask, "What are the forms of Otherness in a predominantly white community?"

Some white students had difficulty accepting themselves as white and wanted to disassociate from white people entirely. They felt both guilt and helpless about their ancestry. They looked to class discussions as opportunities to reconstruct their social and political locations. It was here that my greatest learning took place. White Otherness made more visible revealed the universality of oppression and domination.

NARRATIVES

The themes and narratives included in this volume were determined by the students' willingness to publish their work. Students were eager to contribute their work reporting that the writing of their stories was analgesic. And yet, some students preferred to use pseudonyms because the demons of bullies and oppressors still haunted their present lives. The narratives differed in length and in style depending on writing style, genre, and the space students needed to redeem their memories. Original wording was maintained but some narratives where shortened due to publication limitations. Students' stories were chosen not because they were model representatives of a particular cultural group but because they were cultural authorities of their own personal lived experiences.

They were grouped according to founded categories. In the ordering of stories, I refrained from judging any single oppression as more oppressive than another. That discussion was reserved instead for class. We considered questions like, "Which group suffers the greatest discrimination, Blacks,

Gays, the Disabled?" "Do the groups change position over time?" "What conditions affect the relativity of oppressions?" "The problem with constructing bridges over differences is the risk of equalizing experiences. It presumes that marginalizing experiences are equivalent one to the other — that the alienation of a middle-class white male equates to that of a sexually abused, inner-city black female" (Yeo, 1997, p. 200).

The students and I want to acknowledge to our fellow readers, that in our ensuing discussions of our narratives, we realized that our stories were written from a particular worldview or social construction of race, ethnicity, gender, and so on. We understand that these categories are socially constructed realities, which are dynamic and ever changing. Furthermore, if we accept that these categories are commonly used reference points by mainstream society, we deconstruct the hegemony by recognizing there is as much diversity within categories as there is among them.

This collection of student narratives will be especially valuable to teachers and teacher educators because they reveal multiple forms of otherness in young peoples' experiences. These stories sharpen underscore the dehumanizing school experiences for being different. Kivel (1996) and Duarte (1998) encouraged us to challenge our deeply held belief of the inherent goodness in sameness by seeing more acutely and insightfully the difference that difference makes in the way people are treated. Educators who use this book as a resource may want to choose narratives from categories that best suit the curricular needs of their own students, whether that means selecting a narrative that closely resonates with heretofore unvoiced identities in their classrooms or picking narratives that are seldom heard in their community as a way of demystifying new voices.

MY VOICE AS AROMATIC INCENSE

My reflections on the narratives reflect my own longing to be heard. As you read the stories of otherness in this chapter, I accompany you with my reflections and interpretations as an Asian American woman educator. Clearly, these sections include my biases, beliefs, and worldviews. The idea to include reflections was partly inspired by Stanfield's (1992) question to the research community, "What happens . . . when the life worlds of the dominant are investigated and interpreted through the paradigmatic lenses of people of color" (p. 183). Because of my intense desire to know my students and to understand the phenomenon of white otherness, I became increasingly familiar with the concept of *multiple identities*. I learned that one could be a member of a group accepted by the mainstream but could still be dehumanized by Otherness (e.g., white and large sized). This revelation helped the entire class resolve to dismantle all forms of othering.

My intent was not to upstage the student narratives but to accompany this literary journey like aromatic Asian incense; voiced reflections to stimulate the senses to see more. My inner voice reflects both my positions as an involuntary minority "other" and as a privileged "model minority" instructor. By offering my own voice to the collection of narratives, I am member of the composite transformation as well. The *italicized* sections represent my internal reflections that stimulated the dialectical exchange between students and teacher. They reveal the often disguised, afraid-to-disclose subjectivity that one uses to cognitively process stories of difference. This is the gift of difference that I offer to you the readers.

CONDITIONS FOR DIALOGUE

Fundamental to the narrative experience is the sharing of stories within a safe, mutually supportive environment. The storytellers and the community of learners were bonded by their mutual vulnerability and s stance of humility to their own experiences and knowledge (Kanpol, 1995). Similar to Giroux's (1993) border pedagogy, the sharing of otherness was not just about opening up curricular space but it meant preparing one's self to address a variety of languages, experiences, and voices; that "will not fit easily into the master narrative of a monolithic culture" (p. 34). It also meant respecting the courage it took for fellow peers to move from the margins of society to the center of the classroom to speak new truths that we needed to hear (Palmer & Livsey, 1999). Quotes like the following facilitated our openness to new inscriptions on our consciousness; new imprints on our mental pages of consciousness.

> What appears to be new,
> may in fact be familiar
>
> What appears to be familiar,
> may in fact be new.
>
> So question what you know,
> because you may not really know it all.
>
> (Author unknown)

COLORISM—3A

If you're white, you're all right;
if you're yellow, you're mellow;

if you're brown, stick around
but if you are black, go back!" (Halprin, 1995, p. 192)

Students of color teach us there is a hierarchy of skin color—the darker
the skin, regardless of heritage, the lesser value of the individual. They
explain that it has been their experience that this view is widely held by the
greater society and to some degree inside one's own community. Blacks,
Latinas, and Asians have stories about family members and friends who place
different values ok skin pigmentation.

One black sorority sister told us the light-skinned black boys at the fra-
ternity tasted different than the darker skinned boys when she kissed them.
One Latina shared with us how she was often hidden and dressed in long
sleeves because she was dark, whereas her sister, who was light-skinned, was
socially acknowledged and wore sleeveless dresses. Within Asian cultures, dark
skin infers that a person might be a peasant or laborer who works in the fields.
Light skin indicates wealth and status that could not be acquired outdoors.

Some people of color have also used skin color as a social chart to distin-
guish one member of the community from another. "How Black was she?
Sometimes I can recall colored faces that way," reported one black woman
(Walker, 1995, p. 204).

One Latina student described in my class the great lengths she went to
fitting in:

> When I took a bath, I scrubbed my skin so hard that I irritated it. One
> day my father told me that if I drank a lot milk , my skin color would
> turn white. He meant this as a joke, but I took him seriously. I drank a
> gallon of milk a week for a few weeks until my mother caught me. She
> told me, "Sweetheart, you're beautiful just the way you are." However,
> her words were not enough to dismiss the pain I felt from feeling so dif-
> ferent. (Castro, 3/21/00)

In the 1970s people of color called for a radical rethinking of color within the country's metanarrative. Identity and color were inextricably woven
together for many of them. Skin color was not just a palette of hues but, for
many, it was how we viewed our positions in society. hooks (1990) captured
the critical demand for new aesthetics:

> My sister has skin darker than mine. We think about our skin as a dark
> room, a place of shadows. We talk often about color politics and the way
> racism has created an aesthetic that wounds us, a way of thinking about
> beauty that hurts. In the shadows of late night, we talk about the need
> to see darkness differently, to talk about it in a new way. In that space of
> shadows we long for an aesthetic of blackness—strange and oppositional.
> (p. 113)

From a position of learned ugliness came a celebration of dark skin tones. People of color assumed a "proud to be" stance to their relative positionality in the social hierarchy. Affirmation of color contested the prevailing condemnation of darkness. Poet Sandra Cisnernos (1991) seized the moment:

> God made men by baking them in an oven, but he forgot about the first batch, and that's how Black people were born. And then he was so anxious about the next batch; he took them out of the oven too soon, so that's how White people were made. But the third batch he let cook until they were golden-golden-golden, and, honey, that's you and me. (p. 152)

Some students shared that ethnic pride sometimes led to a balkanization as evidence in their observations that whites were not welcome at university ethnic clubs such as the Black Student Union or Meccha or the Asian Pacific Student Association. Several white students described how they were regularly interrogated by both white students and students of color for taking ethnic study courses. Another student in my class described the color lines drawn for dating:

> The Black girls at school gave me a hard time. They said I should, "stick with my own and leave Anthony alone," that there weren't enough Black men to go around and that he would be a lot happier with one of them. I got the message. (Ante, 10/10/97)

White students also had strong opinions about color. One white student wrote about her childhood realization of the difference between her and other children in her Hawaiian classroom. "For the first time, I really saw how pale my own hand was in comparison to the children's brown hands. I wanted dark skin and dark features so badly. They nicknamed me 'Vanilla.' I remember using lemons to scrub freckles off my face" (Dawson, 4/17/04). Another white student in my class who lived in Hawaii wrote:

> My way of "fitting in" was to do silly superficial things to prove my allegiance to anything the whiteness I was. I would spend hours straightening my curly hair and tanning my moley Irish skin so I could look more like Jean Nishimura or Kimberly Chun. . . . I am paying today for what I did to my skin in childhood, fry and peel, fry and peel, fry and peel. I'm still not sure what that was all about, but I always wished at least one of my parents could have been Asian. (Rowntree, 1999)

In another moment of realization of difference, Naomi Wolf (1995), a Native American describes her first thoughts of blackness and whiteness:

I thought of blackness of licorice or blackboard slate, and the whiteness of Casper the Ghost. . . . I looked around me at my class of Chinese, Philippine, Japanese, "Afro-American," and scattered Nordic children, and what I beheld was ivory, biscuit, buff, brick, sandalwood, clay, tobacco, peanut, hazelnut, walnut, chestnut, and Moroccan leather. . . . What am I? I asked, and was informed that I was "white." I stared at my hand, darker and sallower than the unpleasant peach-beige "flesh" shade in the crayon box. . . . It was clear, though, from something in the voice that explained these things—or perhaps from the images around that were starting to filter in, that I was my skin. (p. 38)

Being white in a multicultural world creates a feeling of "otherness" for white students, they reported. "What multicultural world?" asked students of color? Students of color were blind to the trendy multicultural magazine covers and diversity media that white students had cited as indicators of a color-changing world. Both agreed white had been the standard historically. They disagreed to what extent whiteness prevailed as the standard today.

Subsequently, student discussions moved to asking which social indicators specific groups were reading to determine the prevailing thinking. Some white students pointed to reified sun gods and goddesses in our southern California habitat as evidence of a color as beauty. Students of color noted legislation against Affirmation Action and bilingual education as evidence that people of color have little intrinsic worth.

Anecdotally, biracial students, with white backgrounds, described the various conditions in which they used their ability to self-inscribe a white identity over their colored one. In what instances did they feel it necessary to blend with whatever group was dominant? Likewise, students of color reported on the social conditions in which they were accused of "being white" and called names like, "coconut," "banana," and "oreo" because their peers perceived their a behavior or attitude being one that implied one was too good for the group or was a sell out. Color consciousness was accentuated for everyone whenever students dated across racial/ethnic lines because they felt a need to defend or deny their color. Halprin (1995) tried to explain why

light-skinned people of color pass as white; Jews pass as Christians; old people pass as young; lesbians and gay men pass as straight; women, for centuries, have passed as men, and men have passed as women. Passing may be seen as living a lie, denying one's own identity, or it may be seen as surviving, even growing, in a hostile environment. (pp. 233-234)

In a country that focuses primarily on black and white relations, yellow gets minimal coverage in the media or in public policy. "Confining race in the U.S. to a "black-white" thing render Latinas/os, Native Americans and Asian Americans invisible" (Thompson, 1996, p. 103). Although I ethnically represented almost one fourth of the world's population, media and my experiences inform me that I am politically small in this country. The invisibility of my social and political influence is in part culturally ingrained. Imprisoned in the Asian stereotype as one who is quiet, passive, and compliant, I seek to break out of this "accept everything and do nothing" outlook that permeates my Chinese upbringing.

Currently, society has conferred on me the status of model minority, with all the rank and privilege of my white counterparts. I feel as if I am a snake who has molted and slithered out of my colored encasing to emerge as some unrecognizable albino mutant. This quick-change artistry of identity is facilitated by both fellow Asians who feel this is the way we must prevail or by hegemonic social architects who map the fate of all minorities. As a model minority, I am a social lab experiment who is positively reinforced for assimilation at the expense of the status of other minorities. Every step I take "forward" toward the "American Dream," cripples the steps taken by my black and brown brothers and sisters who choose alternative pathways. Junichi P. Semitsu exposes the strategy of holding up Asians as models to other minorities in the last stanza of her poem "Super Model Minority," read January 18, 1996 at a University of California Regents' meeting in protest to the ban on affirmative action:

> and in this hazy shade of lazy
> if you stand accused
> hope you ain't used
> by the majority
> like me
> your super
> model minority

As Asian Americans we are a minority group who has learned to shed its color via generations of assimilation. We are institutionally defined as white. We are led to believe that we are longer discriminated against or exploited and therefore do not require differentiated consideration. Some call this social progress. Others see this designation as a convenient construct to prevent the expenditure of tax dollars. The concept of the model minority is used by dominant white ideology to implicitly denigrate other minorities (Lee, 1996).

Oliver Sack (1996), a neurologist, studied colorblindness on an island community diagnosed with achromatopsia; congenital colorblindness. He wondered what was it like to live in a completely colorless world. He was curious to find out if achromatopes "developed heightened perceptions of visual tone and texture and movement and depth, and live in a world in some ways more intense than our own" (p. 6). One of his colleagues, an achromatope, responded by asking the following question, "Might the colors *of things have dominated my experience, preventing me from knowing so intimately the other qualities of things?" (p. 209). Was colorblindness then, a biologically desired state and not a disability? The implications of Sacks' research to the social sciences are questions like, "Does color preventing us from coming to know other human qualities?" "What could people of color learn from those who are colorblind?" On the other hand, if color is used for seduction, protection, and camouflage by living organisms from the plant and animal kingdoms, does society disable people of color if society self-induces colorblindness? Will I become endangered without my color?*

You Would Have Me White
Herb Sanchez

Brown is the color I am.
Brown is not White.
Brown, the color of worn leather.
Brown like the arms of the men who stand at the corner looking for work.
The men my mother does not want me to see.
The men my family never wanted me to be.
Brown is the color of the gardener and the busboy.
Brown, the man who picks up my trash.
Brown, the man working in the lettuce fields.
Brown, the lady hocking flowers off of freeway on-ramps.
Brown is abandoned and pregnant at sixteen.
Brown is no skills and no future.
Brown is minimum wage.
Brown is limited English.

We will not let you be Brown, my son.
For Brown reminds us of our indigenous past.
Brown is the conquered, not the conquistador.
Brown, our homeland we left behind.
White, the land of opportunity.
White, our dreams.
White, the color of clean hands that never knew work.
White, unstained by Brown (the color of dirt).
White, for whom we pick the fruit.
White, for whom we mow the lawn.

We will not let you be Brown, my son.
For we wish to spare you the pain and degradation of a crushed people.
For we wish you success and respect.
We wish you White.

But I cannot change culture as I would a pair of shoes.
Brown is the color I am.
And Brown is not White.

Brown is the color of shit.
Brown, the color of my hands. My skin. My face.

Brown, the color of shit that my father had to clean out of the bathrooms.
My father, the teacher, coming to America to mop and scrub toilets.
My father who always wished more for his sons.
My father who understood that America sees but two colors.
My father who knew that Brown is not White.
My father who let us know that we were Brown.
My father who taught us the importance of a good education only to
    discover that knowledge is not bleach.
Learning does not whiten.

My brother is a lawyer, and I will be a teacher.
But we will forever carry a racial prefix.
The Latino lawyer.
The new Hispanic teacher.
As if to bring into question the merit of our work.
As if to remind me that Brown is not White.
As if to remind me that I am Brown.
Brown like the men who stand at the corner looking for work.
I am they, and they are I.

For together, we are Brown.
We share the White dream."
The dream that we might be counted.
That we might be respected."

For we recognize in ourselves that we are more than the color of our skin.
We are more than minstrels and entertainment.
More than sombreros and Macarena.

We are the product of centuries of mestizaje.
Of crossing and blending.
We are the children born of the mixture of Old World and New.
Spaniard fathers penetrating Aztec wombs.
We are Montezuma and Cortes, both and at once.
Heirs of two great cultures.
We are thinkers and poets.

Doctors and lawyers.
Scientists. Business owners.

Just like you.
Except for my Brownness.
The Browness that I can no longer escape.
The Browness that I am.

Brown if the color I am.
Brown is not White.
But Brown is not lesser.
Brown is just darker.
Brown the color of freshly hewn lumber.
Brown like damp earth.
Brown, the color of coffee or dark chocolate.
Brown, the color of baked bread.
Brown, the first seed that springs forth into the first tree.
Brown, the Earth's first color.
Brown is the color I am.
Brown, the part of me, which I once detested.
Brown, the part of me in which I now rejoice. Brown, the color God
    gave me.
Brown, the color I am.

Female and Black
Nsiza G. Senga

In the eyes of my professors and fellow students I was black, yet somehow
they did not understand why I was in constant conflict between my homeland in Africa and my new environment in America. The paradox was
almost deafening. I come from a line of very proud people and my mother
always told me that I was blessed to be born a female. She said that I was a
"carrier of life" and that I should never forget or abuse that privilege. I wear
my hair in braids because it is easier to manage that way. I am the way my
mother, my grandmother, my aunts and almost all African women wear
their hair. Hairstyles generally separate women from men. All my life, I
knew that if I was anything at all, I was female.

   Four years of living in America began to take a toll on me. I no longer
saw myself as a woman, but rather as Black. My identity as a woman was
slowing being replaced by my blackness. Today, I AM a Black Woman. The
seed was planted a long time ago, and has since been growing inside of me.
At first I resisted. I did not know what it meant and I was not ready for the
added on responsibility. Being a woman was hard enough. Now I was Black
too?

A Dash of Paella and Soy Sauce
Katherine Borras

I am the daughter of a war hero, a Puerto Rican man. My bedtime stories were his comical interpretations of his days serving in World War II, Korea, and Vietnam. I loved hearing those stories because he was an American war hero . . . my hero.

A dash of paella runs through my veins. It is the trilling r's that so easily roll off my tongue, the love to dance, growing up with tapes of Julio Iglesias in the background, the love to sing, to talk, and rapidly move my hands when I converse. It is the expressive body language and the love to mingle and socialize. It is the Catholic influence and my acquired religion. A dash of paella runs through my veins.

I am the daughter of a hero, a Chinese woman, who disobeyed old Chinese customs and fled to America to wed an American man. She tells stories of how my parents met in the army base in China. She was the administrative secretary and my father, the Western soldier. This went against all Chinese custom, where arranged marriages were still an integral part of my mother's culture. Yet, she defied culture and rooted herself across the Pacific Ocean in America.

A dash of soy sauce runs through my veins. It is the Chinese grandparents, who stressed the importance of learning Chinese, the long noodles that symbolize longevity, the rice cooker always steaming with fresh rice, the clacking of bamboo chopsticks, the red envelopes on Chinese New Year, the pouring of tea into porcelain tea cups and waiting last to eat until I had served the elders. It is the loud clicking of my "Po-Po's" mah-jongg tiles and the fast Mandarin language to which I did not understand. A dash of soy sauce runs through my veins.

I am a mutt, a happa, an ethnically mixed female, the daughter of a Puerto Rican father and Chinese mother. I am the cooing of my mother and grandmother's Chinese friends who say I am so, "qua-I" or cute and my nose bridge so high and beautiful. It is the naturally curly hair that I have, mixed with almond shaped eyes. It is the comments that I look exotic and tall for a Chinese girl. A dash of paella and soy sauce run through my veins.

I am confused; I grow up not knowing what bubble to fill in on tests that ask for your ethnicity. Do I fill in half of the bubble for Chinese and half for Hispanic? I grow up not wanting to be Chinese, but to be fully Puerto Rican or white, because no one can tell what I am. Are you Philipino, Chinese, Japanese, Korean, Spanish, Hawaiian? The list goes on.

A dash of paella and soy sauce runs through my veins. I am 10 years old and my father passes away. With him goes the presence of my Spanish culture. All I have left is my Chinese side. My mother, a strong woman, left alone to raise two children becomes my hero. Chinese talking and culture surround me now, but I am American. I am mixed. I am not just one ethnicity. A dash of paella and soy sauce runs through my veins.

At college, I get asked the question that I can never avoid, "What are you?" I say that I am half Chinese and half Puerto Rican. People seem shocked, as if they have never heard of ethnically mixed people before. I vow never to date an Asian, because I was American, I was mixed, and I wanted to immerse myself in my white culture. I join organizations that are comprised of mainly Caucasian women and pick up that ever so infamous "valley girl" lingo.

A dash of paella and soy sauce runs through my veins. I graduate from college and I begin working. I am faced with that question that has followed me through my life, "What are you?" Now it has become a spectacle, "Wow, that's so different," I hear, and I take pride in being unique. I meet my boyfriend, a Philippino man, to whom I find my greatest joy. My vow to never date Asians had been broken. He allows me to be who I am and to embrace my "Asian-ness." I feel proud to have a mixed heritage. I straighten my naturally curly hair so that I may have the staple silky straight hair of Asian women. I highlight my hair with blond streaks so that my other half can stand out.

A dash of paella and soy sauce runs through my veins. I am proud to be who I am. I am happy to be "different," because there is too much of the same in our world. Two cultures brought together have made me appreciate my heritage and who I am. I am able to see the world through two different eyes, yet I feel lucky to be "dissimilar."

A dash of paella and soy sauce runs through my veins. I am the fast clacking of tongues speaking Mandarin and Spanish, the social but yet reserved, the white rice and the saffron red rice, Catholicism and Buddhism. A dash of paella and soy sauce runs through my veins. I am American. I am Chinese. I am Puerto Rican. I am me. I am lucky and blessed because of diversity in my world.

The School Bell Rings
Anita Sweeney

The school bell rang and my heart sang.

I was excited about attending school. I thought the mailman would bring a magical number that would say it was my turn to attend school. I waited every day for the mailman and no magical number ever came. I did however begin attending school at age five. I thought I was in heaven. I was in school and I was sure that I would learn many things. My elementary school was made up of mostly Latin and Anglo students. There were times when the students were split on racial lines. We knew that the Latins mostly lived in the poorer neighborhood and that the Anglos lived in the better neighborhood. We knew there was a difference.

The school bell rings.

Why do the teachers treat the Mexican student differently from the other students?

The school bell rings.
I wondered if they know we were all capable of learning. I know I'll have to be smart (really, really smart). I'll work hard to be smarter than the next person. If I'm smarter than the rest, I'll get ahead or at least they won't frown at me. I'll have to be smarter than the white kids.

The school bell rings.

I won't just be another dumb Mexican. I'll be one of the smart kids. No, I'll be the smartest kid. I'll work hard. I am a Mexican and they don't think Mexicans work hard. I'll prove them wrong.

The school bell rings.

Is it wrong to be a Mexican?

The school bell rings.

Why did many of my friends drop out of school?

The school bell rings.

Why do they rank us according to our skin color? It's not fair. I'll have to work hard so they do not frown at me or think that I am a lazy Mexican. Why do they get to push us around and influence our lives the way they do? How come they aren't teaching all of us? It's not fair! I'll work harder and maybe they won't mind so much that I'm a Mexican.

The school bell rings.

I'm taking the Mentally Gifted tests but I'm glad my mother decides to keep me in regular classes. The gifted students are bussed off to another school. How come so many of them are white? None of the kids from my neighborhood are on that special bus? They are not like us and we are not like them. We aren't treated like we're special. I'm glad I'm not on their bus. I get to stay with my friends from my neighborhood.

The school bell rings.

I've been given the MGM stamp of specialness. The teachers treat me like I'm different from the other Mexican children. I'm too bright . . . to be a real Mexican, but I know this is part of my heritage. How come they think it's not?

The school bell rings.

Does she have an Anglo father? Oh yeah, that's right she does. They think I'm different from the other Mexican children. I'm not. I'll work hard though (really, really hard).

The school bell rings.

Why are all my teachers in elementary school white? How come every story I've read has only white characters in them? Why don't we learn about other people? Is the only world the white world? Do you have to be white to be successful or to be in a book? Books are important aren't they? The teachers tell us that they are.

The school bell rings.

I'm in junior high now. Many of my Mexican friends have become low riders. They are loyal to their neighborhood and to their race. I'm not a low rider.

The school bell rings.

[Girl], you're not like the other Mexicans. You work hard and pay attention. I begin to feel that no matter what I do I am a Mexican and yet people are telling me I'm not. My ethnicity hasn't changed has it? I look in the mirror and I'm still the same color. I'm brown like the other kids from my neighborhood. I'm still brown. They think I'm different because I'm successful at what they think is important. I'm still brown.

The school bell rings.

The lines have been drawn between the low riders and the surfers. Where do I stand, I don't belong to either group. Where do I fit?

The school bell rings.

How come none of my friends are in my classes? They're in the remedial classes. What does that word mean anyways? It's rumored that those are the classes for the dummies. I'll work hard. I don't want to be in those classes. How come so many brown kids are in those classes?

The school bell rings.

I can't believe it. Someone from my neighborhood wants to have me jumped because I have become too upity. I am not like them because I don't wear makeup and baggy low rider clothes. They call me a school girl and think that I'm trying to be better than them. The fight never happens. My good friends from the neighborhood stand up for me. They know I'm not conceited and that I like to read. Even though this threat disappears I feel like I've been moved further away from the kids from my neighborhood and from myself. I look in the mirror. I'm still brown. I know I am. I'll work harder. I know I have to.

The school bell rings.

I'm in high school. I'm attending a school named Los Amigos. In English this means friends. I think that's pretty funny. It's a real laugh a school called friends.

The school bell rings.

The year before I was to attend this school there were violent racial riots. The tension was between the Anglo students and the Mexican students. Anyone who wasn't white was lumped in with the Mexican students. My two brothers and my sister were attending the school at the time. They said that it was just all out fighting and that even some of the teachers had been beat up. I can't believe they were beating up on the teachers too. The school was closed down for a couple of days and the racial tension never quite subsided. How come they still call it Los Amigos? It's funny really funny.

The school bell rings.

[Girl] you're a beaner.

The school bell rings.

[Girl], you're a dirty Mexican.

The school bell rings.

[Girl], your mother is the scum in the bottom of a barrel.

The school bell rings.

[Girl], Mexicans don't go to college.

The school bell rings.

Advance Biology—apologize for calling her a dirty beaner. I heard you call her that. The apology never comes. I won't hold my breath. I've learned not to.

The school bell rings.

I am the only Mexican or person of color in the college prep courses. I work hard because they do not expect me to succeed. I know that if I slip up too much they will place me in the dumping ground we know as the remedial classes. After all, that is where most of the other minorities are or the trouble makers.

The school bell rings.

I am graduating a year early because I can't wait to get out of this school. I'm tired of the tension and many of the classes have been boring and or not challenging. A couple of students laugh when they hear that I have applied to UC Irvine. They laugh and tell me didn't I know they don't let Mexicans attend there. I don't pay attention to them, but of course I hear what they are saying. It makes me more determined to educate myself and to prove that I am smart. I look in the mirror. I'm still brown. I'll have to work hard really hard.

The school bell rings.

I'll work hard here really hard. I look in the mirror. I'm still brown.

The school bell rings.

What are you doing here?

The school bell rings.

Don't most Mexican carry a knife in their sock?

The school bell rings.

I didn't know they let Mexicans go to college.

The school bell rings.

It must be that affirmative action thing.

The school bell rings.

I look in the mirror I'm still brown. I'm not a charity case. I'm not some sort of social project. I won't hold my breath. I'll just work harder really harder.

The school bell rings.

It's my senior year and I finally have a professor that is a Mexican. The rumor mill has it that he did not really attend good colleges. Why aren't these things said about other professors? Maybe they are and I haven't been around to hear them? Does it have anything to do with him being a Mexican? I wonder? I'll wait to find out, but I won't hold my breath. I've been taught not to hope for too much.

The school bell rings.

My friends and I talk about who has been followed or stopped by the police this week. They are letting us know that we do not belong in Irvine and who do we think we are attending college anyways.

The school bell rings.

It must be that affirmative action thing. I look in the mirror. I'm still brown. I'll work harder. I'm not a dumb Mexican.

The school bell rings.

I'm graduating from college. I am the first person in my family to graduate and there will be others to come. I sit in a sea of black graduation gowns and their are few Mexicans graduating this year.

The school bell rings.

I'm in the neighborhood that I grew up in and I am set apart because I am one of a handful of college graduates that grew up here.

The school bell rings.

Coconut. Coconut. Coconut.

The school bell rings.
I'm an educated Mexican. I'm not pretending to be white. I look in the mirror. I'm still brown.

The school bell rings.

None of the classes I attended or books I've read have lightened the color of my skin. They have not changed my ethnic heritage. Why do they believe that education has made me somehow less of a Mexican and less of a member of our community. I choke on this thought. They have bought into the lie that real Mexicans don't go to college. [Mexicans] do! I did.

The school bell rings.

I am a teacher. I welcome my students into our classroom and we will try to learn to value each other as human beings.

The school bell rings.

The children on the playground are laughing, sharing and playing together.

The school bell rings and my heart sings.

Blend
Jason Milton

I was born in Berea, Ohio. My mother, an immigrant from the Philippines, moved there when she was in ninth grade. She used to joke with me that she was the first Filipino the town had ever seen. Whenever I asked her how it felt to be the "foreigner" on the block, she always responded with horror stories. She said that the other kids would ask why she looked differently, and some even told her to go back where she came from. Nevertheless, she managed to make friends and even wed her high school sweetheart. She married my father, a white son of a blue-collar, steel-working family, just after they both graduated high school.

When the time came for me to attend school, my mother was determined to provide a better educational experience for me than she endured. Unfortunately, she believed that the only way to accomplish this was to strip me of my Filipino ethnicity. We never ate Filipino foods, never practiced Filipino customs, and, worst of all, she never taught me Tagalog, the Filipino language. In fact, I had no idea that I was even Filipino; that is, until I went to school. I can't really blame my mother, however, because she was just trying to protect me from the discrimination that she faced.

My mother did not realize that I would soon encounter a challenge unfamiliar to even her: I was of mixed descent. I have struggled with my mixed ethnicity throughout my life. I understand how some may say that two cultures are better than one, but two cultures also bring twice the problems. I have to suffer discrimination that both whites and Filipinos face. Also, I've never been able to claim one culture. Being half-and-half leaves me with half a culture—at least that's how I've been treated. Throughout my educational career, I tried desperately to fit in. And unfortunately, my desperation led me to commit some shameful acts.

Just like most kids, my favorite part of the school day was recess. Ironically though, recess is where I experienced my first cultural awakening. One of my friends asked me why my eyes were so small. I was speechless. I had never realized that my eyes were small at all. In fact, I couldn't see a difference between this boy's eyes and mine. Other kids heard the boy's question, and this resulted in a snowball effect. Seemingly from nowhere, kids were asking me all sorts of questions, to which I had no answer: "Are you Chinese? Can you still see as well as I can? Do you speak Chinese?" I just stood there silently. Of course I was not Chinese. I looked just like all of them. I was white. Wasn't I?

After school that day, I ran home and told my mother what happened. I asked her to look at my eyes and tell me if I really was different. Seeing how worried I was, my mother told me for the first time about my Filipino ethnicity. She told me I was not Chinese and that if the other kids asked me similar questions again, I should tell them that I am half Filipino and half white. Then she told me how special I was because I had two nationalities while most people only had one. This comforted me and she sent me off to play. Looking back, however, I can tell that my mother was devastated. She had hoped that she could hide my ancestry and keep me from the taunting she faced as a child. But kids saw right through the facade and wasted all her efforts.

The next day I felt much more confident at recess. I was even able to respond when another kid asked me about my appearance. "Why is your nose so flat? he asked. "Because I'm half Filipino and half white," I replied. "That's not why," he said. "Your nose is flat because you picked all the boogars out and it fell down." All the other kids laughed and pointed at me. The humiliation was so terrible that I ran off the field crying.

Fortunately, I can look back on the incident and laugh, but on that day, I wanted to crawl away and hide forever. Even worse, I blamed my Filipino heritage for my embarrassment. If it weren't for that, I reasoned, no one would laugh at me. I ran home and told my mother what happened. Devastated again, she tried the only way she knew how to make me feel better: She tried to hide my culture. She told me not to listen to them because I was white, just like them. I was an American just like them. I was born here and I only spoke English, just like them. She said that even though I was technically half Filipino, I was more white because I'd never been to the Philippines and did not know a thing about that country.

Eventually the kids found someone else to tease and I didn't have to explain my appearance. In fact, I had almost forgotten that I was half Filipino. But then it came time for standardized testing. My mother had read somewhere that colleges were now aggressively seeking minority students. She never attended college herself, but she was determined that I would. Before the first day of testing, my mother told me that the test would ask for my ethnicity. "I know, Mom," I told her. "I'm white." To my surprise, however, she told me to fill in the Filipino bubble. I was shocked. I told her that I didn't know anything about being Filipino and that she always told me to ignore that part of me. That was when she told me about colleges and minorities. She told me that I didn't have to tell the other kids, but I should still fill out the Filipino bubble. I told her that I would do it as long as no one had to know because in my mind, I was white.

A couple of years later, my parents divorced and my sister and I moved with my mother to Fremont, California. This move accounted for another cultural awakening. When I walked into my new school for the first time, I was scared to death. All of the kids were Asian. How on Earth was I going to fit in? I was positive that all the kids would tease me for being different. Indeed, during the first recess one of the kids asked me about my nationality. I told him that I was white. "No," he said. "There's only a few white people at this school, and you don't look like them." I realized then that if I wanted to fit in, I couldn't be just white. That was when I remembered how my mom told me told me how lucky I was to have two cultures. Maybe she was right after all. I could choose which one I wanted whenever I felt like it. At my old school, it was better for me to be white. During testing, I should be Filipino. And now, I thought, maybe at this school, I should be Filipino all the time. "I'm also Filipino," I told the boy.

"Yeah," he said. "I can see that. Cool." Everything went fine for the rest of the school day, but on my way home I began thinking about what I had done. I was scared to tell my mom what happened because I thought she would be mad at me. All this time she told me to tell the other kids that I was white, and now I disobeyed her. I wanted to make up a different story, but when my mother asked about my day, I couldn't help but tell her the truth.

"So, the other kids are all Asian?" she asked.

"Yes," I said.

"And they liked it that you are half Filipino?"

"Yes," I answered.

"Great! Then you should just tell people that you are Filipino when they ask. It's important to remember your ancestors, you know," she advised.

It wasn't until years later that I realized that my mother wasn't teaching me my culture; she was using it. She taught me to use my mixed ethnicity to my advantage. She taught me to pick and choose between my Filipino and white nationality as if I were choosing an outfit for a job interview. If my audience wanted a white person, then be white. If they wanted a Filipino, be Filipino. Unfortunately I followed this trend for the next several years. I changed schools many times, and I always used this "pick-and-choose" technique to my advantage.

Everything worked fine until I reached high school in 1993. Despite the fact that my school tried to teach diversity and racial tolerance, our campus looked like a lesson in segregation. At lunch, the school seemed to be broken up into ethnic groups, and everyone knew where they were accepted and where they were not. To this day, I can still point out exactly where each racial group hung out. To make matters worse, there was an unsaid rule across the campus: You only stayed with your own people. This law was obvious just by looking around the school. People gathered everywhere, but the groups were strictly limited to one particular race. Even though I noticed this right away, I wasn't really intimidated because I had my trusty pick-and-choose technique.

By the time I graduated high school, I was so tired of trying to blend with everyone else. I was sick of picking and choosing. I finally realized that the more I tried to fit in, the more I became an outsider. I saw college as my chance at a fresh start. No longer would I follow my mother's pick-and-choose technique. No longer would I worry about what people thought I was. I am who I am, and I refused to make apologies for it.

The result was astounding. I felt confident around any group of people because I was confident in myself. I knew people wondered about my nationality, but it didn't bother me. In fact, I am proud to tell them that I have two cultures and I respect each one of them equally. I am proud of my mixed culture; not because I can pick and choose to my advantage, but because that's who I am.

Eternally "Other"
Frank Perez

I have an assignment
Called the "Otherness" paper
Describe my feelings
That's my caper

I descend from two cultures
How can I explain this?

I was raised as a kid
Speaking Spanglish
Freckled face
They called me "huero"
The same nickname given
To my abuelas perro

Do we stick out in a crowd?
We always find each "other"
We must be distinctive
When father's not like mother

My cousins are pure Mexicans
They said I wasn't the same
Our only solid connection
Lies within our last name

"You're lucky you're gabacho
You won't have to struggle"
They have no idea what it's like
When there's two cultures that I have to juggle

As we've gotten older
It seems we've all matured
But I put up with years of pain
From labels I endured

"Half-breed," "Mutt,"
"Confused" or "Mixed-up"
I'm an experiment of two cultures
Scrambled in a cup

I went to a private school
My counsin said that I acted White
Well, my mother descends from Scotland
So I guess that she was right

When I went on to public high school
My old private buddies said I changed
I looked more Mexican
Because my clothes had been rearranged

I went out with a Mexican girl
She said I sounded White.

Embarrassment shot through my veins,
I was bummed all night.
I went out with a White girl.
She said I sounded Mexican
My whole mind was in turmoil
Everything was complex again.

I unconsciously became two people
To fit in with the majority crowd
Always being the minority
Never made me proud

I am finally proud to be bi-cultured
It is no longer an issue
I won't cry you a river
I don't need a tissue.

However, I have assumed a natural defense,
Depending on the nature of a person's descent
I have constantly been known
To alter my own accent

This is not international
Or even cool to do
But apparently my subconscious
Wants to wear the right shoe

I can't speak fluent Spanish
I don't really like the food
Skipping my grandma's menudo
Makes me feel rude.

Christmas is always interesting
We eat pan Mexicano and tamales
We go to my other grandma's house
And have apple pie from Polly's

I love the closeness of
My Mexican family tree
All of my mom's relatives
Are scattered across the country.

This poem has opened scars
That I thought had all but healed

My mind drifts off to the awful reunion
In an Illinois corn field
My brother and I went to my mom's reunion
Back in Illinois
In an uneducated town
Where a black person is still called "boy"

For once in my life
I really tried to act White
Not because of embarrassment,
But instead it was pure fright

My goatee is red
My hair is brown
When the kids at work stare me
I feel like a clown

They actually think it's cool
And tell me I look dope
They have no idea
How hard it was to cope

Interracial children
Are becoming less unique
But they still have to reckon with
Ignorant people calling them a freak

I remember a confusing moment
When I met my abuelas hermana
She looked at me and said, "Que chulo...
Pero, tienes la cara de su mama"

The first time I met my mom's autnt
She looked at me quite sad
"you're a good lookin' kid,
But you look just like your dad.

I felt like a circle peg
Trying to fit into a square
"Who the hell am I?"
Should I even care?

My first year of high school Spanish
My teacher finished calling roll

"Perez," she asked me with a look of disgust
"Porque no hablas espanol?"
Chillin' with my Mexican friends
I'd get lost amongst their lingo
They'd see my look of confusion,
"Oh, we forgot about the gringo"

I was an easygoing person
I just wanted to be cool
Looking back at the past
I really acted a fool

If I was with White friends
I'd say "Hey bra"
But if I slipped in a "What's up eh"
They'd quickly note my flaw

They thought that it was funny
To say "Hey what's up essay?"
I couldn't fit in as White
Even on my best day.

Don't feel sorry for me
I don't want any pity
Everyone's had their own experience
Of feeling really shitty

Excuse my language
There's no reason to be vulgar
But just let it be known
That you can lean on my shoulder.

We must respect
Each individual's culture
There's no need to pick at one's helplessness
Like a starving vulture.

I didn't get to choose
Who I am today
So I'll respect God's choice
Every night and day

I am a Scottish-Mexican.
I will say that with my head high

But my poem is all finished now
So, instead I'll say "Goodbye."

Color Can Be Deceiving
Stephanie Mips

Color can be deceiving
I am more than what you see.
What do you see?
You see my light skin with brown freckles, my brown eyes, my brown hair.
You hear no accent from my voice.
You see a White girl before you.

Color can be deceiving.
I am more than what you see.
What do they see when the look at me?
They see a person who has lived the White lifestyle.
They see a person who has the White advantage.
They see me as a White girl before them.

Color can be deceiving.
I am more than what you see.
What do I see when I look in the mirror?
I see someone who has been waiting since she was five for her brown dots
to connect.
Then, I will be my color.
I see the half of me that is Latino.
I see my family who has shown me only the Latino culture in my daily life.
I see my grandfather and grandmother who came to this country as immi-
grants.
I hear my mom and dad speaking Spanish.
I see a Latino before me.

Color can be deceiving.
I am more than what you see.
What did they make me see?
I am the dirty White, not the beautiful Brown.
My dots will never connect.
I cannot speak Spanish, so I am not Latino.
My mother is White, so I am White.
I cannot belong to your group.
I see my tears when they laugh at me for thinking I am Latino.
I see a White girl before me.

Color can be deceiving.
I am more than what you see.
So, who am I?
I am half Latino, 1/4 German, 1/4 Irish.
I am what they call a "half-breed."
I am more accepted in my White group than in my Latino group.
I am more than what you see.
I am Latino in my soul.
But, I am not accepted there.
I am a defender of my race that I was raised to be.
White is not me. Latino is not me. So I will struggle to be me.
I am White on the outside and Brown on the inside.
Get to know me ...
Colors can be deceiving.

PHYSICAL ATTRIBUTES–3B

It's What's on the Outside That Counts

Mirror, mirror on the wall. Who's the fairest of them all? How many of us have escaped ridicule of our physical attributes? None of us. But some of us have lived lives imprisoned by imperfect bodies and faces that only plastic surgeons can fix. This "learned ugliness" (Halprin, 1995) starts in our schools and has been a source of pain and self-torture as recounted by student narratives.

Student narratives of otherness disputed the age-old adage that beauty comes from within. The narratives revealed the unrelentless teasing, jeering, and marginalization targeted at atypical physical attributes. Students wrote about body image; how it felt to heavy, too thin, full breasted, small breasted, too tall or too short. They also wrote about physical conditions they acquired as a result of a disease or physical attributes they were born with which invited peer scrutiny such as birthmarks, crossed eyes, hair, crooked teeth, uneven legs, large noses, etc. As children they were either stared at or avoided by other children who claimed they could catch these deformities. By examining how others looked at them, they told classmates how they began to understand that, in the eyes of others, they are their faces and their bodies. Nothing within seems to count.

They believed their physical characteristics deviated from the norm or the standard for beauty. When asked, "What is considered beautiful?" and "How do you know?" students concurred that individuals with blue eyes, blond hair, with light skin, who were thin/physically fit, and relatively tall, while admittedly a narrow interpretation, met the Bay Watch standard of beauty. They pointed to examples of language, images, written and visual representations from media, popular culture, and community practices and the absence of minority role models as signifiers that influenced their assessment. The farther away from this standard, the more likely it was to become social outcasts or victims of otherness. Halprin (1995) explained, "Growing up surrounded by media images of whites can be a devastating experience if your skin is black, brown, coppery, or gold, or if you have a 'Jewish' nose or 'bad' hair," (p. 191). She cited examples of pain and rage felt by women of color over the omnipotent image of the fair, white princess.

> My girlfriends and I imagined ourselves as the porcelain pink princesses: Snow White, Cinderella and, the fairest of them all, Barbie. What a sweet toy for a little Black girl, a rubber-headed, relentlessly white woman with plastic torpedo titties, no hips, no ass, who needed a kickstand up her butt to stand because she was permanently poised on the balls of her feet. My graceless arches were flat next to hers. Barbie's hair never had to be straightened. She had no burn scars on her tiny pink ears. I liked to pull her head off, spike it on a pencil, or poke out her Barbie blues with a straight pin. (Lampley, 1993, p. 144)

Children learn to consider themselves ugly by comparing themselves to mainstream standards. They learned to forget their ethnic origins and values in order to "fit into" the mainstream.

Chu (1980) studied co-eds at the University of California in Los Angeles and found that Asian co-eds have, in a single generation of Western influence, acquired a preference of Western attributes over Eastern attributes in men. Asian co-eds revealed that they were attracted to some of the same physical attributes in men as their western sisters—body hair, strong-framed physiques, and large hands in men. Whereas in China, their mothers desired civilized men of strong character with long thin, uncalloused fingers that signified scholarship rather than labor.

The Western concept of beauty demonstrated its stronghold over our worldview again when Negro children made preferential choices for white dolls over Negro dolls in studies carried out in 1940s and again when the study was replicated in 1990s (Clark & Clark, 1947). This dominant ideology is further reflected when adults recall their mothers' influence on their self-images; "My mother seemed happy that I didn't look Jewish" (Halprin, 1995, p. 188). "My younger daughter is prettier than her sister because she has rounder eyes," claimed an Asian friend of mine.

Bodies

Roghenberg (1992) noted that women in this country live under the tyranny of slenderness. Girdles and corsets were invented to reshape us. The prolifer-

ation of diet ads, the sale of diet products, and cosmetic surgery are at an all time high and indicate that we are ashamed of our natural bodies. Large-sized students, both male and female, described in their narratives the regular scrutiny they succumbed to at restaurants and grocery store checkout lines. "I am the fat one. Shelly, belly they call me, " reported one student.

Discrimination and otherness as a result of weight and their struggle to achieve the "right" body size forced some students to "almost die to become thin" as they gave their anorexic and bulimic histories. A recent article in the newspaper reported a ballerina who literally starved herself to death to achieve the "ballerina figure." "Slim is in" applied to men as well as women who recounted how their large size caused people to question their physical prowess as well. This fixation on changing our bodies in order to be accepted by society obscures the possibility of changing the culture to accept our bodies

There is a social conspiracy, unknown even to those who participate in it, that prevents individuals from developing their own bodies and power. A poignant example, specifically for women, is Eve Ensler's off-Broadway show "Vagina Monologues" (2000), which brings attention to the abstract social constructions of the vagina. She makes visible the multiple ways society has exiled the vagina to a dark place that is forbidden and taboo. By euphemizing the vagina, by mystifying it, and by not talking about it, society tries to sever it from our senses of knowing and being.

Hair-Raising Tales

Curly, full-volume tresses described by Jewish, Black, Polynesian, and Latina students as "Big Hair" could make a woman instantly vulnerable. Students described how a mere walk across campus on a humid day transformed hours of straightened flat hair, into a large, uncontrollable mass that burst bandanas and popped off hats. Girls ducked for cover, too embarrassed to talk with anyone. Humidity, rain, or sprinklers could mean instant tears.

Did blondes have more fun? The increased popularity of "color highlights" seems to indicate that blonde was better. Blondes countered by sharing how their seemingly privilege position was often a disadvantage because of the associated personality defects of blonds "dizzy, dingbats, airheads." Redheads complained about hot-tempered attributes attached to their hair color. A girl who was teased about her curly hair wrote:

> *Everyone in the restroom began to laugh. I ran inside one of the stalls feeling ashamed of the way I looked. Tears ran down my cheeks. "Why was I not born with straight hair like my sister?" I asked God. I thought that if I looked White, I would not have any problems. (Castro, 3/21/00)*

Bathrooms were sometimes places of assault and sometimes places of refuge. In order to "blend in" and feel safe, female students went to great lengths, from taking bleach baths to consciously seeking the right genetic constitution of a future mate in order to avoid public judgment of these perceived physical deficits.

Beauty and the East

Department store dolls: golden hair Cinderella, ivory-skinned Snow White, large breasted, slim Barbie—are you my role models? When I turn you over, you are stamped, "made in China." Which one of us was made in china? How is it that you are the norm for beauty and the 3 billion people in the country of which you were assembled are not? Where are the Asian-faced dolls? And when someone decides to produce them, will the doll features look Asian or will they merely put a Chinese dress on a Western-featured Barbie? How many voluptuous, full-bodied, Asian women do I know?

I remember, as a young girl, going to a predominantly white school thinking my hair was as conspicuous as black tea. I watched my Chinese mother marry a white man and lighten her hair each year until it was almost blonde. When my mother gave me a home permanent, it fried my silky black hair into frizzy straw. Instead of feeling traumatized, I was euphoric and proceeded to parade my brown hair in front of all my friends. I no longer looked like a China doll, I was Westernized.

Other Asians, often elders, have scorned what we had done to our heads. Our light-colored hair has been perceived as disrespectful to our Asian roots. It communicated that we were ashamed of our origin. Recently, a newspaper article described how a Japanese grandfather in Japan swiped the head of a teenager with blonde hair in public, reprimanding him for not being proud of his black hair and for trying to look like a Westerner.

When my daughter was born, she had brown hair, a sign of weak genes I was told. My son, influenced by Dennis Rodman, has dyed his hair orange. Now at age 50, I hate it when my gray hair stands out like piano keys against my black hair. Baldness is the only answer. For Chinese monks, it is a sign of spirituality.

My height at 5'2" limits my ability to assert myself at public meetings because I tend to be visually out of range. I have learned how to project my voice to make my presence felt.

My cousins from China acknowledge how "healthy" I look. This is a nice way of saying I am their fat and therefore, wealthy American cousin. Fat is an indicator of social economic status, of eating well. When I visit Hong Kong, all the clothes and shoes are too small for me. I feel they need a "porky" section for American-born Chinese.

I wonder, "Is it incumbent for me to search for a society of large-sized people so my particular abnormality seems trivial in comparison? "When will social conditions evolve when I will be able to traverse between large-and small-sized people and not be judged to be "more or less than?" Do we augment our bodies to fulfill society's prescription on beauty or should society expand its acceptance of difference? How can we, in good social conscious, continue to see individuals victimized for their physical differences?

Eyes, from an Asian American woman's perspective, means familiarity with cosmetics and cosmetic surgery. Expensive eyelid operations have helped these women acquire rounder, Western eyes. I am told that the pain of the operation is less than the pain of being called "slant eyes." If beauty is within the eyes of the beholder, why do we apply corrective measures to those with physical variations but do nothing to correct the vision of the tormentors?

Coping

Students who have suffered otherness as the result of physical attributes write that their low self-esteem has persisted over the years, even though their physical attributes have changed. Late-blooming boys told how their low self-esteem had endured even though their height had changed. The crippling experiences of feeling vulnerable and socially inferior still prompts now-adults to avoid photographs or activities that reveal their physical variations. Physical education activities were among the scarred memories of students who wrote about weight, breasts or debilitating physical capacity due to illness. 'Oh no!' could be heard every time a fly ball came my way" (Keating, 2/11/97). They recalled their feelings of inadequacy from being the target of mockery in locker rooms and the humiliation suffered from being the last person picked for teams, recognizing that the order of teams was also their fate in the order of life.

A few students felt they were culturally disadvantaged to remedy a situation. "The boys teased and call me a man for having a mustache. While the girls laughed and gave me disgusting looks. What could I do since my parents were strongly opposed to the idea of shaving and waxing? It was not in our culture to do such thing" (Figueroa, 3/22/2000).

Some students admitted that these experiences were not equivalent to racism but nonetheless they were tormenting and painful. "I don't pretend for a minute to compare this, to being the only person of one race in a classroom, but I think it helped me see what it means to be set apart all by myself in a negative category. I had been miserable for years. I can understand the pain of ridicule" (Keating, 2/11/97).

Unable to convince others in their childhood that our human worth was more than a cancerous face or large breasts, we take a stand of advocacy now, for ourselves and others like us, to bring attention to the many forms of dehumanization. We challenge the forces that sustain domination and demonize differences. As prospective teachers, we hope that these stories will prompt more caring and ethical treatment of all children in our nation's schools.

Full Sized
Haley

I am a larger sized woman. Larger sized is the term that I prefer to use over the terms overweight or fat. For the politically correct, I am horizontally challenged. I eat when I am fearful, sad, or angry. I have tried numerous diets and have consulted many professionals about my problems with eating. Just sharing about food makes me uncomfortable, but I have much information to share on the subject. I need to share a small part of my pain and my joy in my narrative.

I will begin with the pain. Do you know what it is like to feel the sting of someone's words long after the words have been expressed? I feel the sting when I think about this one episode. A couple of high school students a few years ago called me a whale. Tears still flood my eyes at some moments when I think of this occurrence. Some men and women might think who cares about a couple of insensitive words mumbled by high school students. I care. I repeat. NAMES HURT. This was the first time I was called a whale.

It seems so obvious to me. I am a person. I may look like a creature to those individuals who call me a whale, but I am a person with feelings and thoughts. I have a rich, full life and have plenty to share when given the opportunity. I recollect being called names because of my birthmark, because I wear eyeglasses, because I had a woman confidante, because I am single, as well as other circumstances.

I do not fit comfortably in the turnstiles at the supermarkets or drugstores. Sometimes, I do not fit in desks at school, bathrooms everywhere, or movie theater seats. I cannot shop at regular mall shops. What do you do when you are larger than extra large?

Last summer, I searched throughout my favorite store for the Women's World, which is a polite name for the department that carries sizes 14–24. When I inquired about the department, I learned that the store discontinued the whole department. What do you do when a whole department that carries your size disappears? Note to store managers: Large women are worthy of departments in your stores. We have credit cards, too.

My food is judged by people at grocery stores, from the people waiting in line to grocery checkers and baggers. My food is judged by servers at restaurants. My food is judged much more harshly than my smaller sized friends. I am not imagining any of these episodes. I am so tired of the media telling me what I should look like. I already "shoulda" all over myself and I do not need magazines, papers, commercials and the like to tell me how I should be.

I started to feel *very alone*. My friends would lend a helpful ear but I did not feel like any of them truly heard what I was saying. I have a problem that stems beyond food. I need support. I do not want to butt heads with the next person who calls me a name because of my weight. I was really feeling on edge. I needed to be around people who were going through the same issues. I joined a weight support group.

This is my joy. I found a home. At first, I attended meetings. Taking the first step of walking through the doors was the hardest part. In their stories, I heard my story. The acts that used to make me feel ashamed at times now made me part of the group. I laughed at myself more often. I started to attend group social events, like dances and karaoke nights. No longer was I to be passed over at dances due to my size. I started to make outreach phone calls and to write about my feelings instead of eating over them.

I received some criticism when I first shared about my membership in this weight support group. Some people thought that I was isolating with people who were like me. Criticizers thought that I might never achieve my goal weight because I could stay the weight I was with the support group. I completely disagree. I am accepted the way I am with my weight support group. Being loved for who you are helps you to love yourself and to love your life. I have developed a better understanding on myself. My new approach to life is an improvement over spending my time worrying about what the scale reads and about dieting. Besides, being a member of this organization is only one facet of my life, although an important component.

I used to want to lose weight before becoming a teacher so that no one would criticize me. Then I realized that people will always find reasons to criticize if they want to find reasons. Presently I hope that when students see me, they realize that larger sized people are everywhere. I hope to break the stereotype of large people being lazy. See me teaching or chaperoning a dance and you know I am energetic. I hope that my understanding of anorexia, bulimia, compulsive overeating, and other addictions may even help me to help students one day.

On a final note, I truly believe that sharing our differences and similarities as people will ultimately make us strong, and not separate us. Writing my narrative was one of my stones in the arch. What is or what will be your stone to reduce social injustices?

I Am a Fat Girl
Dawn Griffing

I am a fat girl
No Barbie looks like me.

I am a fat girl.
I don't like to go to the waterslides with my friends because I don't want to be the only girl wearing a t-shirt over her swimsuit.

I am a fat girl.
My mom says she'll pay me one dollar for every time I go to junior aerobics class. Each "A" on my report card is also worth a dollar. But I have a feeling she's happier to pay the aerobics money.

I am a fat girl.
My sister can call me anything and I never cry. I can always think of a comeback. But when we're in the back of my grandma's car one day, on our way shopping, she calls me fat. I begin to sob uncontrollably. My mom gets her in trouble and she apologizes. I don't want to go shopping anymore.

I am a fat girl.
The summer after 5th grade, mom says we are going to count calories. One thousand a day. We will lose weight together. My sister too. For breakfast, we have a Pepsi. For lunch, we eat macaroni and tomato soup. For dinner, turkey sandwiches. Mom buys low-fat everything. Low-fat butter doesn't melt right. Low-fat cheese tastes gross.

I am a fat teenager.
They have to order a new cheerleading uniform for me because there were no fat girls on last year's squad. I am always on the bottom of the pyramids. I can't do the splits like most of the other girls.

I am a fat teenager.
I can barely fit into the clothes at Wet Seal. I want to buy a baby-doll dress there, the bright purple one with big flowers on it. The woman in the store says that I should buy the white one with little flowers. It's more slimming. "Big prints aren't flattering on big girls," she says.

I am a fat teenager.
I am applying to get my driver's license. My dad comes into my room to look at my forms. He sees what I put for my weight, 135. He says, don't you know its perjury to lie on DMV forms? Ha, ha, ha. He shuts the door as he leaves. I flip him off behind his back. He's fat too.

I am a fat teenager.
I never pass the physical fitness test. We have to run the mile on my birthday. It takes me 13 minutes and 51 seconds. I am gasping and out of breathe. I don't want to go out for pizza with my friends afterward to celebrate my birthday.

I am a fat woman.
The summer before college, I do step aerobics every day, for three months.
I am determined not to be fat in college. But the scale still says 191 at the end
of the summer.

I am a fat woman.
I got to college. I think about joining ROTC. The army officer is so
impressed by my test scores. He gives me a helpful hint before I leave the
office: "You should try to lose some weight before you join the Corps. I
don't mean to embarrass you; my wife is overweight too. I only mean to give
you a little advice and tell you that things will be easier for you in basic
training, if you drop a few pounds before you get there." I decide I don't
want to join after all

I am a fat woman.
I go to a baseball game at Edison Field. In the parking lot afterwards, there
is a traffic jam. A man gets out of his car directing traffic. He doesn't let our
line go for almost ten minutes. When I honk at him, he calls me a fat bitch.
I flip him off, tell him to go fuck himself. I go home and cry. I promise
myself that tomorrow I start my diet again.

I am a fat woman.
I watch the infomercials at 1:00 a.m. I buy the Total Gym, Body Flex, Taebo.
I try Metabolife, Slim Fast. I read diet books. The diet industry has me to
thank for at least a couple of thousand dollars of profits.

I am a fat woman.
My college roommate asks me to be a bridesmaid in her wedding. She buys
the dresses without having us try them on. Mine is a size 14. It's too small.
All the other girls are dancers. They wear size 4. I have to fit into my dress
by the end of the summer.

One day, I'm not fat anymore.

I buy my first size 12 black Capri pants, my first size 10 shorts, my first size
8 suit and my first size 6 red mini skirt. My coworkers tell me how skinny I
look. My best friend, who has gotten fat, tells me I'm withering away; I better get some meat on my bones. I can run 5 miles without stopping now.
Less than 10 minutes per mile. I think that all of my problems are solved.
Everything will be easier now that I'm skinny.

But I'm not skinny.
When I look in the mirror, I see a fat girl.
She will always be a part of me.
I am a fat girl.

No, I Don't Want to Be Santa Claus
Marcus

Dear Chris,

Thank you for your letter. I'm sorry that I haven not written for a while. I am still teaching a class for the severely disabled at Granada Middle School. There are five children with severe physical disabilities, one student who is autistic and blind, a new student who has severe behavioral tantrums and several others who require and deserve undivided attention.

With the passing of summer and the dawning of fall, I've begun to hear a whisper in the air, a faint smell of the impending holidays. I'm always drawn back to earlier times when the approaching holidays made me tremble with anxiety and trepidation. For me the holidays always meant one thing. Without fail it would mean that I would be asked to be Santa Claus in the school play. You laugh, I suppose it must seem funny and even trite to someone like you who has never known the misery of being obese. But for me it would mean that Mrs. S., our vocal music teacher, would soon be approaching to ask that dreaded question, "Would you like to be our Santa Claus in the school play again this year?" And just what do you say to a question like that? "No, Mrs. S. I would not like to be Santa Claus again for the eighth consecutive year! No Mrs. S. I do not like to be recognized, on an annual basis, as the fattest person in our school!" For I was always quite certain that the attribute about myself that she saw as the most characteristic of the "jolly old man" was best reflected in the line from the play that said, ". . . and it shook when he laughed like a bow full of jelly." Oh I guess it's pretty funny when I look back, but I'm sure that no one ever knew how terribly that small act hurt me, or how devastated and humiliated I always felt when someone inevitably would say, "And he doesn't even need a pillow."

My weight has always been a cross that I've had to bear. I can remember in physical education classes always being the last one to be picked. Always standing there for what seemed like hours, as every other student in our class was "chosen" to be one of the gang. At the end there I was, standing alone, hurting inside, knowing that I would now be forced on the team that had the last pick. Often there would be grumbling, "*Oh, do we have him on our team?*" And then of course came those damned ropes. Yes, I would always be forced to acknowledge to everyone present that I could not get off the ground. It always seemed to me that Mr. R. took a perverse delight in calling me to take my turn. I always stood in the background, wishing that I could fade into nothingness, but I was always called upon to face my own weaknesses. And last, but certainly not least, were the showers. What an exciting time that was. I only wish that they could have timed me then, as this certainly would have been my personal best running time. If you were first in the shower and first back to your locker, you were likely to be the least noticed. This of course didn't come without its own perils, for if you were too hurried you may slip and fall on the wet floors, and there you would be, lying on the floor, nude, fat, and humiliated.

I was never athletically inclined, though I was always a good swimmer. How unfortunate it was that swimming also meant that you had to disrobe, and wear what seemed to me to be nothing more than a pair of underwear. And did someone actually work at making fabric that clings to your body when wet? This reminds me of a time when I was at swimming lessons at the municipal pool. I had just jumped off the diving board, and I was feeling pretty good about my latest conquest when a boy shouted from the crowd, "Hey fatso, your blubbers falling off." There were snickers and jeers, and I was vaguely aware that everyone was whispering to each other. It was all I could to walk (for what seemed to be miles) back to the shower room, where I sat alone, hurting inside. That was my last swimming lesson at the municipal pool.

You know Chris, this weight thing has continued to be a source of humiliation into my adult life as well. Do you remember when I was working as the Director of Education at The Hope School? I had enjoyed that position very much, and poured blood, sweat, and tears into being the best administrator that I could be. And then came the unexpected with the resignation of the Executive Director. Perhaps I would have a chance at a promotion, after all, wasn't I qualified for that position? I was so excited at the prospect of being considered for this promotion, that I hadn't even entertained the thought that I might not even get an interview. I was devastated that my candidacy had been rejected. For weeks, and months I turmoiled over what I had done, or not done, to be left in the ranks of the "rejected." It was several months later that a professional colleague, and personal confidant, explained to me that I hadn't been considered because of my appearance. That's right Chris, I was deemed undesirable to the Board of Directors because I didn't fit what they perceived to be the professional image they were looking for. They wanted someone with whom they would be comfortable being seen with, in their group which was touted to be politically and socially elite. I suppose I could have remained bitter about this but what good would that do?

Here I am, at the age of 44 and I still find myself the victim of a society that caters to the average-sized citizen, the normal size, and the accepted size. Well Chris, as you of all people know, I have never been "normal" or "average." And at this stage of the game, I think it's safe to say that there is little hope that this will ever change. When you think about it, society (for the most part) simply doesn't like to acknowledge that there are fat people in the world. When I go into most restaurants, and am seated at a booth, I will often find that I do not fit in the space provided. This is always embarrassing; as I am always certain that everyone has stopped gorging themselves and have stopped talking long enough to gaze at my misfortune.

Clothing is another matter altogether. First you will not find large clothing in most department stores. This results in wearing clothing that is often an "off brand." A large person must instead shop at a specialty store. Picture this, you decide that you need to purchase some new clothing; you know that you will not find what you need at department store. You go to a "Big and Tall" store. Now you will undoubtedly find that the sign advertising the store is disproportionately large as the customer to whom they cater. The signs might just as well say, "Fat Clothes for Fat People." For those of us who decide that we are just not in the mood to go shopping at a store that so blatantly advertises to the "other people," we turn instead to a catalogue specializing in large clothing. Now those who have never looked through a large person's catalogue will no doubt be unaware of the advertising schemes that have been developed by the marketing experts, namely the complete absence of pictures of any person who is large. Shocking, but nonetheless true. Catalogues for large men will invariably picture men who are tall, and of average to above average physique. You will not find a fat man pictured anywhere. When in actuality the clear majority of the clothing being advertised is designed for obese and extremely obese persons. I'm certain that the merchandizing premise at play here is, "You may be fat, but see how good you could look if you purchased our clothing."

My most recent encounter of the socially acceptable practice of choosing to ignore the fact that there are people in this world who are "above average" in size was observed recently on my university campus. Upon arrival to my first of two classes that I am taking I quickly realized that the student desks in the room were not large *enough to accommodate me.* Isn't that truly absurd. Now I can perhaps understand that desks in lower grades may be smaller in size, but I think that I should have been able to expect to find adult-sized accommodations at an institution of higher learning. Especially when you consider the fact that each class costs nearly $1,000. You would think that the university could at least buy adult-sized chairs. What I find myself doing, on the night when I have class in a room full of undersized desks, is arriving as early as possible so that I can assure that I can get a seat in the back of the room, in the corner, so that it is less noticeable that I am painfully wedged into the seat.

Well Chris, I suddenly realize that I have been rattling on about my own personal woes. Perhaps my life isn't as burdened as I have made it out to be. When I reflect back on the misfortunes of the students I teach, and I remember the crosses that they have to bear, I realized that I really haven't had it so bad.

I hope that everything is well with you.

Sincerely,

Marcus

PS. I have heard about a new wonder drug and diet as the Phen/Phen plan. Should I give it a try? What do you think?

Through These Eyes of Mine
Katherine Weber

Through these eyes of mine.
I have witnessed ignorance.
"Are you bulimic?"
"No!"
"Are you doing speed?"
"No!"
"Are you eating?"
I walk away before my fist
Has a chance to reach her face.
These were routine comments.
Skinny is an ugly word to me.
I don't want to be skinny.
These people are my friends?
No, they're not.
My friends know I would not subject
My body to these things.
I want people to stop telling me to eat more.
I do eat, I do eat a lot.
Do not put me down to make yourself feel better.
I don't think they knew they were insulting me,
That is until I told them.
Words hurt.
They all have the potential to cause pain.
It is up to the user to use them wisely.
Once you say them,
You cannot take them back.
Remember that point.
To all the word users,
The human race,
Think before you speak.
I live encompassed by ignorance
Every day of my life.

Geek
John Keating

I was a geek. I don't think I was born a geek. I think it was something that took awhile to perfect. Probably more nurture than nature, by the time I was in first grade I had a real problem. How did I know I was a geek? Well, I think that is part of the problem. However successful I was beginning to be, academically speaking, socially I was completely inept. You see, I didn't just look like a geek, I dressed like one, and I had my hair cut like one. I was the whole package.

I can write about this rather jokingly now because decades later I'm pretty sure I'm over the dreaded disease, but occasionally in awkward situations maybe I'm not so sure. I think it all came to a head with those glasses. If you weren't around in the Sixties, you really don't know what I'm talking about. Sure John Lennon made "Granny Glasses" cool in the early Seventies and since then designer eyewear and contacts have become all the rage. But I'm talking Buddy Holly here. He had been dead since before I was born. I think that's why my parents got such a good deal on his old glasses. Of course that piece of tape that usually held them together didn't help either. Those glasses were the focal point of my misery.

From first grade, the year I got my glasses, to the summer before fifth grade, I wore those damned glasses everyday. Of course no one else in my classes wore glasses, except one girl. "Four eyes" seems like such an innocuous and unimaginative phrase now, but for some reason it got to me. Maybe because there was no one around to share it with. I don't pretend for a minute to compare this to being the only person of one race in a classroom but I think it helped me to see what it means to be set apart all by myself in a negative category.

All by themselves, glasses would not have made me the complete geek I was. Clothing was another important factor. It was not until I met my wife many years later, that I learned the most basic rules of matching clothes. You see my mom wasn't really big on fashion, and I'm not sure she knew the rules to teach. Because there were six kids in the family, not a lot of money went into outfitting each us. I remember getting a lot of hand-me-downs from people I didn't even know. Usually the secondhand clothes were better than the ones bought for me. Today, in an era of thrift shop cool, I would have been a trendsetter.

The worst disaster I remember was trying out for football in short pants with black socks with worn out elastic All the other kids had the white tube socks that went all the way to the knees, and I caught a lot of attention for it. As a matter of fact, I think it might have played a small part in why I didn't make the team. Appearances do matter, even with small boys.

I Think About My Breasts Almost Every Day
Charise Harris

"You can see right through those T-shirts you wear," she says.
Who is she? She is my mother.
"You need to start wearing a bra," she says.
This is my mother again.

But Mom, none of the other girls wear bras, I say.
Who am I? I am just a little girl.
But I had to wear a bra anyway.
Who am I? I am the large-breasted nine year old.

"Let's go jump on the trampoline," she says.
Who is she? She's my little sister.
"Okay," I say.
Who am I? I am an eleven year old who wants to have fun.
But soon, I stop.
It's just not as much fun as it was the last time.
But what was different?
It was the same trampoline I loved last time.
The difference was me.

When we visited Grandma the last time, I was only eight.
I could run and jump then, but not now I found.
Now it wasn't any fun at all. So I stopped.
And I said goodbye to being free to move however I liked.
Free to run and jump with the comfort of a child.

"Go shopping with your mom,"
You need a bra that has more support,
So you don't bounce so much, she says
Who is She? She is my 7th grade PE teacher.
Who am I? I am a painfully shy eleven year old.
The one who went home crying to her mom.
Saying that she went bouncy, bouncy, bouncy all over the gym.
We had to buy a D cup with an underwire that night.
A D cup for an eleven year old.

"Come on" she says, "You can do one more."
One more push up, that is.
Who is she? She is my partner in PE for the physical fitness tests.
"You don't even have to go down very far to touch the ground," she says.
You're already half way there.
Who am I? I am a large-breasted high school student.

I am wearing a sweatshirt with the face of a Siamese cat on the front.
"Can I pet your kitty?" he says.
Who is he? He is the sixteen-year-old trumpet player, a friend.
"Do you have to put weights in the back of your shoes to keep from falling
    over?" he says.
Who am I? I am his friend

"Do you need scaffolding to hold those things up?" He says.
He chuckles and grins at his own joke.
Who is he? He's one of the most popular boys in the band.
Who am I? I am the large-breasted teenager who wishes a hole would
    swallow me up.

"That'll be $8.75," he says.
But he doesn't look at me.
Who is he? He is a checker at a store.
"Here's the change," he says.
"Have a nice day," he says.
But he still doesn't look at me, only at my chest.
Who am I? I am a large-breasted customer.

"Buy me! Buy me!" it screams from the rack.
What is it? It is a cute one-piece jumper.
"Not you," I say, "you'll never zip up the back."
I'm right.
What fits in the waist is three or four inches short from closing up top.
"Oh well, no one-pieces for me," I say, resigned.
So I go and look for two-piece clothes.
Ones where I can buy one size for the bottom and another for the top.
No button-up shirts for me either.
Not unless I want to safety pin the front closed every time I wear it.

"Buy me! Buy me!" it screams from the rack.
What is it? It's a beautiful, sleek swimsuit.
Not you," I say, "I have to find extra support models."
But there are only a few. And they are ugly.
And even the ugly ones don't have enough room up top.
So I don't buy anything, again.

"Buy me, Buy me!" it screams from the rack.
What is it? It is a lacy, sexy, forest green bra.
"Not you," I say, "I have to find the large-size rack."
So I find it, but nothing screams out to me.
They are all huge, shapeless, white blobs.
Hours and hundreds of depressing large-size bras later, I find one.
It doesn't come in colors.
It doesn't have pretty flowers or sexy lace.
It is boring, even ugly.
It is the only style in a triple D.
It fits.
It is mine.

I could cut them off or at least pare them down a few sizes.
These bumps that have taken over my front
And my life.
I got to doctors,
I stand naked in sterile rooms.
They take pictures and draw lines and circles on me
To show where everything will be AFTER,
AFTER they make me better.

"That'll be $5000" they say.
$5000 to feel beautiful.
$5000 to wear a button-down shirt without safety pins.
$5000 to be a normal size
$5000 to wear a bra that doesn't hurt.
$5000 to erase the deep grooves in my shoulders.
$5000 to have people look at my face first.
$5000 to see my toes without bending over.
$5000 to be able to run and jump in comfort.
It is not such a big price, it seems.

"No, no!" cries a little voice from the future.
"Don't do it" it pleads.
Who is it? It is my unborn baby.
The baby I will have someday.
"Can I breast feed AFTER?" I ask.
"We can't say," says one doctor.
"Probably not," says the other one.
"And you'll very likely lose sensation," says one.
"And there will be scaring," says the other.

"No!" says the baby who wants the best possible nutrition.
"Yes!" says the little girl who wants to run and jump again.
"No!" says the checkbook. "It'll take years to pay."
"Yes!" says the blouse with buttons all down the front.
"No!" says the risk of losing sensation.
"Yes!" says the stylish bathing suits and pretty bras.
"No!" says the scars.
Yes, no, yes, no, yes ...

Will I do it
I don't know.
What am I?
I am still a large-breasted woman who just wants to be normal.

My Body: A Glass House
Elizabeth Gullotta

I live in a glass house
It is made up of glass and mirrors
It has been under attack for many years
Yet it still stands
The house is in constant state of disrepair
Nothing is in perfect condition.

I live in a glass house
For all to see and pass judgment
Like them, I throw stones at the house I live in
Unlike them I feel the pain it causes
Everyone is in judgment of me

I live in a glass house
It is who I am
Strong, weak,
Damaged, beautiful

She Stands Out
Stacy Wohlers

I'm seventeen, the youngest of six. I have a close group of friends, I am a great student, I am very active, and have a loving family. I have long brown hair, brown eyes, and am very tall. In fact, I am one of the tallest girls in the school. I have sworn to myself and others that I am proud of it, at least, I think I am. Yes, it makes me different, and yes, I stand out. But what's wrong with that, right?

Let's see, I have to stand in the back for all of my dance performances because teachers say, "You're too tall to be in the front." In cheerleading, I have always been the base of the stunts because I am "too big" to be a flyer. I was given the role of G.I. Joe in the school play because I could play the boy role "better" being that I am "so tall."

It is very rare for me to find pants that are long enough to cover my legs, or shirts long enough to cover my waist and arms. Yes, I am too embarrassed to wear high-heel shoes for fear that it will make me so tall, I will get even more reactions from people than I already do. Yes, I am taller than most of all the boys, and yes they make sure to let me know it. And nothing against basketball, I love to watch the sport, but I sure do get tired of people assuming I play basketball or telling me I should, because I am, "so tall!" I do not play basketball. I dance. Just because I am tall does not mean that basketball or volleyball are my main activities.

Yes, it does hurt when people let their mouths drop open and gasp, "You are sooooo tall!" or "You are sooooo big!" Don't they know how awkward I feel when they say it like I'm some abnormal being? For some reason, it's okay to say it like that. On the other hand, saying, "You are sooooo fat!" or even "You are sooooo short" isn't considered appropriate. My mom tells me to say these things back to people and see how they like it.

Carrot Top
Heather Johnson

"Carrot top, Carrot top!" Why does she keep calling me that? If she had half a brain, she would know that the top of a carrot is green, and I do not have green hair. When I was younger, I hated having red hair! I felt like an outcast; I was different and definitely a minority. I was called many cruel names: "Carrot top, Strawberry Shortcake, Annie, Pipi Longstockings, Red, crazy redhead, freckle face, and when I wore green, I was called a 'Christmas tree!'"

Literature portrays red-haired women and men differently. The women tend to be sexy and exotic and the men quite the contrary. The men are perceived as folk-like or farm boys. There is a sense of innocence about red-haired men.

The color red has many meanings and connotations. If one dreams about the color red, it means there will be change in one's life and unfaithfulness. In the dictionary of Symbolism, red hair is often considered "diabolical." Evil is sometimes represented by the color red. Blood, roses, and emergency are labeled red. It is the color that maddens the bull and at the same time, the color for all lovers on Valentine's Day. Tom Robbins wrote a book about the problems of redheads called, *Still Life with the Woodpecker*. In it, he described that redheads tend to be either funny or dangerous. He listed the most famous redheads and their occupations: Lucille Ball (comedian), Thomas Jefferson (revolutionary), Mark Twain (humorist), Woody Allen (actor), General Custer (general), and Van Gough (artist).

There were many afternoons that I came home from school crying. Junior high was the worst, the kids are mean to each other. I tried everything to turn my hair blonde and to get rid of my freckles. Our house has a lemon tree in the backyard. I used to scrub my face with lemons to make my freckles disappear, but it was fruitless. Then I heard if one uses lemons on their hair, it will lighten. So I had to try this, however, I think I got more lemon juice in my eyes than on my hair.

My best friend and I found out that if you put beer in your hair, combined with laying out in the sun, your hair would turn blonde. The next time we saw her dad drinking a beer, we asked if we could use it for an experiment. She poured beer over my head and we laid out in the sun for the rest of the afternoon. When I came home, all I had was tangled hair that reeked of beer. I guess I was stuck with my red hair.

At one point in my life I thought I was adopted. Both my parents have dark brown hair and I have red hair, therefore, they couldn't be my parents. I always told myself that I would marry a man with brown hair when I was older. My children would genetically have a greater chance of having his brown hair rather than my red hair. I would not want my child to go through what I went through. I believe that when children are young they have a need to conform, to be just like everyone else. Since I was not like everyone else, I had a huge complex. I felt like I always stood out. The perception of myself was that I was different.

Cancer
Amy E. Anderson

My mother tells me how she used to set her alarm clock to wake up before I did so that she could run into my room and clean the hair off of the pillow. I guess at night I lost most of my hair from moving around so much. She would run into my room and I would usually be awake, holding the bits of red curls in my hand, and crying. "I don't understand why I am so sick," I complained. "I thought that this medicine was supposed to make me better." My mother tried to explain, again, what it means to have cancer and why the chemotherapy made me nauseous.

I remember having to carry little dishes around with me so that when I got sick, I had something to vomit into. They were light blue like the sky, and they were shaped like a peanut. I remember thinking that they were very strange.

I received a lot of attention when I was sick. People came to visit me all of the time and everybody brought me gifts. My older brother and sister hated that everyone was so concerned about me. My grandmother came to visit and instead of taking my brother and sister to the beach, they had to come to the hospital to see how I was doing. My parents stayed in the hospital with me, sleeping on pull-out cots in my room. That was fun, kind of like my own little sleepover.

After they took out my kidney that was engulfed in the tumor, I returned home to a normal life, I guess. I lost all of my hair. I was afraid that people would mistake me for a boy so I begged my mother to put me in a dress. I must have been moody because my brother and sister did not like to play with me. In fact, if you have ever seen the movie, *Gremlins*, then you probably remember the mean one, Stripe. My sister used to love to call me "purple stripe" and make me cry. She said that I was mean like Stripe in the movie, and I did have a purple scar down the front of my body. I hated when she called me that.

My hair grew back and unless I show you my scar, you cannot tell by looking at me that I am a cancer survivor. I played sports, even though my mother stood on the sidelines and held her breath. Soccer, softball, gymnastics, dance lessons, Brownies, and Girl Scouts, I did all of the typical things that girls do when growing up, except I spent more time in the hospital.

I attended a summer camp for children who have or who used to have cancer. It was called Camp Reach for the Sky. On the first day of camp when the other campers arrived, the counselor called on his walky-talky back to their camp and said, "Hey, the cancer kids are here." Cancer kids? Is that what they call us? Is that what everyone calls me? Do they think we are contagious? I'll never forget the way all of our shoulders sagged, just a little, at that comment.

I had a good friend growing up named Tressa. We rode the bus together. Not really together, I should say that we both rode the same bus at the same time. One day as we walked home from the bus stop, Tressa and her friends were behind me calling me "cancer kid" and making fun of me for only having one kidney. They laughed and joked the whole way home. I never turned around and I never cried. I kept on walking with my back as rigid as an iron rod. When the girls all went into Tressa's house, I ran as fast as I could, shaking with convulsions because I cried so hard. I was devastated because the only way that those girls knew anything about me was if Tressa had told them. She was my best friend.

I think that it is strange how someone else can make you feel so small and insignificant. I was no different from any of those girls but they made me feel as though I was less. I didn't like feeling that way and I never want to be the cause of someone else feeling that way.

Grey Eyes
Elizabeth Randal

I have grey eyes like my daddy. And my baby brother has grey eyes, too. My right eye doesn't work though. I was born that way. The doctor and my parents make me wear a patch over the eye that does work and they got me thick glasses to see with they eye that doesn't work, but now I can't see. The teachers at school think I'm stupid, but I just need extra help. I don't want to wear the eye patch.

I told Mommy that I didn't want to be in the Early Bird group anymore. She asked why and I told her because I didn't want to be stupid anymore. I want to be a Late Bird because they're smart.

Mrs. Porter, my new teacher at the Catholic School, helps me. She told the other kids not to make fun of me because it's not my fault I have to wear the eye patch. I have trouble seeing a lot, but I can usually get my work done in the same time as the other kids. If I don't finish in time, then I get to finish my work later.

When we were making bar graphs in class today, we had to raise our hand when Sister Mary called out our eye color. She didn't ask for grey and I had to put myself under blue. I'm offended because my eyes aren't blue. They're grey. Probably no one can see my grey eyes because of the stupid patch and the thick glasses.

People tell me they don't believe that I have a lazy eye because it doesn't wander all over the place, because it looks like a normal eye. I just stare back at them in one-eyed disbelief. They think that amblyopia only looks one way. They have no idea what I had to suffer through as a child.

I don't like when people I am trying to talk to are on my right side because I can't see them. I try to train everybody to walk on my left so that I don't run into things because I am trying to see their face and walk at the same time.

I am told that I am a stuck up, arrogant b----. In my shock all I can say Is, "What?" I am told that I am too high and mighty to acknowledge people when I walk past them or they walk past me. I try to explain that I really don't see them. But I don't think they believe me.

I often find that when I tell someone that I am not fully sighted, they don't seem to believe me, they sort of gloss over it, or it doesn't register. I don't know. I do know from experience I look and function too "normal" for people to readily accept this, even people close to me. Perhaps I should go back to using the incorrect term, telling them that I am legally blind in one eye. Of course, they didn't always believe that one either.

It is difficult for me to spend a lot of time at the computer, the computer that dominates our lives and so many jobs. My eye becomes strained, and sometimes I think my other eye becomes tired out of sympathy. I began to wear glasses in order to protect my eye, but now I have a correction for reading. And I still have to sit at the front of the class in order to see the board and the overhead. Sometimes I wonder if my eye will hold up for as long as I need it, but then I can't fault it because it's taken me pretty far and allowed me to see some pretty amazing things, like the view from the top of the Eiffel Tower at sunset and the Old Jewish Cemetery in Prague.

As a child, my mother was my greatest advocate. In addition to limited vision, I had other health problems. My public school teachers were so focused on my limited special needs that they assumed I was stupid. Mrs. Scott told my mother that I would always be an average student and would never achieve more—and that my parents should never expect more because I was incapable of it. And all I really needed was a little more help and a little more time.

My grey eyes and I want to go back to the teachers that said I was dumb, the teachers that put me in the low reading groups, and show them my degree in English literature from the university. I want to show them that I graduated with honors in English and I want to show them the pay stubs that I received as a writer. I want to tell them that I'm not dumb, but that occasionally I still need extra time and extra help to read or find some things.

What advice would I offer to my fellow aspiring teachers? People with impaired vision are not necessarily mentally impaired, and sometimes, we just need a little extra time or help, not to be thrown in to special education or tracked into a lower group where we don't really receive any special assistance. People with impaired vision do not always walk with canes or use Seeing Eye dogs. A person with impaired vision can look and function, just like me.

Banana Nose
Todd Nelson

I wonder what love would be if every person that you met had the same face and body? Who would you fall in love with or what distinct features would you like the most? Although, variety of appearance does create "otherness," it is an important factor of love. If we were all the same, love would never be.

One of the hardest parts of my body to grown up with was my nose and it seemed that my nose was the only thing growing. I was so conscious of my nose in my adolescent years that I never felt comfortable when someone was looking at my profile. Perhaps this consciousness developed over a period of time with quip comments like, "Oh, that one over there with the big nose" or, "Is that a banana you're eating or is that your nose?" Regardless of the humor directed at me, this did have an impact on my feelings about my nose. I always wanted to remove it from my face, but no nose would look twice as strange. I would put the side of my face to a mirror, and, with my finger, draw the outline of my face. I would peel my face off the mirror and look at the profile I had traced and think, "Why me? No one else in my family has a nose like this," but then no one else in my family has broken their nose twice.

Perhaps the most defeating experience came at a time when I was a senior in high school. It was Sunday evening and our family with some friends was playing a game called "Pictionary" and the word that came up was "teenager." Being the only teenager in the room, my brother decided to use me in connection with the word, "teenager." The sand-filled timer was turned over and my brother drew a big, huge nose on a large piece of paper.

We began to say things like, "nose, running nose, smell. . . ." No one could understand what my brother was trying to communicate with his picture. As the last grain of sand filtered to the bottom of the timer, my brother blurted, "Don't ya get it? Nose, Todd, teenager!" The group chuckled over the creativity and humor of my brother, but my blood began to boil. I was so tempted to give my brother the same nose he had drawn of the paper. Eventually, through the nurturing of my mother and the growth of my face, I have come to appreciate my nose. In fact, it is my nose that won the heart of my wife. She thinks it adds character to my face.

Sticks and Stones May Break My Bones But Words Can Scar Forever
Kristan Kirkwood

All my life I've looked at myself through the eyes of strangers. I try not to judge myself by what others think and see, but this has been a difficult task. When I was fourteen days old, I developed a hemangloma between my eyes. A hemangloma is a clump of blood vessels that have broken and clumped together on the surface of the skin forming a bump. Mine was between my eyebrows raised about a half inch from my skin. It was the diameter of a dime and a deep purplish-pink color. Being so young and unaware, I thought I was perfectly normal (which now I realize that I was), but to others, I was a strange looking little girl with a funny face to stare at.

"Bump nose!" "Three Eyes!" "Oh! Look at her face!" "What's that thing between her eyes?" "You're so ugly!" These are just a few of the words I remember. I never knew how to respond to people when they said things or stared at me. My parents always taught me that you are who you are because of what's inside your heart, not just what's on the outside. They told me that I was extra special because I had something different, both on the inside and out, that no one could take away. I would try to remember this when people would call me names, but sometimes it just hurt too much and all I do was walk and cry. Sometimes I would just burst into tears, which made them laugh even more.

Now that I'm older and look back, it really angers me that I let them get to me, but some emotions and feelings just can't be stopped, especially if they hurt. My family has done their share of sticking up for me and taught me to do the same for myself. I found this hard to do especially with older kids or adults. My mom told me about a time when I was just a few months old and we were on an airplane. We were ready to get off the plane and my mom was holding me when a little boy who had been sitting behind us very loudly asked his mom what that weird thing was on my face. My mom quickly turned to the boy and politely (through clenched teeth) said, "This is a hemangloma on her face and it is going to go away. What are you going to do about yours?"

It still amazes me how cruel and ignorant some people can be. I'm not saying that all people are like this because I know they are not. I had many true and wonderful friends that could have cared less if I had horns sprouting from my head. There was just a handful of people that chose to judge me by how I looked, but that handful sure seemed like thousands in my child-hood life. I know that children can be mean and nasty at times, but what still shocks me is that many of these mean and nasty kids grow up to be cruel and ignorant adults. I think that is so sad.

"It will go away as she gets older." "Give it time. It will fade with age." After countless promises and endless hopes, at the age of seven, my parents decided to consult a plastic surgeon for fear that it was not going to just "go away" and that I would eventually go cross-eyed. Being one out of the ten where it doesn't shrink and go away, but rather kept growing, the doctor and my parents decided that we should have them both removed. Having had two surgeries before, I wasn't really scared about that. What I was more worried about was that something that was part of me, something that made me unique and different from everyone else, was going to be taken away from me forever. On the other hand, I wouldn't be made fun of any more (hopefully) and I wouldn't be stared at because of that "bump" on my nose. Needless to say, I was really tired of being called names and being stared at. I may have only gone through it for six years of my life, but that is a long time to a child in a world where you are different from everybody else. So, needless to say, I was both happy and sad about having them removed.

I learned a long time ago never to judge a book by its cover, but rather open it up and see what's inside first. I have empathy for those who have something that classifies them as "different" from others. I've walked along that path before and know how it feels to be treated differently and I vowed a long time ago, never to make anyone feel the way that I felt then.

GENDER–3C

The absence of talent in a woman is a virtue.
— A Chinese proverb

Although it has been said the girl baby ponds in China have dried up, it's no secret that boy babies are still valued over girl babies in this patriarch cal soci-ety. My relatives used to joke that long ago girl babies were thrown away when they were born. The not-so-funny present-day reality is there are more boys than girls being raised within China's one child per family birth-control code. So where are the spirits of those girl babies? Are they better off than here on earth?

> *A little girl never questioned the commands of Mother and Father, unless prepared to receive painful consequences. She never addressed an older person by name . . . even in handing them something, she must use both hands to signify that she paid them undivided attention. Respect and*

order—these were the key words of life. It did not matter what were thoughts of a little girl; she did not voice them. (Wong, 1950, p. 2)

My feminist conscious is veiled by my cultural consciousness. I do not know feminism the way white feminists have written about it because my perspective is tightly interwoven with culture. It is hard to distinguish where the silk of feminism differs from the satin of culture. I am a third-generation Chinese-American woman who has listened obliquely to the stories of exploitation and discrimination of aunties and grandmothers. Unlike the Western tradition of storytelling with a moral, these stories were never relayed directly but are the result of a patchwork of eavesdropping opportunities by the younger females, who discretely listened and retained every morsel of folk history whenever the women gathered to cook, to eat, or to do needlework. It was here that you learned about picture brides and how they had no choice in the selection of their husbands. Parents selected marriage partners based on social standing and wealth. Every bride's sole concern was that they would be blessed with a charitable mother-in-law for it was she who inherited an indentured servant and it was she who would determine the bride's future happiness. I was lucky. My mother-in-law is a reincarnate of Kwan Yin, the goddess of mercy.

In the news: On Monday May 25, 1999, the Los Angeles Times reported that the Supreme Court ruled that schools can be held liable in cases where they are deliberately indifferent to sexual harassment. The National School Boards Association and the Education Department's Office are in support this ruling. School officials who turn a deaf ear to complaints of serious sexual harassment and violence are now vulnerable to damage claims against their district, cited a legal advisor (p. A1).

Students wondered why their genitalia warranted different treatment and different expectations. Some women passively agreed with Halprin (1995) that the clearest path to power was simply to be a man (p. 234). Other women openly resented "the arrogance of men to speak for all humanity and to attempt to ascertain from their limited basis anything universal about human being" (Walsh, 1989, p. 38). Through it all, both women and men used our classroom forum to rediscover their gendered voices or to repair themselves spiritually from wounded gender identities. They desperately needed this opportunity because those who have been tormented in our public schools tell us that no one ever listened to them (Simmons, 2002).

I am a Woman
Sheri Hannaford

I am a Woman,
I know what that means

I see how they stare, and think things unclean.
Everyday I'm reminded of what sits between my knees,
The size of my breasts, and just who to please.

Growing up with fairytales and ideas of womanhood, I truly believed I was lucky to be a girl. I thought it was fabulous that I would one day be beautiful like those princesses or my mom. I was taught to be polite and to never speak up, to be a lady. To be a lady you must always cross your legs, you must smile and smile even if your heart bleeds. You must always be thankful and sweet as can be. You can never be angry, or ugly, or mean. You don't ask directly; you never confront. You clean and you cook and you love everyone. As a woman you nurture, you're a mom to the world.

I am a Woman,
I know what that means
I see how they stare, and think things unclean.
Everyday I'm reminded of what sits between my knees,
The size of my breasts, and just who to please.

They told me stories of princess who came on white horses. A prince who would love me and marry me "till death do us part." I would be his world, just as he would be mine. All of my toys, everything, taught me exactly what I was to be. But as I got older, although still naïve, I started to see what men truly believe.

I am a Woman,
I know what that means
I see how they stare, and think things unclean.
Everyday I'm reminded of what sits between my knees,
The size of my breasts, and just who to please.

As I grew older I started to see how I was growing and just what that means. Boys started grabbing and groping. Still I try to hang on to the idea of some prince who will never come. It's interesting that I feel like I need a man to complete myself. Perhaps all those years of gender brainwashing had their effects. Sometimes I wonder if it matters at all that I am smart and kind and compassionate. I look at my life and I see how hard I tried to show to myself and to the world that I am more than what they have reduced me to. I worked my ass off in college to prove that I really had a brain that I had something more than what was between my legs. But no matter how hard I try to be something else, I'm reduced to a sex object and nothing more.

> I am a Woman,
> I know what that means
> I see how they stare, and think things unclean.
> Everyday I'm reminded of what sits between my knees,
> The size of my breasts, and just who to please.

I wish I were pretty, and perfect and more. I wish I never had to choose between the Madonna and whore. Maybe if I took the Italian out of my nose, or grew legs that were long, I wouldn't care about being reduced to an object anymore. Maybe I could become numb to the hollers and stares; the pinches; the whistles and just not care. Maybe my beauty would wash it all away, like a magic pill for forgetting the truth and what's real.

> I am a Woman,
> I know what that means
> I see how they stare, and think things unclean.
> Everyday I'm reminded of what sits between my knees,
> The size of my breasts, and just who to please.

Sometimes I wonder if there will ever be a man who can see us as equal and love me for all the great things I am. I wonder if the world will ever come to terms with the fact that women are as human and worthy as anyone else. They tell me I'm lucky to be born here and now. I know it is worse for women all over the world. I can't understand how it ever came to be this way. How things could be this ugly and cruel is beyond me.

I am reminded every time I step outside, each time I turn on the television, or look at a magazine that no matter how great I am. I am limited by one thing and one thing only, my gender. So am I lucky to be a woman? Am I lucky to be subjected everyday to hooting, howling and creepy stares? Am I lucky to see this and how it's not right?

Finding My Feminine Voice
Kathryn Henry

I was born the sixth of seven,
So my voice was seldom heard.
Above the din of constant talk
My meaning came out blurred.

At High School for only girls
A nun helped me to see
A woman's voice can be important
In her quest to succeed.

I was not like Helen Reddy
"I am woman hear me roar"
I was not like Billie Jean King
Trying to even the feminist score.

I had a small yet special voice
Which I had not learned to lift.
Till a female college professor
Gave me a priceless gift.

She praised my writing on Thoreau
With personal comments so strong.
This vote of confidence in me
Was what had been lacking for so long.

My voice came from a pen it seemed,
And so from that time on,
I learned to keep a journal
As if it were a friend of long.

I won't forget that little girl
Whose voice was seldom heard
Nor will I ever forget
Those lessons so hard-learned.

To have your voice heard
You needn't shout nor scream
You must always speak the truth,
And never forget your dream.

The Man Thing to Do
William Horan

I can never remember my grandfather giving my grandmother a kiss or saying he loved her in front of the children. It was as if he took his emotions and just put them all in a closet. It must have been the man thing to do.

My first experience with death and sadness came when my Grandfather died when I was about 8 years of age. A year or two later, my other grandfather died suddenly. My father and uncles showed no emotion . . . "don't cry, men don't cry." It was as if they took their emotions and just put them all in a closet. I was totally convinced now, it must have been the man thing to do.

My father and I spent a lot of time together. It is amazing how few words we exchange over the course of a day. It was exactly like the silent hours my grandfather and I spent on the porch swing. It was as if my father took his emotions and just put them all in a closest. It must have been the man thing to do.

The Vietnam conflict was at its peak and the draft was implemented. When my friends were wounded or killed, I treated it like they were "gone." I created my own closest and stuffed everything I had seen or done in it. It seemed like the man thing to do.

A few white males described the obstacles in constructing their male identities and their efforts to deviate from the norm. A student recalled, "One of the oddest things that set me apart from other boys was an extreme aversion to violence." Even at the risk of ostracism, he decided, "I would always stand my ground (of nonviolence) and continue to play by myself." For others, finding that middle ground upon which to stand was not as easy.

I'm a Man, Whatever That Is
David Crissinger

My father would grab me by the wrist and drag me to the living room to show me his latest wrestling moves. Other times he'd enjoy grinding my face into the carpet while twisting my arms back behind my head. He takes credit for making me a man, whatever that is.

I played tackle football in junior high. In high school I wrestled for a while; the "manliest" of sports. I didn't really like sports. I was a survivor, a chameleon. I guess I wanted to be a "man."

I really began to believe that women wanted men who were more macho, a little on the rude side. Encouraged by alcohol I made my case overly clear. I was pretty rude to her. I am a Chameleon I adapt but I just wanted to be sensitive, caring me.

I wanted to study literature; I was told that literature was a chick major. "You're not turning into some kind of faggot are you? Pretty Boy Faggot."

Being a male feminist, talking to other men is probably where I could do my most effective work towards creating positive social change. I will stand out and stand up. I'm red on a green carpet. I hope I have the strength to stay that way. I am a Chameleon. I know I'm a man, whatever it is.

Some students felt comfortable enough in our learning communities to authenticate their sexual orientation and to bring light to their closeted lives.

I Feel Like a Woman
Christine Hunt

I feel like a woman.

Was it because of the beer? Was it because of my skirt? Was it because he was almost twice as big as I was? Why did I have to go with him? I could have stayed with everyone. We were just going to get more beer from his room. I said, "No, Let's get back to the party." I tried to push him away. His hands hurt my wrists. Why was this happening? I said, "Stop." I said, "No." I tried to push him off me. I felt small. I felt voiceless. I felt nothing.

I feel like a woman.

I have great legs. Lots of people tell me so. I always wear a
short skirt when we go out. I get a lot of attention when I do.

Smile, honey. You're so cute when you smile.

It is amazing despite how hard you try to push a thought or experience into oblivion; it never really goes away. It stays there seemingly invisible but leaking out into your life bit by bit. I work out almost daily, to be stronger. I usually drink a little too much, to be braver. I hear stories of other women—I wonder what did they wear, what did they say? What does it mean when they say, "she was asking for it" or "she should have known?" I feel confused and push it away.

I feel like a woman . . .

Because I'm getting married! My mother is so happy!

Smile, honey.

I am exhausted but overjoyed. I hold this beautiful baby in my arms. His forehead scratched from the monitors. His eyes peering at me. His ears listening to my cooing words. My body feels completely foreign to me after the past 24 hours of labor and delivery. I felt so privileged as he grew in my belly, feeling his kicks, squirms and hiccups. But there are no words for my feelings now. He is my son. I am his mother.

I feel like a woman

I knew I would miscarry that day. I was alone all day except for talking with my O.B. on the phone. He reassured me. He promised to see me in the morning for a D&C. Twelve weeks along I was looking forward to the end of morning sickness, to a burst of energy and to feeling my baby grow. Cramping and bleeding. I am overcome with pain and dizziness. I am losing blood. I barricade myself in the bathroom. I scream for my husband who takes forever it seems to answer me. I lose consciousness. He tries to get me to the car. I pass out again. I awake to the sound of the siren of a fire truck. My hands and legs are numb. The paramedics can only get a pulse from my throat. They try to calm me because I don't understand why I can't move. They say it is the blood. They take me to the hospital and I go into surgery. My husband is with me as I wake up. He says, "Well, it is best. It wasn't a good time for us anyway." I feel dead inside.

Smile, honey. You are so cute when you smile.

I feel like a woman.

"Mom, I got the job! I am going to be the Executive Director of the YWCA of North Orange County"

"You're going to be the secretary?

"No, Mom. I will be the boss. I'll have a secretary!"

"Oh. Are you sure you can do that?"

Smile, honey.

Ten years later, I say the words. My counselor urges me gently and I feel like a dam that has overflowed. The water spilling over freely. Free is really how I feel. Fear had quieted my voice. Fear had consumed my body for years. I was done with fear. I feel dizzy, overwhelmed and now I can move forward. I was raped. And it was not my fault.

I feel like a woman.

Sitting in a room with almost 900 women, a small handful of men and lots of coffee cups, I feel the energy of strong spirits, powerful voices and many backgrounds. "Should men be allowed to be members of the YWCA?" is the question on the floor. The debate is heated. Passionately, we make our case that without men how can we truly move forward? How can an organization that prides itself on inclusion exclude half the population? If women cannot be empowered working with men, then are we ever truly empowered? Fear of change and the stories of the past are powerful advocates. "But won't they take over?" they say. "Where can women go to be leaders?" I can't believe successful and intelligent women are asking these questions. The vote is taken and fears win out. I realize the YWCA is not an organization I can fully support. I know I will leave within the year.

I feel like a woman.

I sit in my house alone. My boys are at their father's house for the first time. It is really quiet. I realize I will be divorced and a single mother. I feel like a statistic. I feel lonely and ashamed.

Smile, honey. You are so cute when you smile.

I feel like a woman.

When a man touches me for the first time and I am not afraid.

I feel like a woman.

Without these experiences I would not be who the woman I am today. I would not have worked with battered women and children. I would not have met the most amazing women and men who inspire me daily. I would not have grown to make choices I believe in and to love myself. I would not be here pursuing my dream. Although, recently I was told by a former colleague, "Teacher, huh? That's a good career for a woman."

I smile and have to say I agree.

To be Queer
Eddy Haskill

That year many things changed in my life . . .
I'm no longer married
I'm divorcing my wife.

That phone call with the ominous voice was right.
I had spent so many years
Living in absolute fright.
Since lifting the weight of the world
I feel so light.
I've gone back to school
Centered and focused.
Cause I'm no longer running
Or hiding from myself,

Or those phantom phone calls
In the night.
Sometimes what appears to be isn't!
Not all things are as they appear-sometimes.
To be queer,
Isn't a negative,
And can be a positive.

You asked, "Have you lived with prejudice . . ."
And I'd have to say "yes."
But mine came from within,
From a need to impress.

In my effort to run from my Father,
And all of his woes.
I almost became him,
Like him and all of his brothers.

I believe I am, who I am because of Biology.
No one made me this way.
I wasn't recruited.
I didn't choose this lifestyle,
Because who would choose this . . .
To be hated, instead of loved.
To be rejected, instead of accepted.

The religious RIGHT,
Thinks that I am WRONG.
The conservatives blame me,
And the liberals patronize me.
Rush Limbaugh scorns me,
And Bill Clinton lies to get my vote.

Now as I prepare to become a teacher.
Something I've been all of my life.
I worry about how my "news" will be accepted
Now that I have done what I've never done before . . .
Come out.

Blending In
Tiffany Voss

"Blending in" is not hard for me,
My difference is one you cannot see,

It's part of me, right under the skin,
Near the surface, yet deep within.

Although sometimes hidden, it's always there,
Frequently crying from hurt and despair,
Condemned by those lacking this part,
They fail to see what's in my heart.

"Blending in" is not hard for me,
My difference is one you cannot see,
It's a part of me, right under the skin,
Near the surface, yet deep within.

Been told many times I'm a huge disgrace,
Bringing shame upon the human race,
Hated by many who don't know me,
I don't understand, how can that be,

"Blending in" is not hard for me,
My difference is one you cannot see,
It's a part of me, right under the skin,
Near the surface, yet deep within.

I've hurt no one, and cast no blame,
Why is it you cant do the same?
Everyday a newfound slur,
Where is the remedy, where is the cure?

"Blending in" is not hard for me,
My difference is one you cannot see,
It's a part of me, right under the skin,
Near the surface, yet deep within.

It's part of my soul, not something I chose,
No different from having two eyes and a nose,
Yet still I am othered every day,
Simply because . . . I am gay.

Primary Document on Otherness
Ryan Ramirez

Although I've had various experiences with otherness in my life, the most vivid and intense experience was during my senior year of high school. Having no friends, I spent breaks, lunches, weekends, and vacations alone. I felt as if my isolation was a result of being gay; I felt as if I could not be open with my peers about my sexuality and I did not want to have friends under false pretenses.

I guess I should explain how I ended up friendless. I had a few good friends and one best friend when I lived in Virginia. My best friend moved away about half way through our sixth grade year, which was about the same time that I realized I was gay. After that, I became very emotionally and physically withdrawn. I became very aware of my body and how I moved. Most of my mental energy was consumed with a sudden awareness of difference and desperation to keep it secret.

After sixth grade was over, my family moved to the California Bay area. I had difficulty making friends that year; probably because I was so paranoid about being discovered. That was also the year when the merciless teasing began; the teasing that made me dread coming to school; the teasing that regularly produced suicidal fantasies. I made one friend, however; the pairing of Mike and I was a good one because we were both outcasts. We would bicker a lot—actually, I don't think we liked each other very much—but we would always make up because we knew that we didn't have anyone else.

Changes began to take shape during the summer of our senior year, when Mike tried out for the track team. We had a tradition calling each other on the night before the first day of school to arrange a place to meet the next day. This year, I didn't hear from him. When I ran into him at school, he was with a big group of people. For a week or two, I tried lingering around them, but I quickly got the impression that I wasn't part of the group. That's how senior year started.

During the first semester, I would spend lunch in the cafeteria drawing everything that I could see. In January, my grandma passed away and I spent one lunch period writing about her in my notebook. After that, I spent my lunches writing about everything that I could see. Here's a passage from Valentine's Day when I gave my secret crush a bag of Hershey Kisses—this is about as cheery as my journals ever got: "This morning was so funny. I know it's kinda silly, but I gave Tom a bag of Kisses. I went into Mrs. Beimford's room and asked her if she had Tom in her first period class. She said yes and I said, 'Okay. Can you keep a secret?' She said yes. I said, 'Like, a big secret?' She said yes, so I took out the Kisses. They had a label with his name on it. She said, 'How sweet,' or 'How cute,' or something like that. Then she got out her seating chart and told me where he sat and I put them on his desk. She said that she wouldn't tell him and I thanked her and left."

Here's a more common entry: "It's really cold in the shade today. If only this school was facing the other direction, I'd be in the sun. Lewis just went by. He didn't say anything, but he smiled and waved. Dan just acknowledged me. People always see me and say hi. Why don't they stop to talk or ask me if I want to go eat with them? They don't care. They think I like being alone. They don't want me hanging around them. They don't know how to approach me. Who knows? I don't think I'll ever get to have fun before I get old."

It's times like these when those old 6th-grade feelings come back to haunt me: Why me? Why can't I just be like everyone else? Why do I just sit here feeling sorry for myself? I wanted friends so badly that it hurt. I'm just some creepy guy with no friends.

I remember buying a ticket to grad night. Why did I do that? What was I thinking? I guess I was a glutton for punishment, but looking back, I know exactly why I decided to attend the All-Night Grad Party. I imagined, right down to the wire, that I would finally be noticed. I imagined that my senior year would end like the climax of some cheesy teen movie where the outcast kid finally gets recognized. As one may imagine, that didn't happen, and this time I couldn't wait to get home before I started sobbing.

The whole experience had an eventual happy ending, however. It was the most traumatic period of my life, but once my wounds had healed, I was emotionally very strong and quite independent. I had learned to be aware of my emotions and how to deal with them without ignoring them. Strangely enough, surviving high school without friends gave me a huge boost of confidence. I figured I was tough enough to deal with anything at that point. During my freshmen orientation at college, I met two girls and soon found myself, for the first time, as a member of a group.

Without a doubt, my senior year of high school influenced the person I am today. Whereas before I was afraid, doubtful, silent, and deliberately invisible, I am now confident, thoughtful, pensive, and observant. I hope to use this experience as a teacher to promote those feelings in my students, so hopefully they can skip over the situations that I had to deal with.

IMMIGRATION AND ETHNICITY-3D

I am separated from China by time, space, selective memory, and language. My father's birth certificate lists that he was born in China, not in any province or state, but merely from that vast continent known as China. His birthplace was so vague, they may as well have written, "Born on the Planet Earth."

He never talked about China, only about America and how great this country was. Although he and my mother were bilingual, they only spoke to me in English. Reverence for language maintenance was muted by the forces of assimilation and the domination of English for linguistic space. "Linguistic anxiety is a proxy for racial anxiety" (Matsuda, 1996, p. 90). Although my parents may have been oblivious to the social agenda and therefore let our primary language slip away, I've wondered why they didn't notice that it

*was becoming increasingly difficult for us to talk with PoPo (grandmother).
Rodriguez (cited in Ybarra, 2002) explained this phenomenon as walking "a
tightrope between the personal and the public, between the potentialities of
assimilation and the pitfalls of alienation" (p. E1).*

*The west coast port of entry, equivalent to Ellis Island, is Angel Island.
My mother-in-law was detained there in 1940 when she returned from
schooling in Hong Kong to her birthplace in Oakland, California. It seems
the immigration officials did not believe that she was a U.S. citizen. Although
she will not speak about it, Mai Zhouyi, a missionary from Canton and wife
of a Chinese merchant, captured the experience of inhuman treatment at
Angel Island in her testimony at a public gathering in Chinatown following
her release in 1903:*

> *All day long I faced the walls and did nothing except eat and sleep like a
> caged animal. Others—Europeans, Japanese, Koreans—were allowed to
> disembark almost immediately. Even blacks were greeted by relatives
> and allowed to go ashore. Only we Chinese were not allowed to see or
> talk to our loved ones and were escorted by armed guards to the wood-
> en house. Frustrated, we could only sigh and groan. Even the cargo was
> picked up from the docks and delivered to its destination after custom
> duties were paid. Only we Chinese were denied that right. How can it
> be that they look upon us as animals? As less than cargo? (CSYP Chinese
> newspaper, June 10, 1903)*

*This kind of treatment was not unusual because the Chinese were seen as
temporary drifters not as possible settlers.*

> *The tendency in the past had been to view Chinese as "sojourners" and
> not as European immigrants, "the implication being that the Chinese,
> unlike the Europeans, did not intend to stay but remained unassimilated
> and apart from mainstream American society; hence it was justifiable to
> bar their further immigration and exclude them from American social
> and political life." (Ng, 1987, pp. 53-71)*

*A hundred years later, many of us are still considered foreigners just passing
through.*

America
Jiyoung Kim

America. America. America? Am I really going to America? It sounds so
unreal. Could this really be true? Imagine, me, in America. I'll have to tell
all my friends. I'll have to tell everyone I know. I can't believe I am going to
America. I am going to take a plane to America.

My heart is beating so fast, I can hardly breathe. I think I am kind of scared. What if I don't like America? What if America doesn't like me? What if the kids in the American school do not like me? What if someone says something to me and I can't understand? What will I do?

Gosh, I don't know if I like this idea. I wonder if I'll ever come back to Korea? If I don't like America, I will come back to Korea. I'll come back and live with my relatives. They'll let me. I hope I like America.

I wonder what my relatives are like. I haven't seen any of them in years. I wonder if they'll remember me? I wonder if they'll like me? Will I like living with them? I wonder what my grandmother's house looks like? I wonder if the bathroom is inside or outside? I hope it's inside.

I pressed my nose against the car window and watched the groups of figures walking by, strange creatures of the night, talking, laughing, and running. White faces, black faces, bloody faces with bulging eyes stared into the car, sending icy chills down my spine. Laughing hysterically, a caped villain raced across our car's path followed by a glimmer in white, so fast that had I blinked at that moment, I would have missed it.

Where in the world was I? Isn't this America? I thought that I had boarded a plane for America; instead, I had landed on a different planet, a planet full of monsters.

I wanted to go back to Korea. I wanted to jump back on the plane that brought me here and go back home. My head was spinning like a Ferris wheel, like a merry-go-round, going around and around. I heard something about Halloween.

Becoming an American Citizen
Maria Flores

For me, being an American citizen, means being treated with respect! It means standing up for my rights! It means my voice is heard! It means I can make a difference and embrace another culture as well as my own.

In the United States, the Fourth of July is a day when the whole nation celebrates its independence from the British. For my parents, Fourth of July is a day they celebrate their arrival to El Norte, a day that shifted their lives forever.

Prior to their arrival, my dad had worked in California for two years. He would mail money to my mother to pay for shots I needed because I was born with a shorter leg. Without that money, I would have not been cured. Dad dreamed of bringing us all to the United States.

Mom left her beautiful house, family and relatives to follow my dad to a country that spoke another language and had a different culture. It was not as difficult to cross then but my parents had to pay $700 to the coyotes. We moved into a house where a different family occupied every room.

Mom gave birth to my brother, Isidro and started working soon to pay for the hospital bills. A woman that was very abusive babysat my brother and me. Whenever she got made at us, she would send us to the dark restroom where my brother would eat the toilet paper. Mom and Dad knew, but all they said to me was, "porta te bien my hija, recuerda que te queremos" (behave honey, remember that we love you). I couldn't comprehend why they kept us there then but now I know my parent couldn't afford anything better.

Mom and Dad adored working with plants. Everything they touched, flourished, like magic. Eventually, my parents were offered a job that was connected to a greenhouse in which we would live. The house had three rooms, one bath, a living room and a kitchen. I still remember the first day we say the house, I felt so rich! Gracias Dios mio, thank you God, I said when I saw all the space my brother and I had to play in. Mom and Dad only had to pay $150 a month and work forty hours a week for us to live in the greenhouse.

The house was very old and needed desperate repairs but the owner refused to fix them. The sink, toilet and bathtub did not work. My dad had to dig a deep hole far away from the house and built a toilet for all of us. I was always scared of falling into the hole so I would always squat as I did potty and then grab a shovel to dump the waste into the hole.

I also remember having to boil water in a huge pot and pour it into the bathtub. After we were done taking a bath we had to grab a bucket and remove all of the dirty water and dump it. The house had a big hole in the roof and every time it rained we had to sweep the water out of the house. My Dad had to nail down a plastic bag, which helped the water fall away from the house.

My school days were very hard. I did not know enough English to communicate with the rest of the children and I was also very shy. My first year in kindergarten was very difficult because I was afraid that I was never going to see Mom and Dad again. They told us what to do in case they were caught and sent back to México.

I was originally placed in a bilingual classroom but my parents were opposed. They did not bring me to California to learn Spanish. Before I was removed, I had to pass a test to demonstrate I knew enough English to be placed in an all-English classroom.

The only time I was really exposed to English was in the classroom because at recess I hung around those that spoke Spanish only. I also grew up speaking Spanish, listening to Spanish music and watching Spanish soap operas. Everywhere I went, Spanish was spoken and it was more comfortable to me.

My school was always secondary to my responsibilities of cooking, cleaning and taking care of my brother. My parents did not understand the homework given to me. I always made an effort to bring my parents to

Back-to-School Night because I wanted them to see all that I had learned. As always, my parents felt embarrassed for not knowing English. But how could they learn a language like English when they could not even write correctly in Spanish?

In December of 1996, I became an American citizen. I completed by college education in the United States and my biggest desire in life was to become a teacher. I knew that México was unfamiliar even though I was born there. I cry at times because I wish I were there with my relatives. I want to be where my people are not seen as aliens but as people. However, I thank God for what my parents sacrificed for me, for a better education, and for helping me become an American citizen.

Ni de aqui o de alla (Neither From Here or There)
Victor M. Maciel

Toda mi vida busqùe
un lugar que me perteneciera
Por que nunca fui aceptado
en el pais donde naci
nì en el pais de mi herencia

All of my life I searched
For a place where I belonged
Because I was never accepted
In the where I was born
Nor in the country of my heritage.

It is not my fault that I was born in the gringo country to the North. It is not my fault that my parents sought a better life in a country that will always label me a minority and not see me as just another citizen. Due to this fact I feel that I do not really have a country. I feel as though I to stand on the imaginary line that divides the country of my ancestors and the country of my birth.

Too Mexican, Not Mexican Enough
Rosa Ramirez

I am embraced by Mexican traditions
My first language is Spanish
But I have to learn English before beginning school
"Tomatoes" is the first word I learn
First grade at a private school
I look different from anyone else

Slight accent, darker skin, hair, and eyes
My mom picks us up from school in a Duster
While other parents drive Mercedes and Jaguars
My third-grade teacher changes my name to Rosie
Rosaura is too hard to pronounce
I am too Mexican.

My parents divorced after seven children
My mom refuses to end up in a body bag
Alcoholism took control of her household
Now she takes control
My alcoholic, abusive father is forced to leave
I am raised in a single-parent, minority home
Society says my destiny is to be pregnant and on welfare by age 16
I refuse to be a statistic
I am not Mexican enough.

I go to high school
Most of my closest friends are Caucasian
I don't think about my culture
I change the spelling of my name
Replace the "s" with a "z"
I am not Mexican enough.

My dating years
I don't date many Mexican men
Afraid they will turn out like my father
I make a solemn vow
Never marry anyone born in Mexico
They are all alcoholic, abusive men
I am not Mexican enough.

I meet a man born and raised in Mexico
He doesn't drink
Speaks with an accent
Only kind words
Others ask what I see in him
My last name will be more Mexican then my maiden name
I am too Mexican and so is he
But that is ok

As an adult, I look back
I follow Mexican traditions

More than I thought
1 participate in Posadas at Christmas
I adore and celebrate the patron saint of Mexico
Nuestra Senora de Guadalupe
I celebrate the coming of the Tres Reyes
With pan rosca
I don't eat spicy food
But I have tortillas with every meal
Tacos and tortas over hamburgers and hot dogs for me
I'll listen to Vicente Fernandez
Over Emenem any day
I was addicted to Novelas
But I'm ok if I miss an episode of *General Hospital*
Yet when I am in Mexico
I am different
I am from "el norte"
The north is what they say
I am stuck between the borders
Of two great countries
Mexico, where my ancestors are from
And America, which has been so good to my family

Am I too Mexican?
Or not Mexican enough?
Why be labeled?
Some might ask
After all, this is where I was born
In America
That makes me American
Does it not?
My body was born in America
29 years ago
But my soul was born in Mexico
Thousands of years ago.

Marginalized
Migel La Motte

Marginalized
Their plan to seize my dignity by attacking my birthright.
Rights given that perception takes away
Not safe at school
NO ONE in the world knows who I am today!

Mike, Miguel, Manuel
As my identity begins to fray, I internalize feelings of angst and dismay
As I observe the masses holding the treasure, I learn their game I must play.
Thoughts, appearance and conformity
My individualism stripped away.

The Other
Aleyda Barrera-Cruz

I am the "other" because I come from a different country: Mexico, where language and traditions are very different.

I am the "other" when I speak Spanish and some people just stare.

I am the "other" when I say "Gracias," but receive "You're Welcome!"

I am the "other" when I read Latinos are the targets of hate crimes.

I am the "other" when I walk into my job as an aide, where there are many Latino children that need help, and notice that I am the only Latina and Spanish-speaking person that helps them.

I am the "other" when sometimes I feel the system is telling me that it is a sin to speak Spanish to the children I work with. If it really is a sin, then I have sinned many times.

I am the "other" when schools say, "English only!"

I am the "other" when I remember the day I spoke Spanish to four year old Deborah, whose parents are Mexican, and she responded, "Don't talk to me in Spanish." I knew she understood me.

I am the "other" when I ask myself if my children's children will know about their Mexican heritage.

I am the "other" when in church people ask, "But why do Latinos want their own programs?"

I am the "other" and I know God loves the "other."

I am the "other" when my parents say, "We don't understand you. You should act this way because that is how we were raised in Mexico." I know they want the best for me, but it is still difficult.

I am the "other" when I remember how I wished to be back in Mexico; "Life there was easier," I used to say. But when I went back for vacation, I missed the United States.

I am the "other" when I don't understand what people are trying to say even if I do understand their words.

I am the "other" when I am different from the average, when I don't fit the categories.

I am the "other" when I realize I live on the border between two different worlds; they both form part of my life. If I take one away, it would mean taking half of my life.

I am the "other" and I know it is not bad to be the "other"; it may mean that you are just unique.

I am the "other" when I think that the word "other" applies to everyone, for no one is the same.

I am the "other" simply because I am not like any "other."

"Gharibeh"
Taraneh Djifroodi

It is Friday night. I arrived in Los Angeles at 8:00 p.m. It was a very long trip; I was on the plane for over 22 hours.

I am seventeen years old; I am a teenager happy to be free from my parents and all the parental restrictions. I had to leave my home. I am here to start a new life.

Every thing appears to be different. I look not like anybody else. Everyone is speaking English. I can hear not a single word of Farsi. I need to find my sister who supposed to be at the airport to pick me up, but I do not see her. I do not know how to ask for assistance. I told the information center that I am a Gharibeh; he did not know what I meant, and I did not know how to tell him that Gharibeh means a foreigner. Reality sinks in. I am not home anymore. I am without my parents. I am a Gharibeh.

It is Monday morning. I am starting my new school. I am the only foreign student in the whole school. Everyone is staring at me. They want to know my name. I tell them my name, but they cannot pronounce my name. They ask me to spell my name. I am not used to spelling my name. At home, everyone knows how to pronounce my name. I do not want to know their names. I do not want to make friends who cannot pronounce my name.

They stare too much. I need to find a place to hide and cry, but I do not suppose to cry in public. It is not acceptable. I retreat into silent despair. Reality sinks in. I am different, and it is dreadful to feel different. I did not know it would be like this. I feel like a Gharibeh.

For the first time in my life, I have an accent. For the first time in my life, I cannot express myself I choose to be silent, and my silence is not from wisdom; it is from imprudence.

I am starting a new life for which I did not wish. I do not like to be stared at. I do not want to talk with an accent. I do not want not to be able to express myself I do not want to different. I do not find my new life appealing. This place is not my home. I will make this new life an impermanent life. I will find a way to go home. I want to be me, again.

It is Friday morning. I am a junior at USC. I am going to immigration with a group of other Persians from USC. Iran has taken American hostages, and people despise us for being a Persian. The government demanded that all Persians give up their visas and leave immediately. Immigration demanded to fingerprint all Persians. I think it is so degrading to be fingerprinted for something I did not do. Reality has sunk in a long time ago. I am different and being different is not tolerable. I am a Gharibeh.

Life in the Fast Lane
Kyle Matsuoka

7:30 a.m. the alarm rings
No cheers that ring brings
It's a new day in this world called California.
The last verse of a song on my alarm I hear . . . "To Live and Die in L.A."

Freeways . . . the fast life according to five lanes.
First lane on the right . . . watching your life go by.
Second lane . . . A little faster, but still missing most of it
Third lane . . . Can't decide what to do. Trapped in this uncertain world
Fourth lane . . . Somewhat in step with the fast pace life. Fifth lane . . . The
fast pace life. Everyone seems to be in it. If you're not . . . pack your bags
and leave.
My eyes close
Memories come back in flashes
A feeling that encompasses me
Like a jungle covered by trees.
An easy laid back life
The memory that stays

Life is easy on an island called Kauai.
I look around; most of the people are Asian.

People are friendly.
People are nice, even people I don't know.
Strike up a conversation with a stranger, and you are bound to find
     something in common.
No place is restricted
No place is off limits
I belong
I belong here.

"Eh, where you goin' go tonight?
I don't know. I taught us goin' go movies.
Yeah, but what we goin' go see?
I don't know. Us just go look."

Language that I speak
And I don't sound like a freak
No worries about what comes out
People will understand

Which road shall I take?
Which turn shall I make?
I really don't have to decide
There's only one road to travel on
Fifty miles per hour is fast
Sixty miles per hour and you're insane
Thirty-five is a comfort zone
Want directions to a beach called Poipu Beach.
"Go this way until you hit tunnel of trees. Then turn right at the store, turn
     left at the gas station, then turn right at the sign that says Poipu Beach."

My mind wanders back to a place called California.
First day of college I realize there are less Asians I'm a minority!
I hear others speak up in class, and they sound so intelligent. Using big
     words in complex sentences.
Lunchtime
Something to eat finally. Where's the rice? There is no rice. The only rice is
     Mainland rice. That's not rice
Just getting better and better my roommate comes back from class
I am working on my homework, and he uses my computer I wonder if he is
     done with the computer
"You pau with the computer?"
"What?"
"You pau with the computer?"

"I don't understand what you are saying"
"I'm sorry, um, are you done with the computer?"

Driving . . . driving is scary.
A freeway with five lanes, going 70 or even 80 miles per hour
That seems so fast; I've never gone that fast before
So many cars and people
"Don't honk your horn. Don't cut people off. Don't get anyone mad. You
    don't know what kind of crazy people are on the road," my dad would say.

Directions . . . directions are a whole new ball game.
Go west on Chapman, then south on Main to get to the mall.
Can't anyone tell me different directions than that? I don't know which way
    is north, south, east, or west.

Life here is different,
Not just the people, the food, or the language
But the whole life style.
My life style has just turned upside down.

My walk changed from dragging feet to an up-step walk.
I feel like I'm in the army doing double time walking.
It's not 10:00 and time for bed anymore.
It's 1:00 in the morning and time for bed.
Late nights and early mornings become my routine. I've never had a routine
    like this before.

Life here is hard.
Hard and different
I'm a stranger in a strange land
I don't belong, lend me a hand
But there is no hand
I face this alone

Will I run home to an island called Kauai?
Will I be defeated by this place called California?
I'm in the third lane deciding whether to merge to the far right lane and go home
    or merge to the left lane and live the fast life . . . "To Live and Die in L.A."

LANGUAGE–3E

*My female ancestors had bound feet and led bound lives. But even without
bound feet, new immigrants were bound to San Francisco's Chinatown*

because of language. As we learned English, many Chinese moved to the outer borders. Accents became more faint. You could determine a family's English proficiency by how far from Chinatown they lived.

I have vivid memories of my father penning palm writing across Chinese dialectical borders. When he met someone who came from a different village and therefore spoke a different Chinese dialect, he would use his index finger like a calligraphy pen to inscribe strokes on the palm of his hand. The other person, standing at my father's side, would eventually reciprocate and finger Chinese characters on his own palm to send a message back. Palm telegraphing of the Chinese written language quiets the oral language differences.

> *White light bleaches color out.*
> *White noise dehumanizes you.*

I mourn the loss of my Chinese language. I can make out spoken words in Hong Kong, Canton, and San Francisco. I have a limited receptive vocabulary and have lost my childhood capacity to speak. My speaking vocabulary died when grandmother died. I wish I had learned my language and not been a Chinese School dropout. Did my body truly have a choice to host anything but the English language?

hooks (1994) reminds us that English is the language of conquest and domination of those in power, over those not in power. Darder (1991) added that schools are place where we were made to feel that our own language was inferior to English. The English language is a weapon that can shame, humiliate, and colonize us (hooks, 1994). Even when we acquired English skill, our accents prevented us from being considered real Americans (Chu, 1989). We will always be considered illegitimate as long as we have to accommodate the English speakers rather than having them accommodate us (Anzaldua, 1988). Swindler Boutte (2002) recalled, "I cannot forget what it is like to feel demeaned because my way of speaking is different from the mainstream's" (p. 331).

> *So, if you want to really hurt me, talk badly about my language . . .*
> *—Anzaldua (1988 p. 59)*

In my Chinese family, there was no audible language of resistance, like Ebonics, which was a language, made to speak against conquest and domination (hooks, 1994) but rather a quiet alternative, the language of silence. Silence in Zen is the ultimate communication. Its premise is that the world is so complicated and beautiful, silence transcends words. Words are the communication of mere mortals. Even the most advanced societies in Star Wars *sent their messages through telepathy thus capturing the spiritual as well as the intellectual.*

Therefore, for some Chinese, silence is not resistance as feminists (Ellsworth, 1992) suggest, nor is it the spaces between words to stop the frenzy of Western thought (hooks, 1994), rather it is the language of choice. Silence is preferred over speech. Speech is unnecessary chatter. "Don't say anything unless you can improve upon the silence" (unknown Chinese author).

To not talk has been part of my Chinese socialization. "Don't ask questions." "Why do you always ask why?" demands my mother-in-law. In the culture of silence, one learns not to answer back but to accept the admonishment. A young child learns to know when one should not bother with words but should instead find discrete ways to communicate. One learns how to send meaning silently through the confidence of knowing that words do not tell it all, that meaning becomes deeper with silence. One learns how to read meaning differently. Traditional social protocols involve speechless gestures to convey a message, for example, the tip of an eyebrow conveying interest, the nod of respect (contemporary bow of the head). One learns to know differently, without words, without asking; to know when one should not bother with the words because language is experienced, not spoken. Stop talking and you will hear my silence, my meaning, my spiritual mantra.

Cultural norms reinforce the language of silence. Raised in a culture of modesty (Matsuda, 1996), we are taught, "Don't make waves, don't be rude, don't be obtrusive, don't be self-promoting" (Chu, 1989 p. 413). Consequently, both the language and the culture produce a polyphonic silence. My cultural programming of discreteness and humility prohibits me from using myself as a referent or from expressing "I" in fortissimo! (Even as I write this, I type tentatively.) The obsufication of I in one's verbal repertoire prevents one from speaking up or from speaking out. Sometimes this is a deficit that embarrasses me because it reinforces the Western stereotype of the quiet, compliant Asian. Westerners expect my silence and at the same time are suspicious of it. It is cryptic. They cannot read it.

Silence is a language we all know. It is the language we human beings first learned in infancy, before speech. It's hard to recognize because we don't teach this language in schools. In horror movies, silence is used as a technique to scare the audience. "Does my silence make you uncomfortable?" I ask my colleague. He advises me that I have a responsibility in a democratic society to let others know what I am thinking (Wilson, personal communication, 1992). But I think, "Doesn't he have a reciprocal obligation to learn my language?" Instead of silencing my silence, he has an "opportunity to listen without mastery"(hooks, 1994, p. 172), a language of silence. If he is unwilling, I am forced to translate my silence into speech.

Mayer Shevin (1999), a facilitator of communication, spoke of a similar experience with a friend with a communication impairment with whom he facilitated over a period of time. In each facilitated communication session,

Shevin and his friend started drinking sodas for 45 minutes in silence. After several weeks of this routine, Mayer asked his friend if they could reduce the Coke time so that they could have more time talking. His friend's response was, "When we are talking, I am in your world. When we are quiet, you are in mine." In this instance, silence was not a disability but a language of choice. There are ways of knowing beyond speaking and writing. Intentional silence may be a deliberate cultural practice that aims at facilitating intro-spection and self-discipline (Greene, 1995).

> *Those who speak do not know, those who know, do not speak.*
> *— Lao Tsu*

And yet I know, ultimately, if I am committed to a public position of social justice, I must traverse between the worlds of silence and speech. As a woman warrior, I must use the language of my oppressor as my sword to resist the hegemonic barriers to a pluralistic society (Freire, 1995; Shor, 1987) with the hope of one day retiring my sword in silence.

A LOVE NOTE

Nita Freire, wife of Brazilian educator, Paulo Freire, accepted an honorary doctorate on behalf of her husband Paulo posthumously at Chapman University in December 1998. As she looked deeply into the eyes of a bronze bust of Paulo, she related to the audience how much she loved him, as an educator, husband, and lover. After a brief accounting of his intellectual life, she disclosed how his Portuguese words embraced her entire body when they made love. The audience was noticeably moved by her tenderness and reverence for the man and his words.

Cisnernos (1991) captured the intimate relationship between one's language and human expression in her description of lovemaking in Spanish.

> *To have a lover sigh "mi vida, mi preciosa, mi chiquita," and whisper things in that language crooned to babies, that language murmured by grandmothers, those words that smelled like your house, like flour tor-tillas, and the inside of your daddy's hat, like everyone talking in the kitchen at the same time. . . . How could I think of making love in English again? English with its starched r's and g's. English with its crisp linen syllables. English crunch as apples, resilient and stiff as sailcloth. (Ciscernos, 1991, p. 153)*

Speakers of other languages are perceived as a threat by the dominant language group rather than an opportunity to hear diverse voices in words other than English. English-only policies, like Proposition 227 passed in California in 1998, reflected the people's ethnocentrism and attempt to rid the state of linguistic plurality. Subsequent policies systematically severed people from their culture, their indigenous ideology, their spirituality, and perhaps even their lovemaking. Written as resistance to the silencing of lived expressions of racial and linguistic oppression, student narratives reflect the trauma of otherness experienced by those who did not speak the dominant language.

Speaking Spanish Means Being Poor
Claudia Esquivel

I was in first grade when I first started worrying about my pronunciations. I remember my teachers correcting us when we didn't pronounce something correctly. I started being afraid to talk because I didn't want anyone laughing. This would follow me for many years. I would become a very quiet person. I was thought to be shy, which I started to believe myself.

You see, if your parents shopped at Kmart, Zody's, or Pic and Save, you would be laughed at because only poor people shopped at those places. I would start lying about where my clothes were bought.

I remember my friends talking about their rooms. Well, my room meant mine and Gabby's and Griz' and Linda's. I would lie and say that I had my own room. This was very important in junior high.

I would also lie and say I wasn't sure where my dad worked. I didn't want them to know that he was just a machinist. I would never take my friends home because I didn't want them to see where I lived. I was sure they had nicer houses than I did. I also didn't want them to know that I did live in the barrio.

I remember my dad speaking Spanish to me when we went shopping. I would always respond in English because I didn't want anyone to know I spoke Spanish. I remember wanting to forget my Spanish language because I thought that was the reason we were poor. I hated being different and being teased for the clothes I wore. I remember feeling dirty because I was born in Tijuana. I remember thinking, "Why would my parents have another child if they couldn't even give us what we wanted?" I was so angry with them. I didn't want anything to do with being Mexican.

My parents had been in this country for many years and still spoke mainly Spanish. I still couldn't understand why they didn't speak as much English as I thought they should. At school I would only speak English. I still didn't want anyone hearing me speak Spanish.

I was a senior in high school when my dad was laid off. We had never been on welfare or had received any kind of help from the government but were now forced to because of the circumstances. I remember feeling embarrassed and hoping nobody found out.

My Worth, My Language
Helena Isabel Acevedo

I was born and raised in Santafe de Bogota, Columbia, South America. Fourteen years ago, my husband, the children, and I came to live in the United States to pursue a better life. I had my own identity, and I was proud of my Spanish culture and heritage. I was happy.

The first couple of years were like a nightmare. Even though I learned some English when I went to school in Columbia, I was unable to speak it. I understood a little bit. I was scared. I did not want to leave the house for any reason.

When I was living in my country, Colombia, I was a preschool teacher and taught kindergarten and second grade. But as I moved here, I became nobody. I lost my value. I was not worth anything. This experience affected me to the point that I lost my self-esteem, and my life had no meaning at all. I had wasted the first twenty-five years of my life, and I was not willing to start all over again. I was depressed, sad, and unhappy. I felt like my whole life was only a long memory and was gone forever.

I have struggled a lot by trying to fit in this new society. I know that it would depend on my willingness to make the positive contact, to try hard, and my best to belong here. If I isolate myself and do not accept and absorb the "American way of life," then I better leave. But, I questioned myself, "What if the Americans do not accept the way I am?"

Throughout fourteen years of living in this country, the Americans have put me down either because of the accent I have when I express myself in English, or because I look like a "Mexican," and the idea of illegal immigrant comes to their minds. Some people even think I am stupid because I do not speak English in the right way. If they do not understand me, that is their problem. At least I am smart enough to manage the world in two languages. I think it is time for them to learn a second language, too.

I Struggle
Frances M. Villalobos

I struggle with being brown skinned
I struggle with being a Spaniard and a Mexican
I struggle with being red skinned
I struggle with being an Indian
I'm othered by feeling white souled
I'm othered by knowing I am of a brown mold
I'm othered because I don't speak my native tongue
I'm othered by my native brothers and sisters
I'm othered by the outsider feeling that
Their words have sung.

We grew up in predominately white neighborhoods. My friend Kim was Mexican, but I was a lot darker than she was, and she spoke Spanish. I remember how she used to make fun of me because I looked more Mexican than she did and she spoke Spanish. So, what did that mean? Did it mean that I wasn't Mexican because I didn't speak the native language? How could I claim my identity as Mexican if I couldn't speak Spanish?

I felt caught between being brown and being white. Sometimes I didn't like being called Mexican or Chicana because the only Mexicans we ever came in contact with were poor and dirty. People call me an Oreo cookie, brown on the outside and white on the inside, a whitewashed Mexican. That really hurt. I am othered by my own kind.

I Didn't Feel Mexican
Edie Castro

My father is of Mexican and Native American descent. In a group of Anglo children I felt just a little different. But in a group of Mexican children I felt a whole lot different. Here I was, a dark brown-eyed, dark brown-haired, olive-skinned little girl who didn't feel like she was Mexican but I also didn't feel like I was exactly part of the Anglo group either. I was somewhere in between.

The first time I really felt like I was in between was when I started kindergarten. The school secretary escorted my mother and me to my new classroom. When we walked in, my new teacher asked me, "What is your name?" Being shy, I did not answer her. Instead, my mother answered for me. The teacher then asked my mother, "Does she understand English?" My mother answered, "Yes, she only speaks English." The teacher proceeded to tell my mother that it would be all right for me to stay since the other kindergarten class down the hall was for Spanish-speaking students only. I began to wonder how I was different from other kids. Was I normal?

I wasn't like those other Mexican children back in California. Those children couldn't speak English, but I could. Those children's clothes never matched, but mine did. Those children used special coupons for free lunches, I always brought my lunch in a lunch box. There were so many different things that made me not feel like I was Mexican, but if my mom said I was Mexican, then maybe I was Mexican on the outside and something else on the inside.

On the playground, I met other Mexican girls. As we were playing, they started speaking Spanish to me. When I told them I did not know how to speak Spanish, they looked at me funny. They said, "We thought you were Mexican." They assumed that I should know how to speak Spanish if I was Mexican. Again I began to question how I fit in. How can I be Mexican if I'm not like them? I must not be a normal Mexican. I'm a fake Mexican.

I found myself wanting to be with a different group of girls. Girls that spoke English clearly, girls who wore matching clothes, and girls who I had more things in common with. I wanted to forget that I was Mexican. I didn't like feeling that I was different; so from then on I only made friends with Anglo, English-speaking children.

As I grew up I realized that I was losing out on a very important aspect of my life and that was my rich ethnic background. I had to some way come to terms with the fact that being different among my own people wasn't so bad. In high school, I decided to learn how to speak Spanish and I also joined the Spanish Club. Learning more about my cultural roots gave me a sense of pride I had never felt before.

Being fourth generation has caused me to lose a lot of my cultural background. It's just something that happens. I hope to pass on whatever little cultural customs or traditions I have experienced or been taught, to my own children. However, I think it will be a challenge because my fiancé's ethnic background is both Vietnamese and German. Together we will be creating our very own melting pot.

Speak English
Ji Young Kim

English, speak in English. You are in America now so you should speak English. If you are going to follow those American kids in school, you must speak and write the language better than they can. It doesn't matter if your mother and I can't understand. Your mother and I brought you to American so that you could get a better education and have more opportunities to advance in this world. Do you understand what I am trying to say to you? We want you and your sisters to have a better life than the one we have. We don't want you to struggle like we did. We want you and your sisters to be successful. You can be anything you want to be if you work hard enough at it. English, speak English. Do you understand what I am trying to say? Do you Ji Young?

Korean, speak in Korean. You are Korean so you should speak Korean. It doesn't matter how long you live in America. Your eyes will not get bigger, your hair will not lighten and your nose will certainly never get any bigger. As long as you in this house, you will speak Korean to your mother and me as well as to your little sisters. You are the oldest; you need to set a good example for your sisters. How will your mother and I understand you all if you don't speak Korean?

White students also wrote about language in their otherness papers. Like their classmates, they wrote about exclusion as a result of not knowing the dominant language. The difference between the papers was in the degree of social control the students had over their status. White students could remove themselves from the specific adverse conditions to reduce the feelings of otherness without significant social or economic consequences. Students of color could not easily escape the prejudice, which followed them from home to school and into greater society.

Aspiring To Be a Teacher of Hearing-Impaired Children
Michael Moorehouse

I was interested in working with children with hearing impairments but I was fearful to be left alone with them in this foreign room. What if I couldn't understand what the students were saying to me?

I was panic stricken to find that even some of the most basic signs were escaping me. I had to calm down; take a few deep breaths. In a matter of seconds I had eight little pairs of hands slicing through the air at me. I tried to watch the movements of each little hand, dissecting it down to the placement of every finger. None of it meant anything to me. They would have done just as well to speak Lithuanian, and for all I knew they might have been.

I tried to talk to the students. The words came slowly, my fingers moved begrudgingly, as if each one was weighed down by a boulder. "My . . . name . . . is . . . Michael. Sit . . . down. Wait . . . for . . . your . . . teacher. I . . . don't . . . know . . . where . . . she . . . is. Please . . . sit . . . down. This was my defining moment and I was a failure. I would never be a teacher, at least not for deaf children. My strongest passions withered within me like a rose in the desert sun. How was I going to survive 60 more hours of this torture? I wondered if it would be too late for me to get assigned to a new school where I could complete my observations.

The teacher asked me to walk around the desks and watch the students work, helping them wherever necessary. I wanted to tell them that I thought they were doing wonderful work, but was not sure I could come up with the words.

After hours of awkward silence and furtive glances the final bell of the day rang. My entire body sighed with relief. I faked a smile, turned and walked out of the room convinced that I would never make it as a teacher of hearing impaired children.

SOCIAL CLASS–3F

It's 11:30 p.m. on a school night. I wonder what my fifth-grade friends are doing right now? I am picking peapods and wrapping wontons at my mother's restaurant. I did my homework earlier at a table lit by an aquarium. At

2 a.m., we'll lock up and return to our two-bedroom home over the Broadway Street tunnel.

As a single mother, Mom taught me at an early age that our destinies were tied to the success of that restaurant. Everything we did was dedicated to it—from wallpapering the ceiling with Chinese newspapers to sacrificing every evening of my entire childhood to be with her patrons. We never closed and she was always at the restaurant. When the business did well, I got nice clothes to wear, but seldom did I get to spend time with my mother. She worked 16 hours a day. I would take the trolley to the restaurant after school so I could do my homework and be with her. A waiter would drive me home. Every hug I ever got was in public. She was too tired to hold me when she got home. It seems we gave up so much to get ahead.

We are the model minority, overrepresented at some prestigious universities and therefore we no longer qualify as underrepresented minorities. This privilege is riffled with contradictions however, as evidenced by a 1999 Newsweek article, "I Don't Count as Diversity." Ragaza (1999) reported that Asian Americans are 60% more likely to hold a bachelor's degree than white Americans but have lower median salaries ($37,040 vs. $42,050). Asian Americans make up 4% of the population but only two tenths of 1% of the country's corporate directorships. An Asian-American family is 20% more likely to be living in poverty than a white family.

Slipping to the lower rungs of the social economic ladder is everyone's fear. It can happen to anybody, therefore, we are forever fearful of crossing into it. Poverty is the dark secret of whites who represent the highest group living at or below the poverty line. But media images of poverty show darker colors representing urban or ghetto environments. The collection of inner city images predominantly display immigrants, druggies, and dysfunctional families in economically depressed and racially separated neighborhoods. Urban aura portrays despair, ennui, Gotham-like darkness, and a holding space for people no longer of use to the larger economy (Hamilton, 1991; Howard, 1999; Kozol, 1991; SooHoo & Wilson, 1994, 2004).

"Many children who live at or below the poverty level . . . give up and drop out, recognizing that society and the school are strongly biased against them" (Sleeter & Grant, 1999, p. 204). They lose hope because they recognize that "there is very little in the way of an organized movement against classism as there is in racism because the underlying factors that create vast inequalities in wealth . . . remain largely invisible" (Yeskel & Leondar-Wright, 1997, p. 235). It is difficult to see who is responsible for classism because

> People on welfare are blamed for causing our budget woes; urban young men of color are blamed for crime; immigrants are blamed for taking away jobs; working women and gays and lesbians are held responsible for the breakdown of the nuclear family and the moral decay of society;

> Jews are labeled as controlling the banks and the media; and the
> Japanese are blamed for stealing American markets. (Yeskel & Leondar-
> Wright, 1997, p. 232)

Moreover, "shame at being poorer or richer than others leads to secrecy and
silence" (Yeskel & Leondar-Wright, 1997, p. 232) and further conceals classism.

The following narratives refuse to be relegated to second-class citizens on
the list of social marginalization. As one student put it, "The next time you
think of someone struggling to make ends meet whether they are on welfare
or not, please think of someone like me because we all need help sometimes"
(Webber, 6/6/95).

My World Came Crashing Down
Judy Lighthipe

After college I married a boy from a similar background as my own. We met
at the Friends Church I was now attending and were married before God in
the fairytale wedding I had always dreamed of. I was a substitute teacher. He
worked at a warehouse and finished his education. I worked and washed and
cleaned and cooked and hosted Bible study in our home. I wrote his
Marketing paper for him. He received the highest grade in the class and the
teacher copied it and handed it out to all the class sections as an example of
a thorough marketing analysis. While nine months pregnant I walked
around Beverly Hills and researched his second paper. This one my husband
was asked to read to all the class sections. He was given another A. I gave
birth to our first child. Soon, he left his warehouse job and began an insur-
ance agency. I promised that if the agency were not viable I would go back
to teaching and support us. I designed his business cards and the logo for his
stationary. I picked out and arranged his office furniture as well as his
clothes. I planned and wrote the letter accompanying his first marketing
campaign. His district manager asked if he could copy it and distribute it to
all the agents in the district to use as a standard marketing letter. My husband spoke at a seminar as the key speaker telling about the letter and the
marketing strategy he was developing. I gave birth to our second child. I
became a stay-at-home mom and he became one of the first agents to make
the top sales convention in his first year.

As his business prospered we moved up the social ladder. Eventually we
moved into my dream house. I hired an interior decorator, an art decorator,
a landscape architect, a plant service, a personal trainer, and a Peruvian
housekeeper who came twice a week and did all the laundry and ironing. I
designed the swimming pool and the hotel-size Jacuzzi which looked out on
a magnificent view from Catalina to Los Angeles to Fashion Island, and
instructed the Filipino gardener to plant seasonal flowers in my garden. We

sipped Chardonnay from our wine collection which we kept in a private wine locker and watched the Disneyland fireworks every night from our balcony. My children went to private school and Cotillion where they learned manners and ballroom dancing. They danced classical ballet and entered dance competitions. We drove a Mercedes and a BMW and used the Suburban only for excursions to our 37-foot sailboat, which we kept in a permanent slip at the marina. We went on Caribbean vacations and to a dude ranch each summer. He bought me diamonds. I wore them when I lunched with my friends and volunteered at my children's school. They were thrilled that I had a teaching credential and gave me a reading group of my own. I never considered teaching again, even after my children were both in school. I quietly felt sorry for my acquaintances that had to work and raise their children, secretly believing that their family and children must be suffering. I began to spend more time with my friends in the new neighborhood and less time with my old friends. My new friends enjoyed the dance series at the Performing Arts Center. We always bought the sixty dollar seats and dined before and after at the nicest gourmet restaurants. My husband and I enjoyed our church, made up mostly of upper middle class, college educated families like ours and were active in our Sunday school class, whose theme was building strong marriages.

In the midst of this prosperity our marriage, however, was crumbling. The stresses of his business along with many other factors eroded the fabric and the trust until he became abusive and silent. I went into therapy and he became more distant and secretive. There was nothing left to build on. One night after he was violently abusive to me in front of our daughters something inside of me snapped. The idea that they might think that this was acceptable behavior was more than I could bear and I left the marriage that I had stayed in so long because of my belief that God hated divorce. My husband eventually agreed to let me stay in the house so the children could remain in their home. My therapist agreed that had I stayed in the marriage I would have had a breakdown or become suicidal. That was before I was no longer able to afford his one hundred dollar an hour fee.

Over the next months my world came crashing down around me. My husband's business was experiencing a downswing because of the recession and he had borrowed and mortgaged and creatively financed in hopes of riding it out. This strategy had failed along with our marriage and soon the dikes were crumbling and we were overcome with a flood of financial disaster. I had never been involved in the financial affairs of our marriage, naively believing that he had our best interests at heart and that he had the savvy and know how to manage things much better than I. I was pathetically unprepared for what was about to take place. Because he was no longer living in our home and had conveniently not left a forwarding address, I stood alone against the barrage of creditors who descended upon me, along with the IRS, for unbeknownst to me, he had not sent in our prepared and signed joint tax returns for several years. They sat in the bottom drawer of his desk at work in the mailing envelopes. How could I tell each one that I had no control of or prior knowledge of what was going on with us financially? How could I make them understand that I was really a good person and not some cheat? Day after day I suffered humiliation and anguish and fear at what my insecure future would bring.

The cars were repossessed out of our driveway. My neighbors called the police because they thought they were being stolen. I was unaware he had not made the payments for several months. He took my wedding rings and the diamonds he had given me and pawned them without telling me. I no longer had a credit card to show as an ID when writing checks. I could not make hotel reservations, or rent a video. I wanted to apologize and explain to everyone what had happened to me. I wanted people to forgive and not judge me. I felt desperate for some reassurance that I had not failed miserably at everything that was important to me. No one wanted to hear. The house went into foreclosure when we couldn't sell it. I had two weeks to find a house to lease for my daughters and myself. My husband didn't answer his phone. On the final day we were moving out my next door neighbor confronted me in the driveway and demanded to know who was going to maintain the pool, since the pumps and filter were now turned off. She was worrying about seeing algae in my pool from her bedroom window. She harangued me as if I was just an irritation in her day. I sobbed and mourned the loss of my marriage, my house and my life. The next time I was to see her in the grocery store she avoided my eyes and turned down another aisle rather than speak to me. I no longer lunched or shopped and I cleaned my own house and did my own laundry, and planted my own flowers when I could afford a few in the front yard of my now very modest house. What did inspire those qualities however was the journey I was about to take in my life. A journey I am still on. It is the journey for my name.

Stepping down in social class did not prepare me for what I was about to experience as a single divorced mother. The ranks of privileged society in America, that is, of white upper middle class males and their wives, do indeed close ranks quickly. In fact, I can still hear the echo of the door slamming shut reverberating in my ear. Because the business my husband owned was borrowed against and because we lost almost everything else in our financial debacle, I was left with no assets and because of the bankruptcy I had no credit as well. My now ex-husband had taken my wedding rings but left me with his name. In the midst of despair and grief I clung to my small shred of dignity in a community of friends who now avoided me and silently endured my daily humiliation, all the while staring into two sweet faces who needed reassurance that everything would be alright. Each morning I smiled back into their eyes and gave them what little courage I could muster, always trying to keep them on track, balanced and optimistic about the future. Each night after I kissed them goodnight I would sit in the dark in the chair in my bedroom and cry for hours, feeling like a failure, feeling like an outsider, living a life that I had not chosen and did not know how to lead, angry with God in front of whom I had made my sacred vows. I felt like He no longer cared, nor was he listening to my prayers and as a result I experienced a profound crisis in my faith at a time when I needed all the faith I could manufacture. I thought of my children and how I could not prevent nor shield them from the hurt and anguish they were feeling and would feel the rest of their lives. What might someday be a new beginning for me was a permanent ending for them. They would always be children of divorce and as much as I longed to take this burden from them, it would be their burden alone. The guilt and responsibility I felt because of this was overwhelming. It reinforced my feeling of failure and my sense of helplessness that my life was now careening out of control toward a destination that I could no longer imagine.

My ex-husband in the meantime bought a Porsche and lived in an apartment at the beach. I spent hours driving my girls to their activities and went alone to school meetings, back to school nights, dance competitions and banquets. The chairs were always arranged in groupings of twos at the tables, I never knew where to sit. The information from school was addressed "to the parents of" no matter how many times I told them I was just Ms. now. My Sunday school class politely informed me that I might enjoy the single parent fellowship or the single woman's class now that I was no longer married. It was the same me inside. I wanted to scream it at them. I felt a constant gnawing in the pit of my stomach feeling that my life had become surreal, that this couldn't be me. I looked forward to the solace of my bedroom chair in the cool darkness late each night where I could indulge my grief, my profound sense of loss and separateness, and my humiliation at becoming someone I no longer knew. While desperately trying to keep my little family ship on an even keel, I was lonely and confused. I was no longer invited to the usual barbecues and parties, card games and get together. I was no longer part of a couple and my old friends did not know how to talk to me. The fun trips that we used to take with three other couples were no more. I had no one to go to the movies with on Sunday afternoon. Society is arranged for couples. I had taken these things for granted. I could never feel excluded or discriminated against or disenfranchised. I was a white upper middle class married woman. My pastor stated in church one Sunday that he wanted to make our church one of strong marriages that would reflect God to the community. I sat alone and wondered what that meant my life would reflect.

Rain
Margarita Adame

The storm
continued for nine months
as we moved
from home to home
with our relatives.

The worst part come
close to the end of the nine months.
We left an uncle's home
and it was raining
endlessly.
We all got into the car
and it hit us.
We were homeless.
Other family members
had protected us from the storm.
But,
this last one,
didn't care what else
the rain
washed away.

My Stomach Was Always Empty
Christine Clark

Growing up as the youngest of six, my parents were exhausted and so I raised myself mostly. It was expensive to raise us. My brothers were gigantic and never stopped eating. Also my father had spinal surgery and could not work for two years. Our friends would help us out and sometimes put food on our front porch like bread and pastries but that was rare.

My stomach was always empty. When I did manage to get food my brothers would eat my food before I could finish it. I learned to eat fast and never leave my plate to go to the bathroom during a meal.

Lunch money was a privilege not a necessity—and if I did pack my lunch it was always a pickle sandwich with mayonnaise. I learned to hide food in the house. I would save any food from school I could get my hands on and keep it in my purse. I loved the days when they served apples, wrapped cookies and orange juice.

Anyway, grooming was the next issue. Or should I say, "lack of grooming"? I was supposed to keep my hair long for some religious reason—what I never knew. But I was responsible for my hair and so dread locks became of me. Ratty ratty hair and so it was. I didn't care because I had no self-esteem because when you're a child and you don't have money, you don't think you have any value.

My parents work two jobs and deal with guilt on a daily basis. They always think that they aren't good parents because they could not afford what we needed. They feel badly that their youngest daughter has no bed nor a birthday party. They never wanted us to feel differently, but we did.

My teachers would ask if I would like to go home with them on the weekend. I asked my mother and she was more happy than I. She needed a break and also wanted me to do well in my life. So I went.

And so I would go with anyone who would take me. I moved out young and grew up fast. I met several people who took extreme interest in me and believed in me. They told me to "reach for the stars."

The cycle will not continue. I educated myself and will not have more kids than I can give attention to. My brothers and sisters will not have many children either. They struggled with our reality more than I for they tried to kill themselves repeatedly because they just never felt worthy enough.

I will never return to the house I was raised in because it is infested with mice, rats, cockroaches and fleas. So now, as future teachers, maybe you want to know what you can do for students like me? Give them love, they need it. Hug them, compliment them, they eat it up. Look beyond their smelly hair and dirty clothes and do not judge them because, believe me they have already written themselves off.

Shame
Stephen Windes

The school was familiar, though all along my family was different. We lived only three blocks away, walking distance. It was a Catholic school, and it always seemed as if every other student got a ride in a flashy car; everyone else's parents seemed well dressed. Tuition at the school was costly. My mother worked to make ends meet, and I don't remember anyone at home when I got back from school. My father worked nights and I didn't get much help on homework. I took pre-algebra in eighth grade. When I asked my mother questions, she never knew the answer. I learned quickly not to ask her.

The mother of a friend who was one of the lunch-moms noticed how often I came to school without a lunch. She stared bringing an extra one for me. At first, it was great. I'd never had such snacks. There were juice containers, chips, cookies or candies, sandwiches I had never seen before. It took awhile for me to realize that I was the only one who needed a lunch. I don't know if my mother ever realized where my lunches were coming from. It wasn't the first time school had taught me something about shame.

You should understand, there were nine people in my family. It was wonderful to have siblings sometimes, instant friends and companions, partners in play. It's just expensive. I never had a costume for the parade on Halloween. I shared my bedroom with my younger brother by five years. Our house attracted many of the neighborhood kids, perhaps the appeal of a house without many rules. As I said, there was rarely a parent home. My father worked two jobs for a number of years. My mother did the same.

I was always aware that my bicycle came from a garage sale. When it was new, the paint was faded, the seat torn. It was a few sizes too big. The brakes squeaked. And I loved to ride it.

I had a few friends. Most of them were rejects, some nerds, some social incompetents, some rebels. I was shy, I was attracted to the fringe element from the beginning. With them, I found acceptance.

My best friend never had a father. I never thought it ever made a difference to him. I wasn't very happy with my own dad, I figured, not having one couldn't be that much worse.

After my sophomore year, I switched schools again—from the private school arena to a public school near my home. I wanted to be "in" but certain things about my character and my appearance kept me "out." That hurts. That's when you can sink into a kind of hell of wanting so badly to be part of a group that you would follow them over the edge of a bridge.

Dear Dad
Nicole Joy

Dear Dad,
The kids tease us and say we are the savages, the wild ones. They make fun of us because we do not have all the things they do. They say we are wild and you left us, or we killed you because we are savages. We can't tell Mom because she has so much to worry about, and what could she do anyway? A couple of weeks ago a friend gave me some of her great clothes to wear that she had outgrown. I was so excited that I had them and wore those new things to school.

Cynthia told everyone that we were poor and had no right to live where we did. She said that her mother felt sorry for our family and gave me some of Cynthia's clothes to wear that Cynthia had outgrown, but were like new. Kids were coming up to me at school and asking me if what Cynthia said was true. I did not know what to say. I just ran into the bathroom at school and cried. I could not wait to get home and take those clothes off. Dad, why are people so mean?

I hate being different and people making fun of me. It seems like our family just isn't good enough to live here and go to school here. We can't have kids over because other parents don't think it is right to let their kids come over when there is not a mom and dad at home.

My best friend moved away recently. I miss her a lot since she just accepted me as I was. She was the only one that ever stayed overnight at our house. She did not make fun of the fact that we did not have some of the nice things that her other friends had. Sometimes I thought she felt sorry for me. I really hate it when people pity you. I do not want any one's pity. I just want a chance to accomplish my goals in life.

Mom is concerned that there will be some layoffs at her store. I seem to be helping her more and more financially. I do not have enough money to go to college. Everyone at school is talking about where they got accepted. I can't manage to scrape enough money together to apply to any college. I think I will work for a while and then go to school.

I have so many dreams that I cannot share with anyone at home. They all think I am just a dreamer. I believe that I just have to work harder than others to accomplish my goals because we are different. Would it have been any different if you were here? I sure think so, but will never know.

Your loving daughter,
Nicole

The Uncool Me
Trini Figueroa

My parents came from Mexico to improve their economic situation. With five children to support, they had no choice but to work two shifts. They shared apartments and rented homes with other relatives in order to survive. Owning a home was their only dream.

Going to school became a living torture. I felt myself under a microscope. My appearance suddenly was a crucial part of my life. Of course, nothing about myself reflected anything "cool." My Prowing tennis shoes were no competition to L.A. Gears that everyone wore. All my life I had known K-Mart and thrift stores but nothing about shopping malls. How could I be "hip" like the rest of the kids with second hand clothes my teachers gave me?

Even receiving free lunch became an embarrassment. I hated recess. While everyone played and chit chatted, I would look for a hidden area to sit. I would cry my way home everyday. All I wished was to be a part of them and not to be alienated.

It took me a years before I could find a true friend; a friend that did not place barriers of race and class. My experience, though harsh, taught me to be independent and to believe in myself. At fifteen, I got my first job and bought things my parents could not afford. I put myself through college and proved to others that even a poor Mexican girl can be "cool."

New Kid on the Block
Alix Wu

My mom was a struggling single mother barely making enough money to support the two of us. Because she couldn't afford a babysitter, I had to be a "latch-key kid." I actually had my house key on a string tied around my neck. After school, I would go home and wait till my mom came back from work. She'd stay for a couple of hours to make sure I was okay, and got ready to go to her next job. Working one job wasn't enough to pay all our bills.

After she'd leave, I'd go play outside with the neighborhood kids. When it got dark and all my friends were called in by their moms, I came back home to an empty apartment. I remember crying a lot because I missed my mom so much.

I went to schools where the population was predominantly Hispanic. I remember many times being the only Asian kid in my class. I was teased a lot from my classmates, especially by the boys. They slanted their eyes with their fingers and called me "china." I remember hating it because it made me feel different. I didn't like being different.

This period of time was really tough on me. We moved once or twice a year. I don't know why we moved so often. Maybe my mother was looking for cheaper rent or perhaps we were evicted. Because we moved so often, I always found myself having to make new friends in my neighborhood and in my new school. I was always the "new kid on the block."

INTELLECTUAL DIFFERENCE–3G

My mother told me that her parents would lock my aunt, her kid sister, in the backroom of their business, a little café, so that the customers would not see her. She had a rash (eczema) and was diagnosed schizophrenic. They believed if people could see her, it would drive business away. Not only would Westerners be repulsed by her but so would fellow Chinese, who were superstitious and believed that disabilities were a result of a cursed ancestor. Some ancestral god placed this curse on the family for some wrongdoing committed by a family member in a former life.

"Traditionally, disabilities have been analyzed primarily in medical terms or, by social scientists, in terms of deviance. In the social science literature, deviance is defined as an attribute that sets the individual apart from the majority of the population, who are assumed to be normal" (Groce, 1985, p. 3). Anything that is deviant from the norm has a social stigma (Goffman, 1963) of being polluted or impure (Douglas, 1966). What is deviant varies from culture to culture (Edgerton, 1976).

"They" are called exceptional, disabled, handicapped, and at risk (Banks & McGee Banks, 2003, pp. 296-297). Their differences in academic skills spawn stereotypes, ungrounded fears, and nonacceptance by typical individuals. Tolerance for the intellectually different is limited. The perceived disability is sometimes more disabling than the disability itself. They (students with special needs) are discriminated against for their disabling condition. They are labeled, segregated, seen as misfits, and considered deficient and/or genetically inferior (Amos & Landers, 1984).

Evidence of their otherness status can be found by their social and geographical marginalization at schools. They are located, if not at a different site, in a different building. If not in a building, in some remote corner of the school campus. "My (special education) class and I were assigned a recess spot on the opposite side of the play yard, far away from the 'normal' children" (Aiello, 1976, p. 14). "They" even have their own separate buses.

The Retarded Bus
Dean Wagner

No matter what school I went to, there was always a retarded bus. Boy was I glad that I never had to go on that bus. Unbeknownst to the passengers on the "retarded bus," we would tease and make cruel remarks behind their backs. I was also very glad that nobody from my family went on that bus. I would watch the children get off the bus. Some people were very different. Some would need a wheelchair. However, some looked and acted very normal. Why were they on the "retarded bus"?

One time I had a girl in my elementary class that road the little retarded bus. I never really talked to her. She was always very quiet and never played any of the fun games during recess. She was different because she rode the retarded bus.

Many years later my wife and I had our first son. His name is Drew. Drew is very smart, active, coordinated, and really loves life. One amazing thing about Drew is that he doesn't forget a thing. At three years old we enroll Drew into preschool. We are so excited for him. After several weeks had passed, Drew's preschool teacher asked my wife and I to come and observe Drew at the preschool. She stated that she was concerned about his ability to communicate with others. While driving down to the preschool, my mind was racing with anger and denial. How could anybody think my son couldn't communicate? How could anybody think my son isn't smart? How long has Drew's teacher been teaching? Maybe Drew's teacher was hard of hearing? There is nothing wrong with Drew, somebody else must be wrong! The anger and frustration continued to grow as we approached the preschool.

Drew's teacher recommended that a professional should evaluate him. She then ushered us to playground where all the children were playing. My eyes searched for my son. He was playing with the other kids. I was relieved. I knew that there was nothing wrong with my son!

As we walked closer to within hearing range, I could hear the other children's conversation. They were trying to get Drew to chase them because he was different. He would catch one of the children only to be pushed away. "Let me go you weirdo!" they shrieked. Drew didn't understand and started to cry.

I have never been so hurt in my life. I grew up being well liked, athletic and intelligent. To see my own son, my own flesh and blood, not being accepted by his own peers was very difficult. It was as if somebody had pierced me in the heart.

We started with all different types of testing. While we were waiting for the evaluations and the testing, we had him in private speech lessons. We had several doctors evaluate him. Finally, the doctors came to the conclusion that he had a processing disorder. The best news was that he could possibly overcome this disability on his own with a lot of hard work. My wife did some research and found out that the school district had a program to help Drew's disability. We went through another battery of tests with the school district. After six weeks of meetings and testing, the school district decided Drew qualified for the program. I was so relieved until the principal said transportation is provided by the district. Drew will have a bus pick him up and return him home. Immediately I realized the retarded bus was coming to our house.

That evening, I insisted that my wife drive Drew to school in our car. I did not want him labeled. All of those memories from my own elementary school haunted my mind. For the first time, I felt like an outsider wanting in.

Would Drew be labeled for the rest of his life? Would our family be labeled as well? I wanted him and our family to be classified as normal! How could we be normal if the "retarded bus" was coming to our home?

For the first time in my life, I realized I didn't fit into the norm. We had a child that needed special attention. I felt a sense of embarrassment when the retarded bus came to our house. With time I realized that I was the only person who thought this way. Nobody said anything about the retarded bus coming to our home. The topic of discussion was always about the progress Drew had made. With time I realized how much easier it was to converse with my son. I realized how well he was able to express himself. Drew has overcome his disability without any mental scars. I learned to overcome my own prejudices that I had carried with me since elementary school. I eventually looked forward to the little yellow and white school bus coming to our house because that little yellow and white school bus was an instrument in helping to correct my son's disability and my own insecurities and narrow mindedness.

Dumb, Dumb Reading
Stroller White

As I proceeded through elementary school I remember enjoying it less and less each year. In second grade I was placed into the dumb dumb reading group. A phobia of reading out loud started to form at this point. By fourth grade I would go to a remedial reading class. A pullout I remember as super dumb dumb reading. I remember running down the long hallways at school yelling and screaming then sliding on our bellies into a stack of chairs at the end of the hall. We went to super dumb dumb reading but we never went quietly.

This reading problem was starting to get me down. A feeling of frustration was developing; a frustration that was starting to become part of my everyday existence. The last few months of that year I spent every recess sitting under a little bush with my back against the wall watching the other kids play.

Fifth grade I had a great teacher. The bush was no longer an option. I started to get in a lot of fights. By the third month of school I was the meanest, most frustrated motherfucker in the school. I was fighting everyone. I made a daily trip to the principal's office. I fought girls, friends, it did not matter. I could, in no way, control the rage that was engulfing me. I was scared to death of myself. I tried to control my anger. I remember going to the edge of our playground away from anyone else and repeatedly yelling, at the top of my lungs, "FUCK." I would yell so loud that the sound FUCK became my world. FUCK was in me, coming out of me, and with eyes shut tight fuck engulfed my entire world outside. I remember yelling louder and louder, fuck becoming more my world and reality slipping away. Like a cross between a hallucination and a dream, my reality would shift. I would envision the earth pulling away from me. The earth got smaller as I yelled louder, eventually I could roll the world around in the palm of my outstretched hand. Frustration and rage were all around me. No matter how hard I tried I never made the world disappear entirely. I would have, if I could have, destroyed all of humanity in an attempt to ease my frustration and pain. Worst thing was I didn't know where it was coming from and it was obvious that no one else in the entire school felt the way I did. I felt like this everyday.

Toward the end of fifth grade we were required to take a test to see how as a school, we were performing. As I stared at the page, all of the rage that I usually released in the playground comes shooting up through my spine. It nearly rips my head off and the next thing I know I'm standing up. My test booklet is torn and crumpled. "FUCK THIS TEST!" Throwing the booklet in the trash, I head outside. I feel dangerously volatile. I don't want to kill anyone when my body explodes with the force of an A-Bomb. Once outside I start to feel better. I'd been in trouble enough times to know I would eventually wind up in the principals office so I made my way to his office.

The following summer I took tests to figure out what was wrong with me. My mother and I would drive for hours to different doctors at labs and hospitals. I would get hooked up to machines that had needles that rocked, special do-hickies that tested my eyes, hearing, and equilibrium. It was all tested, my reflexes, reaction time, and IQ. I drew pictures of people in my life, plants and animals and again the circles.

I got into the special school with flying colors. I got into a fight every day with a kid named Trevor. Me kicking the shit out of Trevor every day was the least of this school's problem. Every kid there was the craziest motherfucker in his or her real school back home. This place was the illest of the ill. I'm eleven at this point.

I absolutely hated this school. I had some friends and tried to make the best of it. The main problem was the atmosphere. It was as if the school was electrified. At any given time the entire school would erupt into an every man for himself eraser fight, or a giant all school dog pile onto one unfortunate kid. We had dumpster fires, we took the hinge pins out of doors, so the entire door would fall down when the teacher would open it, we would jump or dangle out the window when the teacher turned her back. The school was an oppressively tense place for both teachers and students.

I was putting in my time, learning to read, waiting for the day I could join my friends in regular school. I told only my closest friends where I was going to school and what it was like. I avoided doing sports of any other activity were I was likely to see an old school mate. Whenever I saw someone from my public school days it was always the same thing "Where have you been? I thought you moved? Where are you going to school?" That subject always came up and I was ashamed.

I never did enter the public school system again. My parents told me they were scared I'd fall behind. They liked the individual attention offered by private schools. Plus they had learned not to trust the public school system. You see if a child is diagnosed with a learning disability that the school can't handle, like the one I had, then the public school system must pay to send that child to a special school. All the frustration, agony, hell and alienation I was put through was to help a school system stay within budget. The school system would never acknowledge that I had a problem beyond their capabilities. This is ridiculous given the fact I couldn't read in 5th grade.

I will always be indebted to my parents for staying by my side, never giving up hope, and laying down some cold hard cash to set me straight. I can only hope I will be as persistently warm and giving if this kind of thing should ever happens to any of my children.

Ditz
Jill Edelberg

It all began the day I was four
and first walked through the kindergarten door,

I realized I wasn't like all the others
who stood excitedly with their mothers.
I was frightened, I was scared,
I didn't feel at all prepared.

But in I went and mommy left,
I stood by the door all day and wept.

I cried every day I went,
I hated the time there that I spent.

I couldn't keep up with the rest of the class,
In and out of my brain information would pass.

I couldn't do things that the 5- and 6-year-olds could do,
My teacher would ask "what's wrong with you?"

You're a terrible crier and a horrible student,
She didn't even try, to her I was translucent.

And so every day I felt a little bit worse
And so began my life-long curse.

For through the years my self-esteem fell,
I didn't feel that I could do well.

My teachers would lecture and I'd begin to shake,
all that information was too much to take!
And when I was made to feel stupid for asking the teacher "Why?"
I would immediately lose it and begin to cry.

And then inevitably someone would say,
"Oh, that's just Jill. She's always that way."

I had lots of friends who took me under their wing.
They thought they were doing such a generous thing,

Because "Jill simply couldn't stand on her own two feet.
She's not at all bright but she's cute and she's sweet!"

So I was proclaimed as the "ditz" of the crowed,
and although I fit in, I didn't feel proud.

The years went by and I just couldn't shake,
the dim-witted position I was forced to take.
And I started to believe that I really was dumb,
and I took on the role as if it were fun.

I figured being thought of a ditz isn't too bad!
think of the worse luck that others have had.

It wasn't that awful being pampered and protected,
but what made me feel bad was when I was neglected.

I was never included in intellectual debating.
They shunned my opinions and it felt so degrading!

My ideas and thoughts were never taken to heart.
What I had to say was usually dismissed from the start.
But I would get patted on the head for at least trying.
They had no idea that with each pat I was dying.

Did it make them feel big to make me feel small?
I didn't think they meant to hurt my feelings at all.

And the most ironic part is that of all of my friends,
I'm the only one that graduated from college in the end.

So who is the smart one and who is dumb?
I've had the last laugh and, I admit. It's been fun.

Slower Than Other Students
Melissa A. Martin

I know what it is like to struggle with a math problem or feel like every student in the room is staring because they're waiting for you to finish the assignment. I spent years in elementary school feeling like an outsider for these same reasons. I was always much slower than other students and always had special books and special tutors that took me outside of class to help me understand what the rest of the students in the class already knew.

I can remember on several occasions feeling like I wasn't like everyone else, and that is a hard concept for a child to adjust to. My memories of school begin at a very early age.

One of my first recollections of elementary school was a time when I was sitting in Ms. Harris' first grade classroom learning how to create sentences using proper punctuation. I remember Ms. Harris showing some concern about my work and raising her voice out of frustration. It was not long after I started the first grade that I had what my mom called helpers to come and assist me with my grammar and math or whatever I had trouble with. For at least an hour each day I would sit outside the classroom in a sunken area of the carpet and work with the tutor. Although it was very helpful, the idea of being separated from my class just made me feel different, or slow.

It was at the end of the first few months of first grade that Ms. Harris requested a conference with my parents. A grade report consisting of Cs and Ds was sent home and my parents were obviously concerned. Although I had always tried my best and both my parents and Ms. Harris knew this, I was still struggling to stay on top of my work. She suggested that I repeat the grade, strongly believing the extra year would be helpful. Although my parents agreed that retaining me might make second grade a little easier, the idea of separating my twin sister and I really bothered them. It was the decision of my parents and not Ms. Harris to let me continue, I would somehow be labeled or that I would not be given the proper opportunities like the other students.

I continued on to the second grade, struggled with most subjects, was pulled out of class for testing and sent to special programs after school for help. I cannot remember a time in which I did not have tutors or I was participating in class without special help or special homework. Being young I do not believe the segregation from my class bothered me or upset me as much as it did when I was older. But as the years passed, I felt like my parents had exhausted the idea of a tutor and I was simply tired of spending each Saturday practicing my math and completing worksheets. I was a normal kid who just wanted to play with my sister and be with my friends. It is hard for a young child to admit that the extra help is really necessary, but deep down I knew this was true. I knew the only way I could keep up with the rest of the class was if I did have the tutors and special help.

I remember being very frustrated and sad at times because I was not like my other friends who caught on so quickly. I was one of the few students (along with the class discipline problems) that would sit in during recess and work on my unfinished homework. I felt so sad that all my friends were out playing and sad that my friends knew the reason I wasn't. I can remember the one week which I did complete all the work assigned and went out to play at recess. It was one of the best weeks in fourth grade.

I Was the Smart One
Sharee Pfaf

My teachers referred to me as a "model student" who was a "ray of sunshine in class." They always called on me and were always pleased with my performance. As a result of my positive experiences, I loved school, and I loved to learn.

By the time we reached third and fourth grade, the dynamics of our group of students was beginning to change. Socially, strong cliques were forming, and strict standards for admission into each group were being established. Being smart usually was not a respected quality nor was it a means to acceptance. I began to find myself losing friends because I was not willing, or allowed from my parents' point of view, to give up my academic success. To further my inappropriateness, I had the misfortune of being in a carpool with three of the most outspoken boys of our grade. These three took it upon themselves to successfully set me apart as "the teacher's pet," a separation which many others readily acknowledged.

By the time our class reached junior high, I was labeled as "the smart one" and was not offered many social opportunities. Having that one label seemed to imply an open door, or open season, for teasing that related to me; whether it was about my relationships with teachers, my clothes, my looks, my parents' cars, anything. Any part of my life was fair game, and all students tolerated any jokes about me. Still, I maintained my grades. I began to resent being the "smart one" because I was ostracized from my whole class. Junior high is a difficult time period as it is. To have to deal with social isolation in a class of only 40 students was extremely difficult. I started wishing that the teachers would not call on me or would not read my papers in front of class, because I could almost feel the glares of other students on the back of my head. These instances only further hindered my acceptance by my peers, and I wanted desperately to be accepted. I broke off a relationship with a good friend as a result of trying to prove myself to the "in" group. I tried to live up to their standards and to base my thinking on their ideas. I gave up what I could, but I could not give up academics, so my situation remained the same. The teachers still loved me; the students did not.

Needless to say, by the end of junior high, I had a very low self-esteem. I could find no comfort in being "the smart one" or "the teacher's pet." I remember the day when I was walking with my head down looking at my knee socks and I reached the decision, "It's OK. I don't need any friends. I have myself. I'll be fine."

I was sure that wearing those silly knee socks was another reason why nobody liked me. I never did share with my parents all of the emotional turmoil I experienced. As long as I brought home good grades, they were happy. Keeping them happy was my one opportunity to have some control over at least one area of my life.

High school intimidated me. While I was relieved to be away from junior high, I felt completely incapable of making any friends. At this new school I knew only one person, someone I had known since second grade, but this was our first time at school together. She was frustrated with me because I would walk around campus with my head down, fearful that someone would look at me. Ultimately I was afraid of being judged or teased again. I sat in the back of classes and did not participate, because I certainly was not about to come across as "the smart one" at this school. I even toyed with the idea of changing the pronunciation of my name because I thought it would be more acceptable. I knew that I was a good student, but my abilities caused me so much heartache at my previous school that I wanted to do all that I could to blend in and to not draw any attention to myself.

RELIGION–3H

Every Sunday when I was a young girl, we read the Sunday comics while other families went to church. My family attended no church and claimed no affiliation to any known religious group. Who were we spiritually?

I only know that "our ways" were Chinese and it was hard to decipher where culture starts and ethics or spirituality ends. They were commingled and a conglomerate of ways of life. Elders, ancestors, and superstitions were our moral guides. We knew to pay reverence to our elders and ancestors and to go to them when we were unsure. We didn't need anything else. When I was young, I would ask my Christian classmates, "How could Jesus be my god if I'm not white?" They didn't know either.

In the past decade, and then catapulted by September 11th, there has been a growing realization of our social responsibility to understand religion's multiple forms in multicultural education. Harvard professor, Diana Eck (2001) claimed in her new book, The New Religious America, *that the United States is the most religiously diverse nation on earth. Islam is the fastest growing religion and yet it is shrouded in mystery for most Americans. This ignorance prompted uncharitable logic like, the terrorists who bombed the World Trade Center were Muslims, and, therefore, all Muslims must be interned. Timothy McVeigh who bombed Oklahoma City was Catholic, should we become suspect of all Catholics (Sapon-Shevin, personal communication, 2001).*

In the religious narratives that follow, the concepts of difference and otherness played a major role in the development of who one is, religiously. It was in the face of opposition, that some students affirmed their faith. Many students found it useful to define themselves by defining first who they weren't. In mixed religious households, religions were compared like cousins; held up to regular family scrutiny to determine which did better in life. Other students disclosed that their histories of religious oppression had taught them to hide their religion. Kaye/Kantrowits (1996) reported that some Jewish women have had nose jobs performed so as to not look Jewish. This is done not only for cosmetic reasons but also to escape religious or cultural prejudice. "Many Jews can walk safely down the streets of North America because our Jewishness is not visible . . . If I need to, I can hide" (p. 129).

Green Eggs and Ham
Elan Goldmann

> I will not eat them in a box!
> I will not eat them with a fox!
> I will not eat them in a house!
> I will not eat them with a mouse!
> I do not like them here or there!
> I do not like them anywhere!
> I do not like Green Eggs and Ham!
> I do not like them, Sam-I-Am!
> —Dr. Seuss

We had just read the book *Green Eggs and Ham* at my preschool, and as a follow-up activity, we were going to eat green eggs and ham. The green eggs (eggs with a little food coloring), I had no problem with, but the ham, I simply could not eat. This was because I kept kosher.

A typical conversation about my eating habits will usually start like this: a friend or acquaintance, noticing that I am consistently ordering fish or vegetarian dishes while eating out will ask; "Are you a vegetarian?"

"Well, no, not really . . ."

"What do you mean, not really?"

"Well, I keep kosher."

"What's that?"

"Do you really want to know?"

"This is really good. Too bad you can't eat this steak/shrimp/ Twinkie/bacon-double-cheeseburger."

My Jewishness
Heather Meade

Heather Meade does not sound like a very Jewish name, nor do I look like what seems to be the stereotypical Jewish woman. I do have curly hair, but I don't necessarily have a large nose or talk in a loud "Jewish" tone of voice. I am Jewish though.

In my youth we went to temple every Friday night for Sabbath (Shabbat). I prayed at a young age and even went to Sunday school. Being virtually the only Jewish child in elementary school classrooms was difficult for me. Especially when my teachers would not acknowledge my religion or holidays. I felt weird not being in school on Yom Kippur and Rosh Hashana.

Peers would ask me, "What's Jewish?" There is no reason why I should have been embarrassed, but I was. The lack of understanding among others and the neglect of my celebrations made me sad and confused inside. Why at the holiday season did the teachers only talk about Christmas, Santa Claus, and trees? What about Chanukah Menorahs, and the eight days of gifts? I knew how beautiful my religion was so why did I hide it? It was not until 4th grade did I open up more and share.

It was not until 6th grade when I began to hear or I should say understand the derogatory remarks about Jewish people. Jokes, slurs, racial comments about "cheap Jews" or "Jew em-down" were beginning to affect me more. My stomach would always sink when I heard these remarks, especially when they came from my supposed friends' mouths. I didn't want to bring attention to myself, my "Jewishness."

Dirty Jew
Shana Brown

Some of the children in her class did not like her because she was Jewish. Although she looked like everyone else, dressed like everyone else and acted like everyone else, she was reminded that she was not. Some children on the playground who whispered and pointed called her a "dirty Jew."

Each day when she got up to go to school, a knot would form in the pit of her stomach. She tried to explain to her mom how it was at school, but her mom would tell her to be strong and proud of who she was and where she came from, whatever that meant. Her family moved following the burning of her father's car.

They would ask her what she did on "her" holiday and she would try to make it sound as exciting as possible, regaling them with stories of the battle that took place hundreds of years ago and the miracle that happened there, which is called the Festival of Lights or Hanukkah.

She knew that for the next two weeks, at school, she would be making Santas, Christmas trees and Christmas stockings, in addition to seeing movies such as *Charlie Brown's First Christmas*. Her classroom was heavily decorated with festive banners exclaiming "Merry Christmas!" It was at these times that she felt that she did not belong. In the Glee Club (known as the "chorus" these days), they would be singing songs such as "Silent Night," "O Come All Ye Faithful," and "We Wish You a Merry Christmas."

As she sang each song and hearing how beautiful they sounded, she wished they were part of her but she knew they were not. During those recitals, she never felt more isolated and invisible. After a few years of being a part of the Glee Club, she was amazed one year when the musical selections had included "The Dreydl Song."

She was now at a point where she was completely involved in clubs and groups, both through school and in Jewish community organizations, living a completely bicultural life. She loved school and hanging out with her friends, but was never completely free of the reminders that she was not fully accepted within her own neighborhood. She and her family found these reminders burned into their lawn and written in mud on the side of their house. Her parents would tell her that these were just teenage pranks from kids who did not know any better. The explanation may have been true but that did not make her feel any better. She was really shaken up.

Dates brought to family functions were truly like a fish out of water. She would watch their eyes glaze over as they would go through the rituals involved in her holiday traditions and she would again realize the depth of their differences. At a time when fitting in was a powerful force, she was incapable of standing strong and taking pride in her culture, so she lived in limbo between two realities. She was sixteen years old.

It is now her passion to convey to her children that differences are a positive aspect of living in this society and should be relished and cherished; celebrated and shared. They are a part of you and a heritage to be proud of. So when my son or daughter comes to me and feels "small" in the eyes of the majority, I tell them to stand strong and be proud of their uniqueness.

My Experience with "Otherness"
Todd Nelson

"I believe in Christ. He is my King. With all my heart to Him I'll sing" are the verses in a hymn written by Bruce R. McKonkie. Not only can you find this printed in a book of hymns, but also engraved in my heart. I do believe in Christ. He is my example, my leader and my hope.

Ironically, in a multicultural class I took at the state university, some people tried to define my beliefs about Christ. A teacher wrote on the board and told the class, "We can group religion into Christian religion, Eastern religion and Other." He then asked the class, "Where does Born Again Christian, Catholics and Protestants go?" The class replied in unison, "Christian religion." Then he looked at the board again and said, "Hmm, what category could we put The Church of Jesus Christ of Latter-Day Saints?" Some replied, "Under Christian religion," but some people in the class were uneasy with this decision and said, "No, Mormons are not Christians." Others disagreed, "Yes they are." I sat there quietly in shock because nobody knew that I was Mormon. Then a girl arrogantly called out, "Oh they believe in Christ, but it is a different type of Christ than what Christians believe in." I replied, "Oh what type of Christ do the 'Christians' believe in?"

The whole class was in turmoil over this question. The teacher finally said, "Hold on! We will put it under both 'Christian' and 'Other' to appease the class." I have been spit at, yelled at, laughed and mocked for my beliefs while I was on a two-year mission for my church, but never have I been so angry, displaced, humiliated and uncomfortable than on this day, in a class titled Multiculturalism in America. The goal of the class was to better understand people of different race, ethnicity, background and religion. The only thing I learned that day was that I was an "Other" in this class.

It's the Same Me I've Always Been
Cindy

Both my parents were raised in very strict Catholic homes and because of this Catholicism has been a very real part of our lives, and I think a place where we as a family have identified ourselves. I can't really remember a Sunday where we missed church, and growing up all three of us kids have been involved in the youth group, retreats, and obtained all the necessary sacraments of the Catholic church. Our religion was us and we were our religion; complete with church attendance on all the major religious holidays such as Ash Wednesday and Corned Beef and Cabbage with green applesauce on St Patrick's Day. The ultimate Irish-Catholic Holiday.

We were a strong close family and still are relatively close, but you can imagine the shock and dismay when I told my parents that I wanted to be baptized into the Church of Jesus Christ of Latter Day Saints, yes . . . the Mormon Church. I had been looking into the church for about six months and I was for the most part pretty honest with my parents, but I think they thought I was just going through a phase. My Dad's first inclination was that he was going to convert me back to Catholicism when my Mom came to me in tears and said, "I just don't know where we went wrong." They couldn't believe that I would be married in the Mormon Temple.

Then the neighborhood was notified of my rebellious behavior and they couldn't say enough about how I was disgracing my family. People I didn't even know were giving me dirty looks, or coming up to me and asking personal questions. Worst of all, my sister told me that she didn't feel like a twin anymore. But how do you continually invite someone into your life only to be continually rejected? Being Mormon in an all-Catholic family has been the greatest challenge of my life. The hardest challenge was the rejection by my own family.

Somewhat Obvious, Yet Hidden
Roselyn Ashton

One of the first times that I remember religion being an issue in my life was in fourth grade. My teacher would "take the Lord's name in vein" excessively. I cried to my mother not understanding how Ms. Anderson, whom I looked up to with such admiration, could say that phrase that I had been taught was worse than four-letter swear words. I knew by this age that not everyone was Mormon, but I thought that in a way we were all at least Christians. "Thou shalt not take the name of the Lord thy God in vein." That made the top ten on Mount Sinai. Didn't she know that? My mom told my teacher that she was offending me. My teacher pulled me aside after class and apologized. I don't know if today I would have done what my mom did. But I do hope that as a teacher I would apologize to my 10-year-old student for offending her and become more sensitive to my student.

My religion has always separated me from the masses. It isn't something that people can know by looking at me. But it doesn't take long for people to notice that I am different. It is a difference that I am proud of and completely happy with. I'm a 23-year-old who has never had a sip of alcohol, never even touched a cigarette, believes that sexual intimacy is reserved for marriage and must stay within those bounds. I don't even swear, and I was always taught to dress very modestly.

In high school when I started going to dances, my mother always had to make my dress. We had a rule in our house, you had to be able to wear a normal bra and it had to have sleeves and fall within two inches of my knee. So you can imagine how many formal dresses I found that fit those requirements. Even though I felt frustrated at the time, I am glad that I was taught the importance of modesty and will do the same for my daughters.

Going to the beach in high school was also a little embarrassing during some of my insecure moments when I just wanted to blend in with everyone my age. It was always obvious who the Mormon girls were . . . the ones wearing one pieces. That makes you stick out pretty good when you're a teenager.

I worry a lot about sounding self-righteous. You see, I have these beliefs that are very different from the rest of the world. I don't want people to feel uncomfortable around me because they don't share the same views. I hope I never make someone feel that I think they are less of a person because they participate in activities that I don't think are right, or say or wear things that I wouldn't. Just because I was raised a certain way, and have come to believe in it on my own as an adult, doesn't mean that I think everyone else is bad who doesn't live the same way I do. I love learning about what other's views are on what they feel is right and wrong. What they are comfortable with. I love people regardless of their beliefs and feel that what I do is best for me, but I understand that you feel differently, and I respect that. I respect that a lot.

Honestly, my religion is my way of life. From the things that I do during the week to my thoughts, goals, and even what I eat. Sunday is the Sabbath Day. We go to church as a family for three hours, and then come home to have dinner together. Many times there is a spiritual speaker that night back at church. That day, we abstain from working, or any other ordinary activities like shopping, or going out particularly to those places where others would have to work. It is a day of resting, and spiritual rejuvenation.

Monday night is Family night for the Church of Jesus Christ of Latter Day Saints. No church meetings of any kind are held. It is the one night that everyone is to be home with their family and spend time together. There was one constant with every Family Night that never varied, there were always treats. That in itself is Mormon culture. Treats after everything. I am not kidding, cookies and punch after every meeting. We love food. The state of Utah consumes more Jell-O than any other state. And after every funeral, there is a meal where we serve a cheesy potato dish dubbed, "funeral potatoes." It is always served with ham, rolls, and of course, Jell-O Tuesday night is "mutual." This is the youth program for the 12–18-year-olds. On these nights we would go out and do service projects or just something fun together, building friendships with other kids our age with the same beliefs. As I got older in high school, being Mormon got harder. I no longer felt comfortable hanging out with friends from school. They were partying and starting to have sex. It didn't bother me that they were doing that, it just made me sad that I no longer wanted to hang out with them.

Every morning at 6 a.m. in high school, I went to seminary. I don't know how but I did it, physically there yes, mentally not always. I studied a different book of scripture each year; The Old Testament, New Testament, then the Book of Mormon. I went to seminary with people my age from four other high schools. It was fun and I learned some great lessons.

Many people have stereotypes of Mormons. I'm glad that as I get older, I talk to more educated people, and many of the old questions have been weeded out like, "How many wives does your dad have?" "Does your church make you have big families?" "What would they do to you if you did have a beer?" "Why are there so many rules?" The first question always cracks me up. Polygamy was abolished a long time ago. And only 1% of the church even practiced. You had to be asked by the prophet at the time to practice polygamy. If you just decided to do it on your own, you were excommunicated. It had a great deal of function behind it. In the early years of the church, there were a lot more women than men. In order to take care of these women and let them own property they became polygamist wives. This practice did not last long, but it was effective. I come from a line of polygamists.

Next question, "Does your church make you have big families?" No! I think it is just kind of one of those things that you grow up in a large family and that is what is normal to you, and therefore, you want it. I am the youngest of seven and I want a big family myself. Everyone always gasps when I say this, but I honestly would love to have five or six children. I just love babies. I'm just being honest with you. But I have never heard over any pulpit that you have to fill some sort of quota with your offspring. We believe that Adam and Eve were instructed to multiply and replenish the earth; we feel that we are to continue this, but not single handedly.

"So many rules, how do you keep all those commandments?" I am asked. It's always strange to me how people see the commandments that I choose to abide by as binding and confining. I see them as what makes me free. They are true freedom to me. I know what God wants for me. I've lived enough to know that it is for my own good and when I do what I know to be right, I have peace and happiness. I have no worries in life. My life is simple because of the way that I live.

Many people think that the Church of Jesus Christ of Latter day Saints are a bunch of white people from Utah. Most don't realize that the church has over 11 million members, which more than half reside outside of the United States. The church was originally organized in New York and the people were forced to move from place to place back east because of persecution. Finally they settled in Nauvoo, Illinois. The people in surrounding areas felt threatened by the increase in the Mormon population.

Mormons lived a law of consecration where they took care of one another and were a tight knit community. The people had not been settled for very many years when the state of Illinois put out an eviction for members of the church. The first and only of it's kind in the history of the United States. It was then that the pioneers put what they could from their comfortable homes, in their covered wagons and handcarts and walked across the plains to the Salt Lake Valley. This is a rich heritage of mine that I am proud of. I don't know if I could sacrifice what they did, go through the hardships, the hunger, cold, and many deaths that they withstood to escape from the persecution. The women gave birth to babies on the side of trails they made, and buried not very many less than they bore. They gave up everything for their faith and walked pushing handcarts from Illinois to Utah, not knowing where they were going or how long it would take. This example has always been a great strength to me in my life. It has made me think about the conviction I have in what I believe compared to theirs, and has inspired me to have the same faith in God as they did. Those pioneers had no idea what an impact they were making on so many lives. It is this pioneer heritage of the church that has shaped my culture.

Growing up I never felt discriminated against, just different. It wasn't until a couple of years ago that I applied to a private Christian University and was denied because "the religious differences were too great." The woman told me that because I wasn't a Christian, I couldn't go to the school. I couldn't breathe. I am a Christian. I believe in Jesus Christ. How could someone tell me what I believe, when obviously they don't even know? For them to not want to educate me as a result of that, completely took me by surprise. I just didn't understand. Although as things always do, it turned out to be for the best.

My religion has shaped my life. I may have been raised Mormon, but I converted on my own. It was on my own that I came to believe what I do, and live my life the way I do because I studied it out on my own. I love my beliefs. They may make me peculiar to the world, but they make me who I am. They give me joy, and make me free. I am proud of my heritage, and the person I am as a result of my faith. Even though at times it was difficult to have such different values as my friends, it has made me stronger. I live my life knowing my purpose and being filled with love.

Life As a Korean-American Christian
Simon Chung

I've never given much serious thought as to who I am. Simply stated, I am Korean and a Christian. My parents sent me to Korean school every Saturday from first to third grade, hoping that I retain my Korean culture. Being Korean meant that I not display or express my feelings and emotions. It also meant that I practice self-control. I couldn't readily share my problems with "outsiders" because it would was deemed shameful. As a Korean-American, I've always felt pressure to reach a high level of "success." I suppose this somehow fits into the "model minority" stereotype. This pressure stemmed from a distinguishing trait of Korean culture, pride.

I was fortunate that my parents never placed any unrealistic expectations that I become a doctor, lawyer, or some prestigious occupation. Many Korean parents brag about how their children are attending some prestigious university, how their children are studying to be a physician, or how their children are making abundant salaries. Though many Asians do seem to have "made it," we are often pushed off to the side. Because outsiders see us driving nice cars, living in nice homes, and children making it into exceptional colleges, they often forget that we are a minority. Where is our Asian-American caucus on Sunday morning television? What acts of legislation have been created to specifically benefit Asians? Where is our affirmative action? Where is our political platform? Is it safe to presume that we our marginalized? Sure, maybe we don't have some of the fore mentioned because we don't take action in the political arena, which is a valid argument. But, maybe our parents are too busy working 12 hours a day that they don't have time to invest in political agenda? Maybe our culture prohibits such activism? Maybe we don't have a common language to bond all Asian groups together? Or, maybe our generation continues to exercise the practice of being seen and not heard?

Having been raised in Cerritos, California since the age of six, I have always been surrounded by Asians. I didn't have any worries about feeling "out of place." I found solace in the fact that there was another person who was similar to me in appearance, culture, or such at my school, church, or community. In that context, I admit that I have lived a sheltered life. Hence, I have never been the target of any "serious" acts of discrimination, or at least, none that left any damaging effects to my self-esteem or psyche. I guess I would consider myself to be very lucky in that sense.

In sixth grade, I was deemed to be a "bad seed" among some of my Korean friends' parents. I admit that I was somewhat mischievous as a child. I was often roaming around the neighborhood trying to find something to do. I really hated studying. I also hated the fact that my older brother was always at home. And, since my parents were always at work, there was no one at home to prevent my brother from beating me up. Needless to say, I was pushed to find new friends because my friends' parents wouldn't allow their children to hang around with me.

In middle school, I made a shift from having Asian friends to having mostly Caucasian friends. One could say that I had abandoned my "Asian-ness" during this period. I related much more with my Caucasian friends (or, at least a certain group of Caucasians) than my Asian counterparts. Mostly, it was our common passion for surfing and going to the beach that drew me into this new crowd. And, because most of my Asian friends were at home studying after school—which raises the common Asian stereotype of being a bookworm or nerd, I needed to find new friends that I could hang out with when school was out. In retrospect, I probably thought that my new Caucasian friends were much "cooler" than my Asian colleagues. Subconsciously, I guess it would be fair to say that I wanted to be "white." I didn't like it when my parents answered the phone in Korean. I was also embarrassed when my mom would ask who's at the door in Korean. I even tried to stop eating Korean food. I would try to speak to my parents in English rather than Korean. My friends never made any negative comments about these things, but I guess it was just something that came about. Maybe I thought I could change my race or ethnicity by erasing my ethnic practices.

Although I didn't especially struggle with my identity as a Korean too much, I did however wrestle with my Christian identity, especially during my late adolescent and early college years. It was difficult to try to maintain my Christian values, and at the same time fit in with the crowd. Being a Christian took a back seat. During my late high school years, I found myself often going along with the crowd whether it was getting intoxicated with my friends, or doing something else that wasn't Christian-like. I pretty much deserted my Christian virtues in order to fit in. Today, I don't face the same dilemma. I have matured much since completing undergraduate school. I work hard in trying not to compromise my Christian practice.

I seem to get some negative reaction from people when they find out that I am Christian. I find that many people become defensive because they expect me to pass judgment upon them. I presume it's because they believe me to take on the "holier than thou" attitude.

This assignment proved to be an arduous task. As mentioned earlier, my culture discourages the expression of feelings, as well as discouraging the disclosure of problems. I have come to terms with who I have become. I try to live up to the "model minority" stereotype. I attempt to represent myself in a positive light because I know that I can be under constant scrutiny of others. This goes hand in hand with what my dad instilled in me at a very early age . . . never to do anything to bring shame to our family. So, I try not to. Similarly, I accept the responsibility of being a living testament of Jesus Christ—Philippians 1:27: "Whatever happens, conduct yourselves in a manner worthy of the gospel of Christ."

FAMILY–3I

We would sneak back to Chinatown for saltfish and steamed pork. Mom couldn't cook it anymore because the smell repulsed my Anglo stepfather. Our bodies lived in the white part of town, but our stomachs were intestinally attached to Chinatown. My mother was a dragon lady; beautiful, charming, bright, successful businesswoman and a second-generation rebel, determined to break away from Eastern influences, eager to carve a Western path. Yung (1995) captured the second-generation phenomenon.

> *Chinese American girls had little choice but to give unquestioning obedience to their parents. However, as they became older and more exposed to a Western lifestyle and ideas of individuality and equality . . . some began to resist the traditional beliefs and practices of their immigrant parents. . . . Like most second-generation children, Chinese Americans experienced cultural conflicts and identity dilemmas when they tried to reconcile the different value system of their home culture with that of mainstream American society. (p. 115)*

Despite the skepticism and disapproval of the Chinese community, Mom married four men over a lifetime; two Chinese, two white. She was certainly no docile picture bride. After my father, husband no. 1, left, family life became turbulent and unpredictable for me. I recall—It was 3 a.m. and this the second time that month I was awakened by the shouting between my mother and my stepfather. I had my eighth-grade exams the next day, and instead of sleeping, I was shivering in my nightgown in the backyard with a flashlight, shrouded by the damp San Francisco fog. My mother instructed me to search for her gold and jade jewelry, which my stepfather had thrown out the second-story window. He was very drunk that night. I was hopeful when I found a bracelet caught in the tree branches but recognized the futility of trying to find Grandmother's gold coin earrings in the dark. Stepfather knew those were my mother's most prized possessions, the only vestiges of her Chinese ancestry. So he threw them out first, to insult her pride as a Chinese woman. Then he threw her clothes out. The police were convinced of his drunkenness to have him sleep it off in jail.

No luck in trying to keep this domestic squabble from our neighbors. In San Francisco, our buildings were so close together that they could hear a feather drop. I walked to school the next morning with a familiar slumped frame, embarrassed that the only interracial couple in the posh Marina district were at it again, as if we didn't already stand out because.

White stepfathers and the resulting cultural collisions left me emotional and psychologically exhausted. My evolving cultural self was continually engaged in a tennis match between high-speed assimilation and stubborn resistance of losing my cultural identity. This start/stop, adopt/abort, affirm/negate cultural volley prepared me for the rugged multicultural terrain in both Asian and White communities to come later in my life and for conscious cultural parenting as a parent.

Silenced
Julie Drogo

My new existence began when I was ten years old. The judge gave me the choice as to whether or not I wanted my step dad to adopt me. In my head I heard myself say no, but I knew I had better say yes. So I did. In what seemed like over night my name was no longer Julie Joanne Schinhofen but now Julie Joanne Drogo. My birth certificate was changed, school records were changed, and my friends and teachers now called me are an awkward new name. The socialization of my new identity began instantly following the adoption. I lost my cultural identity, my genetic identity, and valuable connections with family and friends. To this day if I try to recall memories before him I cannot.

My earliest recollections of starting my new identity were when he made us call him dad. If we forgot and accidentally called him Perry we would be slapped or sent to our room. We had not known him very long and had not established any type or bond or affection for him. It was taboo to talk about life before him or to ask questions about my biological family.

He controlled every aspect of our lives. My mom was no longer the strong person I had remembered her to be. She let him hurt her children. He became very abusive towards my siblings and I, especially to me because I felt that I had him pegged from day one and would let him know. I can remember one time in particular that I disagreed with him in front of a couple of my friends. I can remember his face turning bright red and the green veins in his neck before he pulled me into the other room by my hair and threw me against the wall. The next day my friends never spoke a word about it.

I started to believe that I was this horrible person that he told me that I was. The abuse became a way of life, so it was normal, not something to report to anyone. In everyone's eyes this monster was a saint. I can remember adults in my life saying things like "What other man would marry a woman on welfare with four children?" or "You should be grateful that you can have the nice things he buys for you."

The socialization process that took place in the years to come was sometimes very covert. We started to believe him when he would say that we were Italian, even though we are Dutch and German. We never felt comfortable with his family or with their culture. They are very nice people but there was never a connection. He continuously made comments about how I looked like him and that someday when I had kids they would have a lot of his traits. And although I knew this was not possible, I never questioned it.

I am having a baby this February and I have already let my mother know that he will not be left alone with my son. Needless to say this did not go over very well, but I do not want my son or future children to be subjected to anything that I was subjected to (regardless of his new passive pathetic disposition). My children will know the truth about their cultural identity, genetic identity, and connections to their family. He is still very manipulative and I can hardly look him in the eyes.

I wish I never had to see him but he still holds on to something I value, my mother. I have explained to my mother the reasons why we are all not very fond of him, and she listens, but constantly defends him. In this very succinct depiction of my being, I hope that in taking this risk, I have shed some light on how I have always felt like an "other." I can tolerate my stepfather now because he can no longer hurt me and I see him as being in my life, but in no way a part of my personal life. Despite my adaptation to dealing with him, I feel that he still has some control of my life because in many ways I am still silenced.

The Little Den
Teresita

She was young, beautiful, ivory-skinned, with blue eyes and auburn hair. She had lived in the southern state of Tennessee until age 19. The American dream seemed impossible in the small town of Ripley so in pursuit of her dream, she moved to Los Angeles in 1955.

He was young, handsome, dark-skinned, and athletic, with chocolate brown eyes and hair to match. He had come to the United States illegally in 1946. He had fled his homeland of Guadalajara, Mexico to provide for his twelve brothers and sisters. It didn't matter that he wasn't educated beyond 5th grade, what matter was his brothers and sisters had food to eat and clothing to wear.

In 1956 this woman and this man met and fell in love. Their love seemed eternal despite the many cultural differences and obstacles they would face because of their two different worlds. Within two years of their union they had together birthed two beautiful daughters, Miachelle and Teresa. Their father often called them Mikiella and Teresita.

I'm four years old and my sister and I are sitting in our den in front of Pop's chalkboard. We called him "Pop" rather than papa, dad, daddy or father. It seems to suit him better. It was our evening Spanish lesson and my sister and I would be instructed on new vocabulary words and expressions. My Pop seemed so smart to me. He was constantly sharing a little of his culture with us. I can recall those Saturday morning breakfasts of menudo and pan dulces. My sister and I loved the aroma of that little Mexican bakery which we often frequented on those precious Saturday mornings. We all seemed so happy as we ate our Mexican dishes.

I was five when I made my first trip to Mexico. We went to visit my dad's oldest sister, Tia Pita. Tia Pita lived in Guadalajara and it felt like home. We ate mangos on her porch and fed the pigeons that seemed to come in swarms. We sang and danced and rang in the New Year. It was a beautiful and festive city. I was proud to be able to use some of my Spanish I had learned in that little den back home. We traveled all throughout Mexico that Christmas and passed through Mexico City and Acapulco visiting relative after relative after relative. Pop had relatives everywhere.

We would continue to make our annual trips to Guadalajara for the next three Christmases. I cherished those days and all the cousins that had become a part of my life. My Mexican heritage was brought to life on those visits and I never thought they would come to an end. At age eight you envision that things will last forever. Little did I know my life was about to change.

It was a warm muggy afternoon when Mom and Pop arrived to pick us up from our grandma's house. Despite the heat that day everything seemed normal. My sister and I would soon find out that normal was not on that days agenda. Pop suggested that Mic and I take a trip to the market for a treat. We were ecstatic because he never took us for treats, menudo yes, candy no. As we drove to the market Pop casually informed my sister and I that he and my mom were getting a divorce. As tears welled up in my eyes I tried to understand what this meant. You see it was 1967 and none of my friends had parents who were divorced. In fact few of my friends had two working parents. How would I explain this to my friends? How would one woman and two girls survive all alone?

I remember little about my life for the next three years. My birthday parties, the friends I had, even my teachers all seem blurred and foreign. I do recall, however, the places in which we lived. We moved to an apartment shortly after Pop left and although it was clean and safe, it was not home. I missed my backyard and my dog. I missed my big kitchen and living room. But most of all I missed the little den where my heritage was left behind. As happy as I appeared on the outside my feelings of otherness were locked deep away inside.

As I breezed through adolescence I forgot about those days of loneliness. I was active in school and friends surrounded me with hope and happiness. More "single moms" where surfacing and I became friends with girls who had something in common with me, an absent father. We joked and laughed about the fact that our dads were too busy to visit, but deep inside I know we were in pain . . . we wanted to belong, but how could we without a family complete with Mom, Dad and siblings? Whether we liked it or not, we were different. So we accepted our differences and tucked the pain away once again.

My Mom dated a few men and finally met a new husband. She remarried close to my sixteenth birthday. What a present that was! We finally were able to move into a "rental" house, but a house nonetheless. It was great moving into a real neighborhood, and out of apartment living. I finally felt like I belonged. My life was going in the right direction, with or without Pop, and the divorce.

As I grew into an adult I didn't ponder much about my childhood. I only saw Pop five or six times a year and by this time, a lot of my friends parent's had divorced or were unhappily married. My feelings of otherness had diminished when society said, "Divorce is okay."

I continued through those early adult years believing that I might have been a victim of divorce but came through it unscarred. I was strong and was not going to let anyone break through that barrier that had been neatly and carefully tucked away.

The key that unlocked my feelings showed up two years ago when Pop passed away. He died suddenly and unexpectedly at age 68. My heritage was recollected when I landed in Puerto Vallarta to bury my father. All the lessons in that little den and trips to that Mexican bakery flashed before me. I wondered how different life would have been if the divorce had not occurred. After all life had been good mixed with many wonderful blessings. I can't help but wonder if there was no divorce, would I be able to recall my birthday parties, those sixth grade friendships and the teachers that could have impacted me?

Deeper in My Heart
Jordon

It has been a while since I dredged up the memories from so long ago, and even though I know the feelings have been dealt with, I wonder if they will return, I guess the best place to start is with the incident, no use in trying to avoid it, I'll try to tell it quickly. Shortly after my tenth birthday, my older cousin, Danny, came to live with my family. I was excited. Being an only child, I had always wanted a brother or sister, and this was the closest to it I thought I was going to get. However, from the very beginning, things did not go well. Danny was an angry and violent person; I remember him calling me names like ugly and spoiled brat and he would often threaten me if I didn't do what he said. He was cruel to my dog and cat and I remember that he seemed to find a lot of enjoyment in squashing the snails on the sidewalk and watching them die. I quickly became afraid of him and did my best to avoid him.

A couple of months after Danny came to live with us I was awakened in the night unable to breath. I tried to cry out, but a sock was suddenly forced into my mouth so I couldn't make a sound. A pillow was over my face and my hands were being held above my head; I couldn't move them. It felt as though the weight on my body would crush me. I was sure that someone was trying to kill me. Then I heard Danny's voice, it was muffled through the pillow and at first I thought he was there to save me but I quickly realized that he was the one holding me down. He was telling me that he had to do this to punish me; it was what I deserved for being so spoiled. He said that this is what happens to bad and ugly kids; it was my fault. I thought he was going to kill me; I had no idea of what was to come. As I struggled to free myself, Danny kept repeating that I deserved this and it was my fault. Then came the pain. I felt my flesh tear and bleed. I thought that a knife was being plunged into me several times; in the place mom had told me was private. I wondered if this was how I was going to die. When he finished, Danny grabbed me tightly by the throat and told me that if I told anyone, he would kill my parents, cut out their guts, and make me eat them. Then he would cut my head off.

I was so frightened, I didn't make a move the rest of the night; I remember feeling like I couldn't even blink. When my alarm went off the next morning, I panicked. I noticed that my sheets and my legs had blood on them. Although I had difficulty standing at first because the pain was still intense, I quickly tore the sheets off my bed and hid them in the back of my closet behind my clothes hamper. Then I took a hot shower. When I came downstairs, my mom was fixing breakfast and Danny was sitting at the table reading the comics. She asked me why I had taken a shower that morning, when I always took a bath at night. I remember that Danny shot me a threatening look from across the room. I told my mom that I just wanted to be clean.

I couldn't focus on school that day. Mrs. Jensen noticed and asked me if I was okay. I said I didn't feel well, so she had me put my head down on my desk. Recess was the most difficult. My friends couldn't understand why I didn't want to play tag with them they knew it was my favorite game. I was still feeling a lot of pain and was really confused. I felt very alone. It seemed like it had just been a dream, I wished it was, I desperately wanted it to be, but I knew that it hadn't been.

When I got home from school that day, I followed, my mom everywhere. I was afraid to be alone. I was thankful that Danny had gone to work with my dad; they wouldn't be home for hours. I couldn't eat much dinner. I was still too upset. I told my mom that I didn't feel well and wanted to go to my room to sleep. I hid a steak knife under my shirt and went upstairs. After putting my pillows under my bedspread to make it look like I was in bed (I had seen that on TV), I crawled under my bed. Before I fell asleep, I remember thinking that I would never again sleep without wearing a pair of jeans and without a knife to protect myself.

The next day at school, I let Mrs. Jensen think I was sick again. This time however, she sent me to the nurse. I had a difficult time explaining to the nurse what exactly was wrong with me. She told me that I could just lie there and rest. I was surprised when my mom appeared in the doorway to take me home. I told her that I didn't want to go, that I felt better, but she insisted.

When we got home, I noticed that my mom had been doing laundry. I rushed upstairs to see if the sheets were still in my closet. They were gone. I panicked and headed down stairs to see if I could find them before my mom noticed the blood. My mom met me on the staircase, gently hugged me, and said that we needed to have a mother–daughter talk. I was scared. At the time, I didn't understand most of what she was telling me. Something about that my body was going to be changing and I was becoming a young lady. At one point she did bring up the bloody sheets, and I was so scared and confused. I couldn't understand how all of this was part of becoming a young lady. I couldn't tell if she knew what had happened. At times she seemed to, but she was so calm, that I thought she must have thought it was something else. I wondered if what Danny had done to me was a normal part of growing up, if other girls had the same thing done to them, or if I was the only one. Could my parents already know? I was too afraid to ask. I didn't want to die, and I didn't want them to die either. My head was spinning when I heard my mom say that we had an appointment to visit the doctor that same afternoon. When I asked her why. She told me that I was becoming a young lady sooner than what might be considered normal and she just wanted the doctor to give me a check-up to make sure that everything was okay.

For the first time, I was afraid to go to the doctor. He was such a nice man; I didn't want him to know what had happened, I didn't want him to know how bad I was. Dr. D. began his examination. He pressed on different parts of my tummy and asked me if I felt any pain. Then he explained to me that he was going to have to examine my private place. I was very resistant. He reassured me that everything was going to be all right. I began to cry. I could tell the Dr. D. was upset when he finished the exam. He called my mother out of the room to talk to her. I wondered if they would hate me or if I was going to die. When they returned my mother was crying. I was scared. She hugged me and kept saying, "Oh, my poor baby!" over and over. I still thought that I might die. My doctor gave me a tranquilizer that sedated me enough for him to examine me further and to repair some of the damage that had been done to my body. I was tested for STDs and it came up positive for gonorrhea.

I was forced to tell my mother everything that had happened. She was horrified. I admitted that it was Danny who had done this to me. I never saw him again. He was arrested, plead guilty, sentenced to ten years in prison, and hung himself while he was serving his term.

He was free from what he had done or so I thought at the time. I was still left to face the consequences. I was kept home from school for a month, to give me time to recover and heal. During this time, my mother gently explained to me what had happened. I know it was difficult for her; she cried a lot. I had a hard time understanding everything. Because I hadn't been able to see on that night, it was difficult for me to grasp what had actually occurred. My memories were vivid. I was certain that I had been cut with a knife. When I discovered what had really happened, I was even more scared. I can't quite explain why. I just felt more violated. The most difficult question I faced was, why? I wanted to know why this had been done to me. I still wondered if I was bad, if I had deserved it and brought it on myself because I was ugly, and most importantly, if it was going to happen again.

To deal with these questions and my emotional state in general, I began seeing Dr. Betty. She was a very warm and nurturing woman and I liked the fact that she spoke to me like I was an adult. She explained a lot of things to me and I trusted what she said. She became a close friend and helped me through so many difficult times.

There were a lot of questions from my classmates when I returned to school. I knew some of them had heard that I had been raped (I lived in a small town and these things always get out), but they didn't really know what it meant. I felt isolated. I was told that I couldn't tell them what had happened and this made me feel like I was hiding something bad. I felt ashamed. I believed no one would want to be my friend after what had happened. Before, I had been very outgoing, full of energy, and extremely talkative. Now I was very quiet and just wanted to sit in the corner and try to make sense of the situation. My friends were told to act as if nothing had ever happened, but it was difficult for them because they were also curious. It took a lot of time before things began to return too normal.

And my life did somewhat return to normal, but it was a different normal. In day-to-day activities, my life seemed no different than anyone else's. Deeper in my heart, however, I couldn't shake the feeling of otherness. It seemed that too often incidents would arise that would take me back to that night. I felt that no one could identify with what I had experienced. Some students thought I was crazy because I had to go to a psychologist. This often made me wonder myself.

Some of the most difficult times were when the subject of puberty and sex would arise. The girls often asked me what it felt like to "do it." I'm sure that my response probably resulted in a few cases of abstinence. And this is where one of my biggest feelings of otherness arose. I felt that I would never have the choice to wait until I was married, like the other girls all said they would, the choice had been taken from me. Although I did choose to wait, I thought that I would never be considered a virgin. I was wrong.

That one night changed my whole life. I felt different. My classmates, teachers, and friends treated me differently. I could tell that people who knew what had happened were very careful about what they said around me and this always made me feel uncomfortable. The repercussions I find the most difficult, however, were the effects it had on my family. My mom felt incapable of helping me. She didn't know how to reach out to me and this left her feeling like she was a bad mother. I was surprised to hear her say this, when I believe that she is the person who got me through the whole ordeal She always gave me the love and support I needed; she still does. My father on the other hand is a different story. The knowledge that I had been raped nearly destroyed him. I had been "daddy's baby" and the guilt he felt for not being able to protect me tore him apart. He quickly withdrew from me and began to drink heavily. I believed that he no longer wanted anything to do with me, that he was ashamed of me. My parents divorced soon after; I knew it was my fault. My father and I drifted further and further apart. I began to hate him for not loving me. But, deeper in my heart, I felt I deserved it. My father accepted my feelings of hate; he felt he deserved it. It has been nearly twenty years since the night that changed my life and my father and I are just now starting to build a relationship. It's difficult at times, but very wonderful. I see this as a remarkable gift from God. Although I spent several years in counseling, it wasn't until I received Jesus into my heart that I was able to truly forgive and put the past behind me. Today, I feel free and at peace. I am no longer filled with the anger and bitterness that I had thought was just part of my being. What a tremendous joy it is.

It always concerns me when I share this story, how it will be taken. I often wonder if the listener will see it as plea for pity. As I see it, there is no cause for pity, but there is a cause for awareness. That is the main reason I wrote this paper. In your classrooms, you may have to cope with a similar situation. In some cases, like mine, you may only face the after effects. However, there may be times when the crime is being committed by a parent or possibly both parents. In these cases, I believe it is so important to be aware, to notice the signals and care enough to investigate further.

Still I Rise (title inspired by Maya Angelou)
Christopher Royal

Otherness has been the only existence I have ever known. I was born with labels that are perceived as numerous strikes against me in this society. I am a black male. I was born to an impoverished teenage mother out of wedlock, and I have no tangible evidence of my biological father. Still I rise.

My mother went on to have four more children, all daughters. She was a single parent trying to rear five children on her own. Often we were left with my grandmother who favored our lighter skinned cousins. We were unknowing prey for our molesting uncles. Still I rise.

As a young child I was often separated from my mother and sisters, living with my stepfather's grandmother or brother. I went to several different schools and was perceived to be despondent, slow, or unmotivated. Thus school to me was more like a holding place until the adults in my life figured out where and with whom I was going to stay with next. Still I rise.

I became a man at the age of thirteen when I was sent to live with my stepfather. He was charming, militant, and refused to work for anyone, especially a white man. He never cursed, smoked or drank in my presence and I found that amazing. However, he was extremely abusive toward women, particularly my mom and sisters. I know my parents love me today especially for having the strength to overcome adversity in spite of weak parental support. As a child, however, their love was not an affectionate or nurturing love. It was a tough and bittersweet love, not easy to understand or embrace. Still I rise.

Growing up with mom and dad, I felt powerless and voiceless. There was nothing I could do to change the way they chose to deal with the adversities they faced in their own lives. I did not know how to tell them that I understood their frustrations and hoped that they would make choices that would uplift our family rather than tear us apart. In retrospect, my parents prepared me for the coldness of the world. I was not broken or defeated when I faced overt racism, evil, or was subjected to unfair treatment in a public place, work environment, or social setting. People have attempted to devalue me purposely or not and I have simply refused to succumb. Still I rise.

My spirit is resilient, and full of hope. I am the eternal optimist. In the corporate and military worlds there has been much resistance to my voice.

However in education, I have always found less resistance, and that is why I teach. I know there are children who feel voiceless and powerless, and I convey in any way I can, that just because people attempt to make you feel less valued intentionally or by mistake, does not mean you have to chose to devalue yourself. Still we will rise.

Lori Bristol
Summer

In the summer of 1971, we moved to the house on Peach Street. I was only four years old and already I thought my life had peaked. The house had a pool, there was a girl my age to play with next door, and my cousins lived up the street.

The next two years were filled with good times and wonderful memories. My father got home from work early enough for us to take a swim together, when the weather permitted. We almost had my dive down to perfection.

Another fun activity was one in which my dad would line tin cans up on the fence beside the house. We would take turns shooting them off with a BB gun. He had quite an extensive collection of guns. My father enjoyed hunting. I remember going with him a couple of times. That was all I could stand because I did not like to see the dead animals. He sure spent a lot of time in the garage cleaning those guns.

In July of 1973, my carefree childhood came to an abrupt halt. My cousin, Shelly, and I were off spending the day with our great aunt and uncle, Bertha and Charlie. They never had children of their own. It was sort of a tradition that first they took my mom and my aunt with them when they were little, then my older cousins and now it was our turn. We had gone out to lunch and shopping with them.

I will never forget what happened when we got back to my cousin's house. My mom was lying on the couch crying and my aunt was sitting in the chair next to her. My mom looked very pale and she had a cold cloth on her forehead. I got down on my knees next to her, took her hand and said, "Mommy, what's wrong?" She began crying harder and said, "Oh Lori, your daddy has died!" I just sat there and cried along with her.

It was not long before my aunt's house filled with friends and relatives. I felt as though I was walking through the house in a fog. I could see all of the people talking, but I could not hear their words. Mom was still on the couch, Dad's mom was in on a bed and I just wandered back and forth from room to room.

The next couple of months consisted of a variety of activities. Friends and family members were knocking themselves out trying to occupy my time. Immediately, I notice the change in the way people treated me. I felt as though all eyes were casting pitiful stares at me. Even at such a young age, I knew my life would never be the same. It was as if I knew I would always be different than my friends who had fathers.

In September of 1973, I began my first grade year. It was difficult for me to get back into the routine of school. I was not being treated like the "Princess of Summer" anymore. It was also sad for me because when I was in kindergarten, my dad would occasionally pick me up. That would never be the case again.

During that year at school, I remember finally feeling the need to address the cause of my father's death. Nobody in my family ever discussed him. I had just wiped my dad right out of my memory bank. The only time I would ask for him was when my mom scolded me. The kids at school would ask me things like, "How come you do not have a Daddy," and "Where is your Daddy?" I must have grown tired of my standard answer of, "My daddy lives in heaven with the angels." I finally asked my mom what I should tell my friends at school. She said, "Tell them your daddy was cleaning his gun and it accidentally went off." I found it hard to believe that a man who spent so much time with his guns would make such a crucial mistake. Being the good little girl that I was, I resumed my vow of silence and did not ask any more questions.

The next several years were extremely difficult for me. My mom did not remarry until I was eighteen years old. The only male influences in my life were my paternal grandfather and my great uncle Charlie. Unfortunately, both of these wonderful men passed away by the time I was twelve years old. My aunt had divorced my uncle shortly after my father's death.

I had many uncomfortable moments throughout my school years. Every time the other children were talking about fathers I would sit there and pray that the kids who did not know me would not ask about me and those who did would not mention it. It was something of which I felt very ashamed.

When they announced the Girl Scout's father–daughter dance, I went home and cried to my mom, "they are going to have such a wonderful time and I do not get to go." My mom had even resorted to asking my cousin Danny if he would go with me. Considering he was eighteen, taking me to this dance was not "the cool thing to do." I was very fortunate that one of my best friend's mothers called and extended an invitation for me to go with my friend, Shana, and her dad. They were so nice to me. I thought it was a very unselfish act for Shana to share her dad with me. He brought me a corsage and danced with both of us the entire evening. I was so glad I did not have to miss this event.

I always felt alienated whenever Father's Day celebrations were mentioned at school or on television. In school, an art project, usually a card would be introduced for us to make for our fathers. I would just sit there and color. Some people might wonder why I did not make one for my grandfather. It was decided after my father's death that I would not give Father's Day cards to my grandfather or Mother's Day cards to my grandmother. My mom thought she was doing the right thing by not giving them any reminders of their loss since they did not have any other children. I think it would have done us all good to have discussed the situation much more and not kept it such a terrible secret that no one was allowed to mention.

If you have not figured it out already, the reason the subject has always been off limits is that my father committed suicide. I always had my suspicions. They were finally confirmed during an argument with my mother when I was eighteen years old. In the course of the argument, she blurted out, "I have just always tried to do the right thing to you because of the guilt I have carried all of these years." She explained to me that before she went to my aunt's house on July 10, 1973, she had an argument with my father. His last words to her were, "Don't worry, I will be gone by the time you get home."

Although I had suspected his death was not accidental, these words were still very difficult to hear. I was disturbed about them lying to me for so many years. Again, I felt like I was on the outside. Everybody else, including my cousins, knew the real story. "Poor Little Lori" needed to be kept in a glass dome where she did not need to learn to cope with things that happen in the real world. I love my mom and my family and I know they thought shielding me was in my best interest. Little did they know that they were confirming my feelings that I was somehow responsible by not talking to me about it. This is a fact of my life that has always mad me feel different from those around me. To this day, I still cringe inside when people who do not know me ask questions about my dad. I still have a hard time just saying, "He passed away when I was six years old." At that point, I know they will either pursue it and ask how or they will just look at me with those puppy dog eyes and say, "I am so sorry."

I often wonder how my life would be different if he had lived. There have been so many times over the years when I have wanted to talk to him. I do know that he loved me very much. At least I had him in my life for six years. Many children never get to know their dads at all.

The Chosen One
Aimee Beitel

When thinking of the word diversity, one usually thinks of race, gender, age, religion, and sexual preference. But my experience doesn't fit into any of these categories. You see I was adopted when I was four weeks old. My birth mother was nineteen when she had me and she gave me up because she was young and unmarried. Having to do this paper has made me understand how being adopted has affected my life.

My parents told me that on the day I was brought home, they read me a book called the *Chosen One*. They have treated me as though they were my actual birth parents. They have loved me unconditionally and I have never thought twice about their love. But I have always felt as though there was something missing.

I have had this feeling of emptiness, loneliness, and uncertainty. When I look at my mother I cannot see me, rather I see someone who I don't look, act or sound like. When I look at my friends and their mothers, I can see a bond that I have missed throughout my life.

All of my life I have searched for a feeling that most others have. This has made me prone to vulnerable situations that I would not have had if I were not sensitive for that love. Men have taken advantage of me because I show them my weakness. This has caused great harm and pain.

When I was sixteen years old and at a very vulnerable time in my life, my dance teacher's husband molested me. I can remember the first time like it was yesterday but what haunts me is the scene of having to stand face to face with him after his wife found out and explain in detail what he did to me while he tried to deny it. I trusted this man and frequently spent the night at their house. I thought I was dreaming when I felt someone standing over me while I slept. Because I would do anything for love and attention, I was blinded to pre-warning signs that were there. It has taken a long time for me to overcome this experience.

Being adopted has also created experiences in school that have greatly affected who I am today. The first experience that I can remember took place in fourth grade. The teacher gave us an assignment to find out certain facts about ourselves; things such as what time were you born, how much did you weigh, who did you get your eye and hair color from. Well since I was adopted, I didn't know any of this information. My parents were never given any information regarding my background except for the age of my birth parents and where I was born so this was going to be a hard assignment for me to accomplish. I was dreading going to school the next day because I knew I was going to have to explain why I couldn't answer the questions. I remember when I got to school all of the kids were comparing their answers and laughing with each other. By the time class rolled around I was sick to my stomach. The teacher asked each of us to tell everyone about ourselves. I was completely devastated by this because I had to explain to the whole class that I didn't know any of this information because I was adopted. Many of the students didn't know what that meant so the teacher had to explain. This was the first time in my life that I felt I was the outsider and that I did not belong. I was ashamed of who I was and embarrassed because my birth parents did not want me. All I can remember from that day are the looks from all of my friends and the whispering at lunch about me being adopted.

For a very long time I wouldn't tell anyone that I was adopted and I even pretended I wasn't. Today when the subject comes up, I still get a knot in my stomach and worry about what people will think of me.

Now that I am in my mid-twenties and am getting married I am curious about who I am and where I come from. I can only make assumptions about who I am. I have always felt that everyone has something that I don't and that makes me an outsider. I want answers to all of those questions my teacher handed out to us in the fourth grade.

What Matters
Heidi Gilman

For better or for worse, I agreed
But how bad does it have to be
To get out of this situation without a stigma?
All of my life I have been one of faith,
The responsible,
The levelheaded.

Where did I go wrong?
I married him with all of the intentions
Of being the devoted,
The honest,
The responsible one I'd always been.
But, what price do I pay to maintain
This reputation?

He jokes harshly about my childhood
I am the bastard child, the welfare child.
No, I didn't grow up as Heidi.
What does it matter?
He calls my family the "Beverly Hillbillies"
The poor, uncivilized family

Displaced in his world.
No, I didn't grow up here.
What does it matter?
He yells at me and calls me a minority-lover
Because I had boyfriends that didn't look
Like him.

I don't understand.
Why should it matter?
I have a scar on my face.

I've lived with it all of my life.
Of all people, why should he care if it shows
Depending on how I wear my hair?

This is not how I pictured it.
This is not what I dreamed.
What did I do to make me
The cook,
The laundress,
The caregiver,
The target?

I am the weak one he *says*.
He tells me I have no spine.
I demand different, I am called absurd.
I tell the priest, I am called the quitter.
I tell the counselor, I am labeled depressed.
I tell his family, I am called a disgrace.
I tell my heart, I am given courage.

I realize I have not given in.
I am not absurd, I am not a quitter.
I will not settle for less when I know
I can do better.
I know I can stand on my own
And stand strong.
That, to me, is what matters.

I Was, I Am
Mary E. Keegan

As a student at the university, I was marginalized by the sheer color of my
skin, at a school where the population is 75% African American. I had never
seen such diversity in my life. I had been sheltered, hidden from the differences of the world. I tried to learn from our differences and expose myself
to those around me. Sometimes I was welcomed and sometimes I was
shunned. I was definitely an outcast that day in the student union when O.J.
Simpson was pronounced not guilty. I was the only one disappointed. I was
a white woman. I am a white woman.

　　While in college, I decided to study abroad in Europe for a year. The
advisors warned us about the culture shock that we would experience.
During my first day in Madrid, I could feel eyes burning through me when
I walked down the street in shorts, clothing that was normal for us, but not

for the Spaniards. I remember not knowing how to order my coffee or buy my bus pass. I remember feeling marginalized and like an outcast, not sure why I had decided to study in the country that did not seem so inviting to strangers. I began to surround myself with Americans to ease the pain of feeling different. I was an ugly American. I am an ugly American.

The shear panic of being different wore off slowly, and I settled into my new place I called home. I learned to dress differently, speak properly and order the right coffee in the cafeteria at school. I made friends, I flirted with and kissed many Spanish boys, and I learned to salsa dance, bien. My feelings of being marginalized were hard and difficult to bear in the beginning, but were almost nonexistent by the end of my trip. I could not believe that I ever felt any sort of marginalization. I was a Spaniard. I am a Spaniard.

Upon my return home to Southern California, I had distaste for the American culture. I was different in my own house because I had returned a different person. I dressed differently and even talked differently. I felt as though I did not belong, longing to return overseas where I had grown so attached to Spain.

I experienced shock by waking up early, driving fast and living each day quickly. In addition to the changes of time and sleeping patterns, I came back a changed person. I was pregnant. I am a mother.

For an entire month I did not sleep because of the anxiety of telling my strict, Catholic parents, who would not understand. During the first few months I decided to look into adoption. I wanted to place my baby in a home that would provide all the things that I knew I would not be able to give him. During this time, people were quick to judge me. My friends did not call. Maybe they were embarrassed or scared, I am not sure. I did not want to go to church because I was shunned. I was such an outcast. People have no concept of what it is like to be me. A mother, a woman, a Catholic, a teacher, a student, a girlfriend, a sister, an aunt and a birthmother, I was and I am.

My Perfect World
Lori Weinman

Crime and violence was very sparse in my predominately middle to upper class neighborhood. I was raised in somewhat of a sheltered way. My family had always protected my siblings and I from the harsh realities. I lived in a little box that was "my perfect world." One day that box was torn open and "my perfect world" would never again be so perfect!

It all started in November of my sophomore year in high school. Soccer practice had just ended, and I was waiting for my mom to pick me up. That day she was running very late so I decided to call and see what was keeping her. When she picked up the phone, I could tell in her voice something was wrong. She told me that my friend's mom was coming to get me and not to worry, but my father had been arrested. The police had been staking out my house for the day. When my dad got home from picking up my little brother, they served him with a search warrant and then took my dad. I can't imagine what was going through my brother's mind at the time, but I know that my dad said to the policeman, "Could you please not handcuff me in front of my son? I am willing to go with you, but please don't let my son see this." They obliged and off my dad went to Santa Ana jail, for what would become my family's largest battle ever.

When I arrived home, my mom was in tears and my little brother was in shock. What was going on? Why did they arrest my dad? Would I ever see him again? Was my family torm apart forever? What happened to my perfect world? All of these questions would soon be answered and my life would soon take the shape of something I had never imagined.

As the night went on, we didn't hear a word from my dad. We tried to go to sleep that night, but to this day I still remember the thoughts going through my head. The next day came slowly and my dad called very early the next morning. He told my mom to post bail and to pick him up.

I remember going to school the next day and my friends and teachers had already heard of my dad's arrest. People looked at me differently, and some of my friends didn't know what to say, so they said nothing to me. Others tried to comfort me, and told me that they would be there for me. Only two teachers to this day pulled me aside and talked to me.

My best friend Nichole asked me what had happened and I told her. The police arrested my dad for embezzlement and fraud. I wasn't quite sure what embezzlement was, but whatever it was, I knew that my dad was innocent.

Days became weeks and weeks turned into months. My dad's attorney worked on his case every day. My siblings and I tried to go on with our normal lives, but we were scared of the uncertainty of what was to come. The trial started a year later and lasted one week. I will never forget going to court and hearing the jury tell my dad he was "guilty." My sister fainted and I broke into tears. My perfect world was now completely demolished and I could do nothing but sit back and watch it crumble. Life for my family and me would never be the same. What would people think of me? I thought. I knew my dad was not a crook and something must be wrong, but I had to deal with the fact that until his appeal came, I needed try my best to keep it together.

My dad was sentenced to four years in prison, and I didn't want to face it. I removed myself from reality and became numb to everything surrounding me. My grades went from a 3.8 to a 2.3, I started to drink and smoke pot just to get away from what was bothering me, and I refused to go and see my dad in prison. What was happening to me? People now looked at me differently, some kids made jokes, and some parents wouldn't let their kids hang out with me. Pictures of my dad were in the newspaper and on the news. Many people turned their backs to us, but my mom remained strong and we carried on like every other day.

The two and a half years to follow were the toughest years of my life and I am who I am today because my perfect world was shattered. When my dad was transferred from Santa Ana jail to Donavon Prison down by the Mexican American border, I decided that I would see him. There were rules that had to be followed in order to visit an inmate; you could not wear jeans, dresses, skirts, low cut shirts, or anything that showed cleavage. Also you could not bring anything into the prison unless it was in a clear bag. I remember filling out a form to get in. My dad no longer had a name. He was now a number.

As I walked through the metal detector, a woman pat searched me. I made my way up to this small window to be about four inches long and three inches wide. There was a phone sitting there and I waited for my dad to come. I remembered seeing small children with their mothers, ladies waiting for their men, and parents waiting to speak to their children. Nobody looked like me. I was the only Caucasian girl in the place and I looked out of place. When my dad arrived at the window, all I could see were his eyes. We talked for a while, but then he had to go. Visiting hours were up and it was time to leave.

A week later my dad would be transferred again, and then again, and again. It seemed as though it would never end. Well one day it did. February 12, 1996, my dad returned home. His time got cut in half and he would now return to a strange place called home.

During those two and a half years my father was gone, my mom's strength carried the family and supported all of us. She'd helped me see that there are lots of things in life that are not perfect, but yet manageable. I feel that things happen for a reason. If I had lived my life in my former "perfect world," I would have not become the strong, independent person I am today.

Scared of Dad
Ann Marie Huizar

I remember a time when I was scared to go home.

Scared of the empty bottles on the table.

Scared of the man passed out on the couch.

Scared he would wake up.

Scared that he wouldn't.

Scared of the angry words.

Scared of the hands.

Scared of the extension cord.

Scared of telling my mom.

Scared that she already knew.

Scared she was being hurt like I was.

Scared of telling my friends.

Scared that they would ridicule me.

Scared someone would find out.

Scared they would take me away.

Scared to be left behind.

Scared of letting the fake smile slip for even a moment.

Scared that my family would disappear.

Scared he would leave us.

Scared he would *stay*.

Scared he would *say* that it was all my fault.

Scared that in some ways it was true.

WHITE–3J

I am jealous about Whites' ability to be inconspicuous, to escape physical self-consciousness. I yearn for the shadows of night where everybody is equally dark. I grow weary of people who ask, "Do you speak Chinese?" They are perplexed at my annoyance and my response, "No, do you?"

I am ironically frustrated about my invisibility and what people don't see in me. I am the tofu immigrant who, like tofu, assimilates every flavor it comes in contact with. The reality is, even with tofu in my veins, I cannot pass as white.

White, a color left out of the multicultural rainbow (Tilove, 1995). What does it mean to be white? Students who described themselves as colorblind found it difficult to acknowledge color categories let alone whiteness. Denying physical or social differences, they declared themselves as color neutral. They tell me this means that they do not take into account skin color in their interactions with people. They don't see themselves as white, as the norm, but rather as just people. They are nonracialized individuals (Fordham, 1996; Howard, 1999). "We do not experience ourselves as defined by our skin color. We especially do not experience ourselves as defined by another race's actions and attitudes toward us because of our skin color." (Scheurich, 1993, p. 6). As Stanfield (1985) asserted, whites do "not even . . . notice they are white" (p. 400). Students of color say they are always aware of their skin color, their language, their cultural heritage, their group membership, and whiteness. Is white then, a color, only people of color see?

Halprin (1995) described her skin a pale ivory color, which she pronounced is lacking in depth, in definition, and in soul. She acknowledged that because she is pale, she has the privilege of being invisible (p. 286). White racial identity is not a biological category but a social construct. Whiteness is an invisible norm and is therefore hard to find. It is, according to Newitz and Wray (1997), a privileged place of racial normativity. "It has been the invisibility (for whites) of whiteness that has enabled white Americans to stand as unmarked, normative bodies and social selves" (p. 3). Media's casting of white as typical and normal is largely responsible for our subconscious worldview because he who controls the media, controls our minds (Chomsky, 1997).

Sleeter (1993) blamed whites for spending most of their time with other white people and therefore they do not see much of the realities of the lives of Americans of color nor encounter their viewpoints in any depth. Nor do they really want to, Sleeter added, because those viewpoints would challenge practices and beliefs that benefit white people. Whites prefer to be spectators and to not name their own complicity or the power differential between Whites and groups of color. We (whites) participate in the reproduction of racial inequity because we are too afraid to talk about our part in racism (Sleeter, 1993). Although whites don't want to discuss racism, blacks can't stop discussing it (Golden, 1995). Students from my class affirmed this observation. Students of color reported they saw racism on a daily basic. White students witnessed none. Scheurich (1993) explained that whites have a habit of not taking seriously what people of color say about racism (p. 14). Furthermore, Kivel (1996) noted that whites see racism as an individual issue, not a racial group issue. Racism is an overt behavior of an individual not a group sentiment or institutional disposition. Whereas, people of color always see themselves as a racialized people, a group defined by skin color because of the difference that color makes in the way they are treated (Ropers-Huilman, 1997, p. 11).

   Scheurich (1993) and Kivel (1996) suggested that individualism eclipses whites' awareness of their racial identities. For many whites, racism is seen as an individual issue, not a racial group issue. Individuals are racist, not groups or institutions. In addition, whites think of racism in terms of overt behaviors by an individual rather than dominant groups and structures that deny access to economic and social opportunity. "Nothing we do is a credit or discredit to our race" because we do not seem ourselves as members of a racial group (Kivel, 1996, p. 29). Whereas, people of color report that they regularly find themselves representing their race and contrasting it to whiteness. They are aware of their relationship to a whole group of marginalized others and the accompanying responsibility they shoulder as the representatives. "Being at the margins where one consciously operates in relation to the center makes it difficult to say this or that because one is constantly concerned with representing the margins to the center. It is not easy to say 'I am' without saying 'we are.' We are always representative of our race" (Taliaferro, 1997, p. 8). People of color learn to see themselves as a racialized people, as a social group defined by skin color because of the difference that color makes in the way people are treated, currently and historically (Ropers-Huilman, 1997).

   Sleeter (1993) added that whites avoid a white identity because they do not choose to see themselves as oppressors. Whites participate in the reproduction of racial inequity because they are too afraid to talk about their part in racism. "Whites don't want to discuss racism, while Blacks can't stop discussing it" (Golden, 1995, p. 1). When racism is talked about, depending on who initiates the talk, it is heard differently by whites. When they themselves initiate the talk, whites hear racism as a legitimate concern (Scheurich & Young, 1998; Tyson, 1998). When whites hear people of color talk about race or racism, they hear people of color as self-serving (Scheurich & Young, 1998). Sleeter (1993) observed that whites also isolate themselves from alternative worldviews. She reported, "Spending most of their time with other White people, Whites do not see much of the realities of the lives of Americans of Color nor encounter their viewpoints in any depth. Nor do they really want to, since those viewpoints would challenge practices and beliefs that benefit White People." "We prefer to be spectators and to not name our own complicity or the power differential between Whites and Groups of Color. . . ." (Sleeter, 1993, p. 14). Therefore, white culpability for racism is left not seen, mentioned, or named (Ellison, 1972). By remaining unframed, whiteness remains invisible and insulated. The naming of whiteness robs it of internal neutrality and counters those hegemonic strategies, which are designed to keep whiteness unmarked (Hill, 1997).

   Some white antiracists/multiculturalists (Hill, 1997; Howard, 1999; McIntosh, 1988; McLaren, 2003; Scheurich, 1993; Sleeter, 1997) suggest it is time that whites take their turn in being framed in their participation toward a democratic imaginary. Those with white privilege, who are responsible for the framing of Otherness must take their turn in being framed and not be excused from marginalization by Others. We can learn to understand whiteness through understanding coloredness. By helping the privileged see the social forces of exclusion and oppression as they are applied to them, they then could magnify how those forces oppress all people. This moment of truth is frequently the catalyst of the realization of the universal bond of otherness shared among all people as well as the collective complicity of structures which other Others. This provocative pedagogy is essential to pierce the hegemony that maintains power inequities; one that liberates the Oppressed and the Oppressor (Freire, 1995).

Making whiteness visible in multicultural studies means moving from unmarked to marked status. In whiteness studies, Thompson (1996) stated, "I am unearthing exactly what I have been taught to forget. From early infancy, white people are taught to deny the centrality of race" (p. 95). Mike Hill (1997), in his work, Can Whiteness Speak?, questions whether white deconstruction has a place at the critical multicultural table. He is sensitive to white dominance and cautions whiteness to not speak louder at this table than those who might best be heard if whiteness was quieter. Speaking louder would grant "oppression privilege" (Bulkin, 1996) the power to speak and be heard, a privilege inherent in white dominance.

In attempts to make whiteness visible, Michael Moore (2001) took an experiential self-inventory and claimed "that it wasn't a black landlord who ever evicted him, not a black person who denied his child college admission, never a black cop who pulled him over, not a black person who denied him a bank loan, and never had a black person laid him off of a job. I don't think I'm the only white guy who can make these claims. Every mean word, every cruel act, every bit of pain and suffering in my life has had a Caucasian face attached to it" (p. 57). Yet, he maintained, every night on the news, it is black men who are portrayed as a menace to society. He maintained that society has become so accustomed to the image of the black man as predator that we cannot see the white boogeyman.

This perspective helps students understand more clearly that identities are not inherent but are produced by social systems. The social forces responsible for power differential become clearer when white otherness is introduced into the curriculum. This is, as Hartigan (1997) put it, when white privilege, which is responsible for the framing of otherness, takes its turn in being framed by its own ideology. An example of this concept is when whites refer to "other" white people as white trash. This reference is a means of "inscribing social distance and insisting upon a contempt-laden social divide, particularly (though not exclusively) between whites." White trash "exists in the fears and fantasies of those middle and working-class whites who occupy a place 'just above' the class divide from poor whites, straddling a line they *are forever fearful of crossing" (p. 53). The use of the term white trash as opposed to poor white by the white middle class is a means to distinguish themselves from the lower order. It is a term that represents "those people" as a group apart and distinct from the white "mainstream." White trash is considered by some as genetic defectives, incestuous hillbillies, violent, alcoholic, lazy, and stupid and the cause for many of the nation's ills (Newitz & Wray, 1997). Because poor whites fail to measure up to the middle-class standards, they are considered "not really white" or "not white enough" (Berube & Berube, 1997)*

White students found it easier to enter the multicultural agenda as an other rather than as an oppressor. Thompson (1996) explained "it is sometimes easier for white women to read themselves into the victim/innocent scenario than the oppressor/guilty one even though white women occupy both simultaneously. In this instance, guilt becomes a safer response than taking responsibility for racial inequality" (p. 106). It is in these instances, that whites are able to see the social forces of exclusion and oppression as these forces are applied to them. It is an opportunity for whites to begin to see the real source of exploitation—those that control the economy. Kivel (1996) said, "Not all white people had an equal voice in defining racial differences. Those with most power-who had the most to gain or preserve—set the terms. Those people were White landowners, church leaders—the educated and successful, who systematically, thought not collusively, defined whiteness in ways that extolled and legitimized their actions and denigrated others" (p. 22).

Differentiating white privilege from white otherness is not to trivialize white privilege nor camouflage hegemonic ideology, rather it is meant to dismantle white privilege by walking through a bridge of otherness. White as Other requires one to understand domination and oppression from the position of one's own experiences of otherness. Making white otherness visible dismantles the concept that whiteness is racial supremacy only. Similarly, students of color are equally responsible to examine their own complicity in the othering of others. They too must see how they contribute to social systems that dominate and oppress others. Ultimately, we need to understand that we all are both victims of racism and systems of domination and agents that reproduce the structures of inequity (Tatum, 1997). Both whites and people of color are the oppressed and the oppressors (Freire, 1995). We must remember how we are all a part of each other's democracy. Martin Luther King (1967) captured this sentiment when he said, "The white man cannot ignore the Negro's problem because he is part of the Negro and the Negro is a part of him. The Negro's agony diminishes the white man and the Negro's salvation enlarges the white man" (p. 101).

Howard (1999) offered a critical question to the multicultural community: "If Whiteness is theorized to be synonymous with oppression, then how do we provide White educators with a positive racial identity and include them in the work of social transformation?" (p. 111). How can the white community become aware of the social and political realities of people of color so that they can be partners in the dismantling prejudice and inequities? "Individuals from the dominant group are usually unaware of their own power and can carry on the daily activities of their lives without any substantial knowledge about, or meaningful interaction with, those people who are not part of the dominant group" (p. 58).

By naming whiteness, we rob it of its internal neutrality (McLaren, 2003). It is an oppressive ideological construct that promotes and maintains social inequalities (Newitz & Wray, 1997). "Whiteness is a concept . . . which holds tremendous power over our lives and over the lives of people of color" (Kivel, 1996, p. 11). To not name it is to buy into an existing system of domination (McLaren, 2003). However, the process of naming evokes guilt and/or denial. "I am defensive about my whiteness, about my legacy of privilege and the hurt it has brought to others" said Halprin (1995, p. 286). "I knew that white people enslaved Black people but no part of me saw myself as part of that white power," admitted Thompson (1996, p. 101). As a white feminist, she could not see her own complicity in racism.

Personally, white students want to know, "Not all white people had an equal voice in defining racial differences. Those with most power—who had the most to gain or preserve—set the terms. White landowners, church leaders—the educated and successful, systematically, thought not collusively, defined whiteness in ways that extolled and legitimized their actions and denigrated others" (Kivel, 1996, p. 22). They must assume their responsibility as the invisible norm (Hill, 1997). Naming this responsibility is the alternative to white neutrality, but the work is not done alone. We collectively must assume responsibility to work against racism because racism "others" us all. Ultimately, we are all victims of racism.

Scheurich and Young (1998) described themselves as both anti-racists and white racists. We "are both inside White racism, deeply and unconsciously affected by it, and working against it—both within and against" (p. 234). We are both the oppressor and the oppressed (Freire, 1995); we are victims and co-conspirators simultaneously. Giroux (1993) added that both whites and others are complex subjects who reproduce and refuse systems of domination; both are complicitous and resistant; both are victims and accomplices; both are responsible for reproducing the structures of inequity; and both are oppressed by any ideological construct that promotes and maintains social inequalities.

Student narratives captured poignant experiences about marginalization and discrimination of whites in a multicultural world as well as opportunities of privilege.

I Am Jeff Brown

I am white.
White, the color of the majority.
White, the color of the powerful.
White, the color that matters.
White, the color of the people in the TV, in the textbooks, in the newspaper.
White, the color of every single one of the presidents of this country.
I am white.

I am also male. I have a penis. I pee standing up. I wear blue, not pink. I have short hair (most of the time), not long hair.

I am male.
Male, the sex of the powerful.
Male, the sex that matters.
Male, the sex of the people in the text books, in the newspaper.
Male, like every single one of the presidents of this country.
I am male.

That's what was taught to me. That's what I learned from school, from TV, from sports, from family, from all of our mainstream social institutions. But, it turns out there is more. A radically different "more." Not the kind of "more" you typically would find in the mainstream media, in church, in history books. Not a "more" the status quo (my group) acknowledges.

I am white.
White, the color of slave-owners and imperialists.
White, the color of racists, sexists, militarists.
White, the color with the money.
White, the oppressor.

I am also male.
Male, the sex of slave-owners, imperialists, rapists.
Male, the sex of sexists and militarists.
Male, the sex with the money.
Male, the oppressor.

Coming to terms with what I was taught in mainstream institutions and what I have learned from people who challenge the mainstream—transformative intellectuals—continues to play an integral part in shaping my identity—in shaping who I am, what I believe in, what I am working for—in leading me off the status quo path and towards my path. So, fortunately, I am more than a white man. I am more than my labels.

I am an environmental science teacher/educator.
I am an environmentalist, an athlete, and a musician.
I am a student, a son, a brother, a friend, a partner.

I am against the war. I am against all wars.
I am against imperialism.
I am against hegemony.

I am for peace.
I am for social justice.
I am for a country where equality is reality, not rhetoric.

I am white.
I am male.
I am Jeff.

Chocolate Chip Girl
Michelle Somogui

When I was in first grade and second grade I was in bilingual classrooms. When the funding was cut, I stopped learning my second language. But, I could say the alphabet, count to one hundred, and sing "head, shoulders, knees and toes" in Spanish.

I didn't learn about people as brown, black, yellow, red or white, those were colors in my crayon box. People had names, Kelly, Enrique, Miss Lee, and Michelle. Not "white-girl." In eighth grade, I found out about "wetbacks" that lived in the canyon and stood on the street corners waiting for work every morning. Brown in San Diego is different than brown in Orange County where they are less normal, less valuable

In class Mary calls me "white-girl," but I am Michelle, her friend. "You don't understand," she says. "You don't know what it is like to be me."

My best friend is half Mexican and half White; we speak Spanish at her house and watch "Sabado Gigante" and the Spanish soap operas. There, I am not a "white girl."

In college, my friends are Maria and Mona who are Mexican, Top who is Cambodian, and Shaughnessy who is Black. Our discussions go past two in the morning, our struggle for meaning are never resolved. "You don't understand," I hear again, "You don't know what it is like." To them I am the dominant culture; White, middle-class, Protestant. They are working class; Catholic, Buddhist, and Jehovah's Witness.

So if I am so privileged, why am I working to support myself through college? Why am I in debt while their families pay their tuition, rent, and grocery bills? They are celebrated and supported for going to college and succeeding. I am expected to measure up. Is this what it means to be a white girl?

A couple of years ago I had a friend who was part Black and part Cherokee, Greg. Greg called me his "chocolate chip friend" because I am white and have little brown moles and freckles. He thought they looked like chocolate chips.

I was advised against enrolling in any Chicano studies courses at college because they said I would be harassed and abused by the Chicano students in the classes. I plan to be a teacher and school counselor in Southern California. How can I develop a knowledge base of cultures different from my own if I am denied access?

I once heard a poem written by a Black woman describing people of color to a Black child. The poem ended with a description of different people of color, and that black is all the colors in the rainbow combined, while white is the absence of all color. How sad that you feel this way, it hurts me to know that people find me lacking because the color of white is what has been attributed to the shade of my skin. If you think I don't understand, invite me into your life; speak freely to me of why you feel this way. If you think I don't know what it is like to be you, you're right. Because I'm not you, and I never can be, but you can tell me what it's like and I'll listen. And then I'll tell you what it is like to be me. My skin may be chocolate chip, but I have a rainbow inside me waiting to shine through if you will take the time to open your eyes and look.

It Can't Be Seen
Susan G. Macleod

My opportunity came upon graduation from college when I was invited to go the Philippines as a Peace Corp Volunteer. I was ecstatic! I would get to seek adventure, and "save the world" at the same time. After spending the summer after graduation white-water rafting down the Colorado River, having the time of my life with my new found freedom as a college graduate, mentally preparing for the separation from all that was familiar, and saying good-bye to friends and family, I was ready to be on my way.

All through my life, I have sought to do things different from everyone else. I have never wanted be just like others or to be stereotyped. I wasn't afraid of the differences I would encounter, this thing they called cultural differences and acculturation. That all seemed obvious and natural that things would be different—that was my challenge and why I sought to go overseas—to see the differences. The challenge was to see how well I could adjust. There was never a fear that I could not!

I had to be culturally sensitive to Filipino ways; I had to make sure I never caused anyone to "lose face." I tired to fit in. For the first time in my life, I was in the minority. But why was it like that? When I looked at Filipinos, I did not see that their skin might be darker than mine. Some were, some were not. I did not treat them differently than I did my American friends and associates. Each person I came into contact with, I treated as an individual, based on his or her own characteristics, not on any stereotype. Isn't that how we all should be treated?

Unless one was born and raised in the Philippines, one could never understand the culture entirely. No matter how hard one tries to fit in, if they are not Filipino, they will never fit in 100%. They will always be different, and never be completely accepted into the "inner' circles of confidence. As Americans, we will always be seen as "cano's," "Hey, Joe's," no matter how well we speak the dialect, no matter how well we have learned our lessons. We will always be different!

Spending four years as a Peace Corps volunteer, I learned a lot about myself, my country and other cultures and the world. No longer do I believe, as most Americans that the United States is in the center of the universe. The U.S. is only a small part of the world and the world does not revolve around the U.S. I started learning about things that went on in the world. I hadn't realized how sheltered I was (how sheltered most Americans are!). I started seeing things on a global basis. I may be Caucasian on the outside but I was becoming a mixture of cultures on the inside! When I would run into another foreigner there or later when I was traveling and I was asked where I was from, I answered, "I'm a Citizen of the World!"

Four years went by and I was successful! I raised funds for a YMCA building, I started a community library, I started a school for the deaf, I led seminars and leadership workshops, and I trained Olympic class swimmers for national competition. I changed the lives of the people around me forever, hopefully, for the better

Even though I knew I was different, I felt I learned to "fit in." I felt like my grass shack on the beach, with only four light bulbs, no modern appliances and no running water, was my home. I was paid the biggest compliment possible by the Filipinos, "You are just like a Filipina. You have become one of us!" I was in seventh heaven! Those Filipinos could see past the color of my skin!

However, shortly thereafter, my American friends said to me, "You are becoming just like a Filipina—its time for you to go home!" I was dumbstruck! How ironic! The same phrase uttered by two different groups with two completely different meanings!

Well, it was time for me to go home! I had stayed twice as long as originally intended. I had accomplished a lot and had made a difference. Why overstay my welcome and ruin a good thing?

Now, I would have to deal with returning home to America. I had survived acculturating into the Filipino culture and I had grown up in the

American culture. There shouldn't be a problem right? Wrong! The saying, "You can't go home again" is so true!

Things were not the same. I was definitely not the same person. I was on a different wavelength than my friends. I didn't know how to act or what to say! I felt off kilter because I was no longer in the fishbowl! No one paid attention to me as I walked down the street.

By the time I returned home in 1988, I had spent almost one third of my life overseas! I had missed out on ten years of movies, music, TV, books, fads, professional experience, etc. I was embarrassed to ask "What is a microwave? a food processor? a telephone answer machine? a fax machine? an ATM machine?"

When people asked, "How was it?" I would be so excited and start explaining until I saw the person's eyes gloss over. They really didn't want to know what it was like. Hearing about a different place was too "foreign" for most people to handle. So I would just answer, "Fine" and then become silent. I had nothing else to say. I had nothing in common with other Americans who tend to look at the U.S. in the center of the world. My otherness cannot be seen and no one wants to hear about it either.

The Good Life
Lisa Wilson Rink

I know what it is like to be the minority. To look at me, it's not apparent that I ever could be. But I was, once.

My mom, my sister and I lived in a middle class Detroit subdivision. The neighborhood was all white. The school we walked to each day was all white. Even our house was all white aluminum siding. The whiteness from the house rubbed off like chalk on your hands and clothes if you leaned against it.

We had the biggest house on the block, with an enormous yard. Naturally, all the kids from the neighborhood hung out at the Wilson's and I was the leader of the pack. Our days were filled with stickball and back-yard plays and hide-and-go-seek.

Every Friday I'd find my $1.00 allowance on the kitchen table and off I'd run to the corner store to spend it all on Swedish fish. They were only a penny apiece, so I could chew for an eternity and still have fish left over. Life was great.

I remember vividly the day Mom came home with a shiny new ring on her finger. It was 1979, on a sunny October afternoon. "Girls, I have a sur-prise for you!" Mom said in a breathless voice. My sister and I already knew —it was all over her face. The year before, she had met a policeman at the wedding of a friend. They were getting married. We were happy and she was ecstatic.

They told us we would be moving to Hank's new house in Benton Harbor, off of Lake Michigan, all the way across the state. We were both sad to leave our friends, our house, our school, and the corner store. But we had a wedding to look forward to and Benton Harbor sounded like such a pretty place—a real step up from the suburbs of Detroit. I imagined we'd be living on the water with the sound of foghorns and dock bells lulling us to sleep each night. I pictured Cape Cod style houses with perfectly trimmed lawns and lots of tall trees. That was cool. Yep, our great life would become even greater!

Euphemisms

Hank's "new house" turned out to be a small lot in a trailer park called Meadow Streams Estates. This was my first experience with false advertising. The "meadow" was a newly bulldozed plot of dirt. The "streams" turned out to be a waist-deep creek (pronounced "crick" by the locals) that regularly swallowed unwary children whole. It was lined with trees, though. And the "estates" . . . well, suffice it to say these glamorous "estates" would be blown away with a strong gust of wind. Be it ever so humble, we were home.

The Bus

It was weird, getting on a bus to go to school. We were forced to wake up early to catch the bus in time. We had to walk to the entrance of the trailer park, where there was a little shelter we could stand under while we waited. It was dark, freezing cold, and snowing. We were both wearing skirts, and our boots didn't go up high enough to keep our legs warm. There were a few other kids already waiting. Two were white and one was black. No one spoke. It was an incredibly long, uncomfortable silence, occasionally punctuated by the stamping of our freezing feet. Roni and I hoped there would be an empty seat so we could sit together. The bus finally arrived, quite noisily, in a smelly cloud of exhaust. When we boarded there were mostly white students. It took about 20 more minutes for the route to be completed, with each stop bringing us closer to the city. No more white kids climbed on the bus. The chatter of students grew louder and louder. The obscenities and the fighting shocked us.

"Ooooooh! We got some chicken, here! Anybody feel hungry fo' chicken?" yelled a girl in the seat behind us. She yanked on my sister's hair and declared loudly, "That means you white meat." Roni and I looked at each other. She held my hand tightly. "Just ignore them," she said. But I saw tears in her eyes. By the time we arrived at school, we were definitely the minority.

The Welcome

"Class, this is Lisa Wilson. She's a new student from Detroit, and I'm sure ya'll help welcome her," Ms. Williams said in a voice that was strange to me, as if she had a mouth full of food. She was beautiful, though, and smiled a lot. As I made my way to an empty seat in the back of the class I heard a girl whisper, "She's a whitey." Someone else whispered back, "She dressed so fancy. Miss La-dee-dah."

I didn't feel very welcome. I desperately wished I had worn the pants I'd wanted to instead of the burgundy velour skirt and top my sister had picked out for me. But the first day of school had always been a dress-up day for us, and we had desired to make a good impression.

From the safety of my seat I scanned the room, while the students took turns reciting their times-tables. There were probably 35 students, half boys, and half girls. All were black. I was the only white kid.

There were no pictures on the walls. The desks rocked on broken legs. I traced my fingers over the dirty words carved into my desktop, and quickly drew my hand back; afraid my Mother was somehow watching. There was an odor in the room I couldn't place. Two boys up front were completely twisted in their seats, staring at me. I wanted to be friendly, so I kind of half-waved "hi." The boy in front half-waved back. The boy in the 2nd row stuck out his middle finger and I quickly looked away.

For the first time in my life, I was unsure of myself. What if I don't fit in? What if I'm not smart enough? What if they find out I live in a trailer park? I was popular at my old school, part of the mainstream. Being so obviously different was a whole new experience for me.

A Simple Question

"Mom, what's a honkey?"
"What?"
"What's a honkey?"
"Where'd you hear that word?"
"At school. What is it?"
"Who said it?"
"Terrance."
"Who's Terrance?"
"He's a boy in my class. He sits in the 2nd row."
"Did you tell your teacher?"
"No. Why? What's it mean?"
"Well, next time anyone calls you that, you tell your teacher."

Recess

I used to love recess. I had so much fun playing dodge ball, swinging on the monkey bars, racing across the playground. Now I dreaded it. Our 15-minute recess would seem like an eternity. That's when Terrence and another boy named Ronald would run circles around us and pull at our hair while calling us names. Lily, Honkey, Whitey, Snowflake. One day, they did their usual circle dance, but this time Terrence dropped his pants, fondled himself and said, "I bet you ain't never seen a black willy before." We high-tailed back to the Recess Lady and told her what happened. The boys went to the Principal's Office, and never returned to class that day, much to my relief. I was afraid they'd get us back for getting them in trouble.

The taunting continued later that week, but Robin and I stuck together and it wasn't so bad. We got used to it, and started to ignore them. None too soon, they found other kids to pick on and began to leave us alone.

The Color of My Skin

Ms. Williams announced that we would be presenting a play for Martin Luther King Day. It was a skit in which Barbara Walters was interviewing King, with several other roles of various sizes. There would be auditions that afternoon to assign speaking roles to the best speakers. I was so excited, because I was a good reader. Then Ms. Williams said with a grin, "Of *course*, Lisa will be playing Barbara Walters." The other girls in the class complained, "She only gets to be Barbara 'cuz she white with blondie hair." I felt cheated.

Another Question

"Mom, what's a crazy Nigger?"
"Lisa Robin, I don't ever want to hear that out of your mouth again!"
"What?"
"Do you want a toothbrush full of soap?"
"What did *I* do?"
"Never mind."

Wake Up Call

Robin hadn't been to school in a week. My step-dad-the-policeman said a girl had tried to stab her on the bus home. She wouldn't be coming to school anymore. Her family was moving. I would miss her every day. Not long after that, my Mother finally woke up to what was happening in the schools of Benton Harbor. We had come to call it Benton Harlem, and were thrilled to hear that next year we'd be attending Lakeshore. It would require another move to another trailer park in another one-horse town called Baroda, but by now we had grown accustomed to the trailer and small-town life.

The Recovery

We had only been enrolled for a single semester, but it was long enough to put us both behind in our studies. For a full year, we struggled to catch up to our new classmates, eventually overcoming the education gap. Beyond that, nothing from our experiences at the school remained with us for very long. The few memories I have of my days as a minority are written here, the anxiety and fear having faded years ago. I was given a unique opportunity to experience life while standing in the shoes of minority. As an adult, I can look without hostility and genuinely appreciate the valuable lessons I was privileged to learn.

Experience of Others
Beth Wickham

My experience of otherness occurred while observing elementary students at an inner-city school in Santa Ana. The school is situated in a poor industrialized area, sprinkled with small apartment complexes and run-down homes throughout the general area. The class I observed consisted totally of Hispanic students without prior educational experiences in the United States. They ranged in age from 8 to 13. This was a very difficult teaching situation because of the students' lack of previous schooling. The teacher, Mrs. Acero, also was Hispanic, and she had many concerns regarding the class's performance and their ability to assimilate into the American educational system.

When I first met Mrs. Colon's class I was overwhelmed. The class was comprised solely of Hispanic students. The kids were nice to me and initially attempted to determine how much Spanish I could understand. In the beginning they acted pleasant and seemed to enjoy my presence, even though most had a look of distrust in their eyes as I worked with them. Perhaps they recognized the uncertainty in my own. I don't know. It is not a subject one discusses comfortably.

I also noticed substantial differences between the students and myself as I watched the Talent Show. I felt alienated as I watched the students perform pop singing, dancing, and culturally based comedy routines. Most of the jokes were about Mexican cultural experiences, and unfortunately, I could not understand them. Instead, the jokes left me feeling withdrawn, wondering what happened to the piano recital, gymnastics routine, and tap dancing that have been a part of every talent show I have attended in the past.

During my observations, I worked with the five students. One student, named Felipe, seemed overly concerned about his English pronunciation. I think that because of our cultural difference, he enjoyed learning about Caucasian people from me. I was able to see his keen interest in taking initiative to learn English. He wanted to understand English more than I wanted to learn Spanish.

Yet, I knew that I was different from Felipe, and the other students, and I felt things accordingly. For example, when they were all speaking Spanish, I could only decipher simple Spanish phrases and sentences such as "How are you?" and "The blouse is white." I was not an integrated part of the class when this occurred, but a curiosity in need of special treatment.

The teacher spoke both Spanish and English so that the student could learn English. Yet, they all looked at me, wondering whether Mrs. Acero did this so that I could understand what was being said. I knew they were keenly aware of our cultural differences and they kept their distance from me.

I was white and they were Hispanic. By simply looking into their eyes and seeing the uncertain look on their little faces I could tell that their lives were not easy. Although I could recognize their pain, I could not know it . . . Or could I?

My pain was caused from being alone in this situation. Only by being in Mrs. Acero's classroom where all the others were Hispanic could I have this experience of otherness. I also felt frustrated at not being able to understand when they spoke Spanish among each other. They could've said anything about me, knowing that I wouldn't punish them if they said something uncomplimentary about me. As it was, I was already unsure of myself as an instructor because this was my first observation experience. The situation made it twice as difficult, and three times as interesting.

Interracial Couples
Rae Afton Wilson

"I think interracial couples are just plain wrong." "Yeah, they're terrible." I stand there saying nothing. In my mind, I skillfully counter each comment. On the outside, I am still just standing there, saying nothing. With each passing moment, guilt is creeping in the way fog does on the bay. I am a sophomore in college.

That year I made friends with an African-American man, a senior, named Leigh Porter (pseudonym). We lived on the same floor in the dorms and everyone there hung out together. Leigh was on the basketball team and often got us special tickets or invited to parties. I look back at that time and remember having lots of fun.

Everything changed when I started dating Leigh. To me, it seemed like a natural progression, we were friends and we were interested in each other.

I was not prepared for the feelings of the people around us. Nor for the feelings I would have toward them.

I experienced racism from both white and black people. A white student on our floor called me a "nigger lover." The black girl that lived next door to me said I was taking "their men." My mother stated," I think Leigh is great but your grandpa would roll over in his grave." Depending on what neighborhood we were in, people would stare or look twice when we were together. I was amazed. I had no idea just how differently people may view what is culturally acceptable. Whenever I could question people about their feelings towards interracial couples, I did. I discovered that often people felt very strongly against it, but didn't know why; they were just "raised that way."

One of Leigh's friends used to tease me that I was from "richville." Where is that? I wondered. I was the stereotypical blond-haired blue-eyed girl. I realized how little I knew about the experiences of people from different ethnic backgrounds. When you grow up in an all white community there is little opportunity to learn about others. Most people I talked to felt that I could not relate to their cultural experiences and they could not relate to mine. The worst part was that I began to feel that maybe it is too difficult for people from different ethnic backgrounds to build a relationship together. This weighed heavily on my conscience.

I began to think deeply about my life. I have heard it said that having blond hair and blue eyes is the "norm." As if having these things is a guarantee of a perfect life and superiority over others. Not to mention you are the "oppressor." But I don't feel this way at all. As a matter of fact I was feeling pretty misunderstood and misrepresented. What was inside this blond-haired blue-eyed packaging was someone who felt "other" than the norm at least 50% of the time.

I have experienced otherness in the forms of being a woman, having a brother who is gay, parents that are divorced, filing bankruptcy and plenty of other ways. However, I had been labeled in the eyes of many people "blond hair = easy life." I felt depressed and resentful about the situation. Who makes these judgments? Who decides light-skinned people should be with other light-skinned people and dark-skinned I people should stay with dark skinned?

Mexican-American History Class
Alyson Palmer

I enrolled in a Mexican-American history class realizing that I knew nothing about Mexican-Americans and I was tired of learning about the U.S. only. I wanted to learn about a different culture and heritage. However, I did not think I would be the only Anglo girl in the classroom. I watched as the class filled up on the first day; many people tried to petition to add but I was still the only Anglo girl. I thought other Anglo people would want to learn about the Mexican culture.

I loved the class, but there were times when I felt myself sinking in my chair. The instructor would discuss the poor treatment of Mexicans by the white people and how we basically made them into slaves with hard work and low pay. I felt bad about the conditions. However, I was not the cause of them. I was taking this class to learn about the struggle and challenges the Mexican-Americans went through to become productive citizens.

I think the people in the class respected me for taking the class and wanting to learn about their heritage and the courage it took to stay in that class. I think the students realized I did feel somewhat uncomfortable, how could one not?

Indian Wedding
Jennifer Vatave

"I have great news. Sunil just asked me to marry him. Isn't that great?" I am so happy. Mom is really giving me a hard time. She thinks I will be "all alone" in India, but I won't. Sunil's whole family will be with me.

She thinks I'll have to cover my face up and bow down to all the men. She says that women are not respected there at all. She is even worried that I'll never return. She said she recently saw the movie *Not Without My Daughter.*

Dad is so angry at me for wanting to go through with this. He even threatened to not pay for the wedding in June if I considered the Indian wedding a real wedding. I never really thought of him as a racist, but he hates the idea of me getting married in another country. He seems really scared of what could happen to me.

Could something really happen to me? Sunil and his family are the nicest people I know. They would never let anything happen to me. He is worried that the family won't like me because I'm not Indian.

Everyone is so excited about the wedding. It is great because they do all the planning, we basically just show up. His family bought me two saris. One is bright pink and green (traditional wedding colors) and the other is cranberry and gold. Sunil is out now buying a special suit for the big day.

We keep getting invited to people's houses for "traditional wedding food." It does not taste very good, but I eat it with grace. They present the food on beds of flower.

The people on the street all stare at me. I guess I really stand out. The children come up and touch my clothes and hands. Sometimes, I will say "Namaste," which also means hello. They giggle and run away.

Even though I feel strange on the street, his family treats me as if I am part of their family. I feel like I am accepted and cared for. They really admire me for coming across the world to meet them and to learn about their culture. They love the fact that I have so many questions and that I try to say things in Hindi. They laugh because almost all of them speak English.

I feel guilty now about getting married Hindu style. I feel like I am betraying God. I have only been thinking of it as a different culture, not religion. In my mind, my Christian wedding should and will be the real one. Although this Indian wedding will be one of the most important days in m life, I just hope God can forgive me.

I have embraced Sunil's culture and traditions with an open heart. I feel like I am lying to everyone about it. To Sunil and his family, it was a meaningful event that brought us all close together. But with my family, I pretend like it never happened. If I or anyone else mentions it, they get all tight in the face. To keep peace I keep quiet and talk about neutral things. They are looking forward to our Christian wedding. It will be a beautiful day.

Name Pain
P. Makzynski

Assuming the role of "outsider" on the stage of life is a part we all must play. Whether real or imagined, to feel less than, different, or set apart from, the mainstream is integral to the human experience. In my own life so many instances from the reservoir of my memory flood my mind that I find it difficult to choose just one. How about being the new kid in town, in school, in the neighborhood? Or being a woman in a male-dominated society? Then there's the part of a single adult in a paired up world. But I choose none of these. For though I claim ownership to each one, none cuts so directly to the core of my being as my ethnicity.

I am American born, but I am NOT one of the Daughters of the American Revolution. I suppose I'd more aptly be affiliated with the Daughters of Ellis Island. Though I fit in the latter group, I longed to be a member of the former. This love /hate relationship with my heritage continues to this day. I have no clue as to the origin of this ongoing battle. But I am cognizant of one thing, that at some point in my life, to be the product of eastern European immigrants was a source of shame. It was that long awkward sounding last name with a mix of consonants that you never see in the English language. Shame. Every time it had to be called out loud I'd cringe as the caller wrestled with it a while then invariably gave up, only to have mangled it beyond recognition. Why couldn't my name just be Smith? Pain. Or maybe it was my nose, my grandma's nose. Shame. I wanted a refined nose, with round blue eyes, and blond hair to match, like the girl whose grandmother sailed over on the Mayflower. But I love my grandma. Shame. Then there were my large hands with knotty knuckles, so peasant-like and unrefined. Shame. But they're so like my Babi's (great-grandma) hands, always covered with flour or holding my face in them. I adored that woman. Pain.

My father had our last name changed, for business he said. It 's an abbreviated form of our real name, with only two syllables. It's real easy to pronounce and it sounds Irish. Acculturation. My brothers each married girls with big blue eyes, and tiny hands and English-sounding names (one of them a direct descendant of Betsy Ross) Pain.

I lied to someone, once, and told them that I was of French extraction. To my mind that sounded more mainstream and therefore more acceptable. Denial. It turns out, though, that this "someone" was my future mother-in-law; so I eventually had to tell the truth. I, too, married a boy with a blonde hair and blue eyes and an Anglo name. Now, it was my name, too. And, for the first few years of our marriage, I would delight in giving my name or hearing it called. I would even feel a little deceitful and, ironically, sometimes sad. Because, with the exchange of that part of my identity, I loathed for another which I thought I so desired. I felt deep loss. And that, I think, is acculturation. Pain.

October 11, 2001, Eye Was in Mexico
Cynthia Hagen

for nearly a month, eye was silenced, engulfed by sounds that had no meaning,
    and, like a thirsty sponge, eye absorbed the strangeness and grew
    with each passing day.
for nearly a month, narrowed ojos fired loaded questions at me: why are you
here? what do you want from us? haven't you done enough already?
    and, through the lens of cultural evolution, my own eyes begged
    forgiveness for the sins of my ancestors.

for nearly a month, heavy laughter from weighted jokes left burning scars
on my eardrums,
    and, like the comic relief in a tragic play, eye sported my laughing
    mask and feigned comprehension.

for nearly a month, the terror of theft resonated throughout every fiber of
my being: ¡Dáme la cámara! ¡Dále un balazo!
    and, as Robin Hood theory danced in my head, eye struggled to keep
    my own eyes from narrowing.

for nearly a month, over and over again, eye watched horrified from afar as
my country crumbled,
    and, like a defeated soldier, eye stood tall, marched on and wore my
    color with pride.

for nearly a month, my pain was met with fireworks and fiestas as eye celebrated their independence,

and, as the death toll at home continued to grow, eye questioned whether mine was still intact.

for nearly a month, warm tears cooled my cheeks as eye longed for my mother's loving embrace,
    and, like a freshly incarcerated prisoner, eye silenced my sobs with
    my pillow.

for nearly a month, eye was silenced, engulfed by sounds so rich in meaning,
    and, like a thirsty sponge, eye absorbed the beauty and grew more
    grateful with each passing day.

for nearly a month, eye was a white girl in Mexico City,
    and eye can't wait to go back.

The Gift of Shoes
Christina M. Boynton

A couple of months after I graduated from college, I started sending my resume out in search of a job that worked with children. I decided that I wanted a job with a nonprofit organization that worked with abused or neglected children. After three or four interviews with different types of group homes, I finally found exactly what I was looking for. They ran me through a variety of tests dealing with my mental and even physical capability to deal with volatile and violent situations that could occur while working with the youth.

I thought I had done really well with whatever they threw at me. I was educated and I had a lot of experience working with children in that geographic community. In my opinion, I had the job. No problem! So when I got the call from the director of the organization to let me know that I didn't get the job, I was confused, shocked, and heart-broken.

The director explained that they really liked me but that they felt I was "too white" for the job and that the kids would take advantage and/or couldn't relate to me. What the hell is "too white?" I thought. Was it actually my skin color or was it a conviction about what I was as a person? I'd almost rather have heard that I was "too small," "too preppy" or even "too middle-class" to work with these youth, rather than "too white"—like that is a quality I can change about myself.

For the first time in my life my appearance became a stone, actually a bolder, in my life's path. I realized that while this was one job lost for me, there are tons of people in this country who face this all the time. People assumed that the kids wouldn't be able to relate to me and that I was not right for the job. I wasn't given the chance to show otherwise.

I felt the sting of discrimination, and it was a slap in the face. When you grow up as a middle-class white kid, society tells you and almost guarantees that you can be anything you want. So it is a rare opportunity/gift to be able to wear someone else's shoes whose been jumping over the discrimination hurdles their whole life. Yeah the shoes hurt and have no support, so you wish you could take them off. But unless you wear them at least once, you wouldn't know what it was like not ever being able to take them off.

4

Critical Literacy

This chapter briefly describes educational implications and acts of social justice taken by future teachers as a result of hearing these stories. The objective of this book was not to prescribe answers to the phenomenon of otherness but to keep the stories of otherness as experienced by school children central on the social radar of future teachers so as to inform their moral compasses to act assertively to build safe school environments that promote social and intellectual growth.

Personal satisfaction came to the authors of the stories from both the writing and the oral storytelling. The process of generating and then sharing, brought public attention to what was known personally and privately. The combined acts of writing and sharing have psychological healing and political ramifications. Students reported that telling the stories helped the scars to heal thus giving credence to Howard (1999) "healing can begin only when we acknowledge the depth of our pain." (p. 48). Sharing the stories with a nurturing, receptive community developed a collective, social, and political consciousness of otherness. Furthermore, they validated students' experiences of otherness and gave rise to pedagogical direction.

We are programmed at very young ages to see difference as negative, which is a reason we have a tendency to want to erase it. In kindergarten classes across the nation, teachers hold up worksheets with shapes and point to circle, circle, triangle, circle and then ask, "Which one is different?" In the next breath, they inquire, "Which one does not belong?" The message is clear, difference is disapproval. Those who are different, who are others, are considered "social flaws" by white dominance (West, 1993). Young children of color enter schools and experience difference negatively (Ramirez & Castaneda, 1974). They subsequently strive to show others they are the same, not knowing they have devalued themselves in the meantime (Ramirez & Castaneda, 1974). Virtually all children learn in U.S. schools that to be accepted, differences must be camouflaged.

Conditions in which certain differences are tolerated vary depending on the social context. From my experiences in southern California, signs in French on restaurants are international but signs in Vietnamese are foreign. The American Grammy Awards are American celebrations; the Latino Grammy Awards are curiously "ethnic." Ivy league colleges, which are predominately white, are prestigious. Black colleges, which are predominantly black (and produce higher rates of black professionals), are segregationists. Fraternities and sororities are normal fixtures on the college landscape, homosexual and ethnic clubs are battle sites for approval. Differential treatment for people with disabilities as evidenced by the availability of handicapped parking spaces is socially acceptable, differential treatment by gender or race afforded through Affirmative Action is not. Heterosexual displays of affection in public is tolerated, homosexual displays of affection invite hate crimes. Children are allowed to play physically assaultive schoolyard games like dodge ball, but African-American children are prohibited from "playing the dozens," a game of verbal put downs. Hence, difference is acceptable when applied to non-blacks, non-browns, nonethnics, and heterosexuals. This sentiment is captured in the following anecdote. When people say, "We're all the same," what they mean is, "I am like them," not "they are like me." Because if "they were like me," they would speak some Chinese, right?

Student authors confessed they were unconscious of how the hegemony of white ideology prevented them from naming the felt difference in their lives. Students of color disclosed they ached to tell their stories, citing limited venues to communicate these truths prior to their college experience. Marginalized groups have resisted telling their stories because they are often made to feel distrustful of their own voices. White students wondered if they had places on the color palette of democracy. They felt a cultural homelessness (Bell, 2001). Most students appear to be unknowing, involuntary participants of white ideology (Kivel, 1996), unaware of their parts as victims and/or oppressors.

"Diversity is a fundamental feature of our human birthright and our cultural legacy as citizens of the U.S." (Gay, 1995, p. 30). Yet difference often engenders fear and intimidation. Many people prefer to be colorblind and whitewash the differences (Meyer, 1995). Ward Connerly (2003), University of California Regent, author of Proposition 209, the California constitutional amendment that eliminated Affirmative Action in 1996, claimed that democracy's goal is a *colorblind* society. Inherent in his stance is the concept that difference is bad. What Connerly failed to comprehend is that the word "colorblind signals a dismissiveness of that translates to one erasing his or her difference to be accepted by the mainstream."

Anecdotal evidence of this discomfort comes up each semester when I ask students how our course on diversitie is different because an Asian-American female teaches it. Their typical response is, "We never noticed you were Asian! We're colorblind." They do admit, however, that they acknowledged my gender. It is socially appropriate to acknowledge gender, but not ethnicity. We are taught not to see color, in the name of tolerance, yet we know color is the "first read" between human adults (Shipler, 1997). Shipler, in his studies, concluded that color triggers white assumptions about blacks in the initial introduction between blacks and whites "before a handshake or a word, before a name, an accent, an idea" (p. 280). Duarte (1998) posited that colorblindness is equivalent to difference blindness, spawned by a fundamental belief that we could all "just get along" if we simply gave up our individual differences and embraced our common humanness.

A well-intended colleague once asked me, "Why do you want to be different? Minorities are always asking to be the same. They want the same employment opportunities, the same housing accessibility, the same number of college placements. Now you want to be different. What *is* it that you want?"

My response, I want my difference to make a significant contribution to a pluralistic society. I want to be accepted without a hegemonic attempt to erase my difference. I want my worth to be judged by my work and not measured by my degree of similarity to others.

In the 1980s, women leaders in education tried to emulate the leadership styles of men. Later, as we learned to renegotiate power with men, we introduced a new genre of leadership skills, born from a feminine paradigm. Women reframed the world through a gender-balanced imaginary that optimized, not homogenized, the unique talent and skills of women and men.

LEARNING FROM OTHERS

And the "marginal" may prove revelatory of a larger complex of questions and issues when situated and scrutinized . . .
—Shirvane (2001, pp. 29-30

Otherness narratives typically brought forth the following conversations.

1. *Cultural surprises*: New social and cultural information about those who are racially, ethnically, and economically different from us, as evidenced by student comments like, "I never knew that." The more diverse the student population, the more likely this is the response.

2. *Differences*: Students concluded after comparing groups and personal experiences that there were as many differences within groups, as there were between groups (e.g., English/bilingual debates within Hispanic communities). We asked ourselves, "What is the intrinsic worth of thinking about people as different but equal?" And conversely, "Why might people be indifferent to difference?"

3. *Relativity of oppressions*: Students inevitably asked, "Is there a hierarchy of oppression?" (Adams, Bell, & Griffin, 1997, p. 65). "Which is worse being a woman or being black?" (Halprin, 1995, p. 195). Are marginalizing experiences equivalent to one another? If one understands sexism, does it mean one understands racism? What is the relationship between someone else's oppression and my own? How is our experience the same or different? Do all forms of oppression use fear, control, and/or hate to subordinate? (Matsuda, 1996). Are all forms of oppression equally destructive to the human spirit? (Adams et al., 1997). Can one be oppressed as a member of a group, but not as an individual? Can one be oppressed as an individual but not as a member of his or her group? Who benefits from oppression?

4. *Invisibility*: Historical influences, social norms, and cultural regularities prevent us from seeing or resisting domination and marginalization. We found there was a relationship between assimilation and cultural invisibility. Those in the mainstream generally control the presence and the portrayal of Others in media.

5. *Inequities*: We studied the inequitable funding among groups of people, which could be explained by discrimination (e.g. men and women's sports). We found there were disproportionate numbers of people of color in education's lower tracks and in special education. We considered how the concept of difference camouflages capitalistic implications of these inequities (Darder, 2002).

6. *Whiteness*: Students explored the concept of whiteness. "Are whites othered? By whom and to what degree? Can whites be victims of racism as well? What forms of otherness exist in an

all-white classroom? What can we learn about whiteness by studying people of color? How is whiteness part of the multi-cultural equation?"

Students mined the narratives like caverns in search of the responsible social forces of oppression and exclusion, trying to make sense of the indignities. The questions students posed revealed a beginning consciousness of their own socially constructed worlds, a curiosity to explore other lived realities and a willingness to question the conditions that may have influenced those social realities. By making narratives of otherness visible, we could critique the dominant narrative, which had marginalized other forms of being.

In the classic, *Border Crossings*, Giroux (1993) encouraged border-crossing discussions to "acknowledge and critically interrogate how the colonizing of differences by dominant groups is expressed and sustained through representations in which the humanity of the Other is either ideologically disparaged or ruthlessly denied" (p. 33). Furthermore, Giroux argued that students should be given the opportunity to engage in systematic analyses of inequality, forced exclusions, and the marginality at the level of everyday life. Scheurich and Young (1998) suggested that looking into "who gets the lowest tracks, the least experienced teachers, the worst hidden curriculum, disproportionate assignment to special education, culturally biased pedagogies, excessive disciplinary actions, under representation in textbooks, the least money spent on them, and the worst buildings" (p. 27), we would better understand the relationship between racism and student achievement. From these investigations there is the hope for oppositional and transformative consciousness (Giroux, 1993).

In the dominant pedagogy of schools, students with self-defined identities as Others, reported that they could not find their places on the social grid that values sameness. What they needed, they claimed, was teachers who could challenge the dominance of sameness and integrate a place for difference. These teachers could help to dispel notions that there is something inherently wrong, divisive, or destructive about cultural or physical differences. They needed foras to critique the social forces that shaped their "less than" lives; those forces that casted differences in a negative rather than a positive perspective. Banks (1993) identified the pedagogical challenge for teachers as one in which the teacher needs to know how to create a cohesion while maintain distinct identities.

Giroux (1993) added that this critique is a moral imperative and a prerequisite for a democratic society. He maintained that when a teacher invites students to bring their difference to a circle of learning, it is an act of utmost dignity, tolerance, and empathy. The possibilities of newly acquired perspectives are the passports to the reconceptualization of our social and political selves. Barbules and Rice (1991) suggested that a democratic ideal would be to hope for one of two results on this journey: new common meanings or nonconvergent discourses; both roads aimed at tolerance and respect.

NARRATIVES AS A TOOL TO BUILD CAPACITY FOR EMPATHY

When I Meet the Other, I Become the Other

Empathy is the ability to share in another's emotions, thoughts, or feelings. It is what keeps our inner bully in check; it prevents us from laughing at someone else's shame; it makes us hurt when we're confronted by another's pain (Howard, 1999).

In this course, we exchanged our deepest secrets of oppression and in return we were gifted with empathy. Classmates reported that they were forever touched by each other's stories. Each story inscribed its mark on the hearts of fellow students. Individuals wept and raged over inhumane treatment suffered by their fellow classmates. Simon (2000) refered to this pedagogy as a "mode of witnessing, a public space in which students learn to be attentive and responsible to the memories and narratives of others . . . the opportunity for students to make connections with others through social relations that foster a mix of compassion, ethics, and hope" (cited in Giroux 2001, p. 8).

> Jill gave me a lot to think about. What had the greatest impact on me was when she said that she was sharing her life experience with us because it was important to make us aware of what our students may be experiencing. . . . I admire all of those who spoke that night for being so open with us and sharing memories so close to their hearts. I left class that night with a very heavy heart. I felt guilty that I had not been willing to share. (Jordan, 4/2/98)

> I felt guilty for being who I am, for what others think that I have . . . privilege. I still feel all this. But I have gained a different perspective. I realized that there are doors that have opened to me more easily than they may open for others. I realized that because my parents are middle class, white and educated, I have automatic membership in a group that wields power. (Somogui, 3/19/98)

The instructor is also deeply moved by the narratives and the communal exchange. Delpit (1988) encouraged teachers to "open themselves up to and allow themselves to be vulnerable and affected by alternative voices" (pp. 318-319). When we listen critically to the reality of dominance and its tragic impact on our students' lives, we are then obliged to struggle and work together to create socially just responses (Howard, 1999). Furthermore, teachers should offer their own narrative to be examined for discourse within the learning community and in so doing; they will "uncover the hidden ideological interests that underlie their own pedagogical practices" (McLaren, 2003, p. 251).

The greatest self-fulfillment in this work was finding out who I was, by finding out who my students were. When they first walk into class, they think they are going to study the "other." During the first semester that I taught this course, both the students and I did not realize until the end that we study others as a way to study ourselves. Narratives jolted us out of unknowingness and complacency. We conducted brutally honest self-inventories of our prior insensitivities and unconsciousness of othering and otherness. We told each other truths, shared mutual pain and revelation at new discoveries, and affirmed each other's feelings. This feminist ethic of empathy unleashed a desire to change the inequitable conditions and dehumanization of others. We pledged to act upon any situations that limited one's participation in school or society.

CRITICAL DISCOURSE

Although empathy is an essential step in one's moral development, "empathy does not necessarily lead to or justice" (Eddy, 1996, p. 7). McLaren (2003) agreed and said that humanism by itself is ineffectual because it "does not educate community members about how power relations in society work" (p. 247). The stories of otherness aroused listeners in different ways. Some felt empathy for the victims; others were angry at the injustices, and some expressed guilt for their heretofore indifference to othering and otherness. Adverse conditions are not changed merely through awareness alone; instead, it is the interplay between reflection and action that remove social barriers.

In critical discourse, students see how people with different social statuses view themselves and their relationship to others. What can be achieved in a community discourse, which cannot be captured in this book, are the dynamic interpretations of the narratives made by the authors and the listeners. It is in this dialectic where students "challenge antidemocratic forms of power" (Giroux, 2001, p. 8) and choose to accept, refuse, challenge, or create alternatives. Here, we can confront our own racist attitudes and intentions that sanction dominant views and behaviors (Ladson-Billings, 1994; Sleeter, 1996). Critical theorists (Kanpol & McLaren, 1995; Reynolds, 1994) have long called for a counter hegemonic agenda in which a deeper understanding of power relationships is dealt with overtly. By naming the inequitable distribution of power and resources that affect our lives, Fine

(1997) argued that we could uncover the way that power, ideology, and culture operate to disempower some and privilege others. The work of naming facilitates healing while at the same time, fueling a moral commitment of reform (Freire, 1995). Some students were so repulsed by the schoolyard bullying that they vowed to do everything possibly to prevent emotionally scarring experiences from reoccurring for a new generation.

These opportunities for critical discourse are rare in teacher education programs. Critical literacy instructors typically report they "have found over the years of teaching . . . that most all of my students lacked critical consciousness" (Kivel, 1996, p. 11). In part, the reason lies in hesitancy to confront controversial issues in dominant paradigm classrooms. Carole Hahn (2003) reported in a 28-nation civic education study, that fewer than 70% of 14-year olds said their classes explored controversial issues over which different people disagree.

Critical literacy does not allow us to dodge the important questions like "How do we, in our roles both as the oppressor and oppressed, reclaim and remake our histories, voices, and visions, in order to change those conditions that limit one's participation in school or society?" "How can our stories of everyday schoolyard victimization lend themselves productively to forms of oppositional and transformative consciousness?" The answers lie not only in the critical interrogation of social inequities but also in the actions we take.

THE POWER OF ONE

Ancient Chinese proverb says that the power of a butterfly's wings can be felt on the other side of the world.
—Briggs and Peat (1999, p. 31)

The flap of a butterfly's wings in Brazil set off a tornado in Texas.
—Briggs and Peat (1999, p. 33)

If one student story can impassion a whole class, can one class influence a whole community? Can our knowledge of difference make a difference in the way people treat one another?

Once we recognized the social forces of domination, we could not ignore them. As a woman, I recognize how I have genderized my democratic participation by taking the path of least resistance (Darder, 1991). As an Asian American, I know I must emerge from my culturalized preference toward social obedience and relieve my black colleagues from their role as miner's canaries in order to take an active role in dismantling inequality and dehumanization. My otherness and inequality shaped my political and social identities. How then can otherness help me become advocate for social justice? How can my cultural and genderize histories inform my anti-racist/anti-sexists agenda? Furthermore, how do I own up to one's part in the reproduction of social inequities? It means asking one's self, "What role do I play in the perpetuation of the 'isms'—racism, sexism, classism, linguicism, ageism, etc. How am I a part of the systemic problem? How might I face my complicity?"

THE POWER OF MANY

Writing and listening to narratives of otherness can jolt us out of complacency but it is in the sharing of these stories that Fischman (cited in Eddy, 1996) claimed that we developed a sense of the potential to transition from individual awareness to collective social action, from individual isolation to collective consciousness. Multiculturalism is bigger than just "coming to know." McLaren (2003) added that the "self and social transformation must be taken seriously within an wider orbit of anti-capitalist, anti-sexist, and anti-racist practices" (p. 250). Therefore, our challenge was to move our commitments from individual merit to social change. Eddy (1996, p. 3) described this type of work as "learning to recognize the exile of others and committing ourselves to make the tasks that face each group into the central topic of public life" (p. 3). "Tolerance of differences is not enough" (McLaren, 2003, p. 251). Giroux (1986) advised that activists must be, "unified in a common struggle to overcome the conditions that perpetuate their own suffering and the suffering of others."

Story sharing gave us a chance to make sense of each other's social locations. We braided the lines of difference and produced a dynamic composition of collective consciousness. The oral reading of these papers was the transformative moment in the course when students became viscerally engaged and emotionally jolted by the terrible and enduring effects of "othering."

Our story-sharing forum became the center to which we could bring our questions, vulnerabilities, and possibilities. It was the place that we spoke as others with each other; the place where we learned from and with others and not just about them. We were able to penetrate the barrier of social positionality and see ourselves from a more realistic perspective. Although story sharing made us vulnerable, the forum was also our lifeline, the umbilical cord from which we gave birth to our new political voices. This meant rethinking the relations between the center and the margins of power structures and visualizing difference as part of a common struggle to extend the quality of public life (Giroux, 1993; Kanpol, 1995). These new understandings are nested in a larger philosophical context where Enlightenment's universalism of an undifferentiated human nature moves to postmodernism's multiphonic, multitextured agenda that honors individual and social differences (Kanpol, 1994; Mouffee, 1988; Yeo, 1995)

Watts (1995) summed up the process of critical literacy nicely:

> The resolution lies in the promise of developing a world which can respect diversity without destroying it or attempting to transform it into one's own image. We do this by first identifying the forms of otherness, analyzing the reasons for this social condition in the forms of hegemony, institutional racism and belief systems, and subsequently, developing a commitment and a plan to actively promote a more caring and socially just world. (p. 45)

SOCIAL JUSTICE PROJECTS

Rather than be spectators, students chose to be agents of collective social change. Their goal was to challenge unfair political, economic, and social practices where human potential might be diminished. They looked for loose threads to unravel the status quo. They sought opportunities to reweave their social and political selves as active players to a new democratic imaginary.

Students in the teacher education program organized collaborative projects that challenged normative assumptions about standard mainstreamed beliefs. Given only a semester's worth of time, the projects were limited in scope but were evidence of thoughtful initiative in addressing diverse issues in the community. Following are a sampler of social justice projects, inspired by ideas from Grant and Sleeter's (1998) book, *Turning on Learning*; Nieto's (1992) book, *Affirming Diversity*; and Steffey and Hood's (1994) book, *If This is Social Studies, Why Isn't It Boring?* For these projects, social justice was defined as collective social movement aimed at deepening social consciousness.

Family

Students inventoried greeting cards at popular greeting card shops. They made lists of what events were significant (birthdays, anniversaries, parties, graduations, promotions, retirements deaths), what social messages were appropriate (celebration, condolences, sorrow, missing) and who was socially represented (photographs/illustrations of people of color, disabled, elderly) on greeting cards. Students graphed their findings and made notes on what was missing. They wrote letters to greeting card companies to inform them of their findings and asked critical questions (e.g., what does it mean when there are no cards to commemorate a foster/adoptive parent? Or were they aware that not one photographed face represented the physically disabled community).

Multiculturalism

Adult students, along with school-age students who acted as co-researchers, conducted a school inventory of multiculturalism (Nieto, 1992). They counted the number of books found in the classrooms and libraries by authors from different backgrounds based on cultural/linguistic, gender, sexual orientation, social class, and physical and cognitive abilities. They examined menus to determine what kinds of school lunches were served. They looked for evidence of different languages on bulletin boards and school communications. Findings were compiled and detailed in a report given to the school administrators. Additionally, students would make suggestions about how to enrich a campus' multicultural dimensions (e.g., a proposal for organizing a multicultural conference, including a list of speakers from different social and ethnic backgrounds from the community, sample flyers; and sample lessons using multicultural literature).

Religion

Students attended services at a Catholic church, a Baptist church, a Buddhist temple, and an Islamic mosque. They compared and contrasted the diverse religious doctrines. They read religious documents and interviewed religious officials and members to identify points of consensus or difference. They explored how these religions differed from their own training and how religion might inform public school policy.

Language

Students interviewed individuals with diverse language histories about their sentiments on bilingualism and English monolingualism. Before categorizing the data from the two interest groups, they asked interviewees, "What message(s) would you like us to take to the opposing political camp?" Then results were shared with opposite camps. Using the acquired data, students developed questionnaires and interviewed public officials who voted for English-only and bilingual policies, respectively. Data was compiled and sent to the participants.

Bullies

Teaching candidates interviewed K–12 children about their experiences with school bullies and held class meetings to brainstorm solutions. Solutions were presented in oral and visual presentations to other teachers and students who shared the same recess period. The audiences were invited to give suggestions to a bullying prevention plan that everyone could agree to (e.g., role-playing interventions to help bullies to interact more respectfully with other children, assertiveness strategies for victims, and community of support for victims).

Gender

Teacher candidates identified and observed single-gender math classrooms. They interviewed school personnel, parents, and students about how single-gender classrooms facilitated or obstructed learning. They compiled their results and compared their findings with the literature on single-gender and single race-schools. A report and discussion of findings were conducted back at the university, whereas a summary of findings was submitted to the participating schools. One school allowed our students to present findings to a departmental meeting.

Social Class

Teacher candidates and their students created a curricular unit on homelessness for K–8 students. In the unit they attempt to demystify the unknown by taking a field trip to the homeless shelter. There, they interviewed homeless adults and children, asking the homeless people what others should know about them. They made a photo essay of the day in the life of the homeless and displayed the pictures on cardboard boxes that simulated makeshift homeless housing. Other classrooms were invited to tour the cardboard box exhibit.

Intellectual Differences

Teacher candidates collected beginning-of-the-year essays from gifted, regular education, and special needs students from the same grade level. Names of papers were erased and essays were posted on a long wall. Teachers and fellow candidates were invited to do a gallery walk to read the essays and label which essays were written by gifted, regular education, or special needs students. Debriefing by those who participated included discussions about the lack of clear distinctions among groups, the overrepresentation of underrepresented minorities in special needs classes, and the benefits of homogenous and heterogeneous groupings. One school used this activity as part of a self-study, which resulted in the reconceptualization of all-day homogenous classes to heterogeneous and homogenous groupings throughout the day.

Beauty

Teacher candidates conducted polls of adolescent and young girls to determine what media influenced their body images. Magazine collages of models were assembled and girls were asked to identify pictures that matched their ideas of beauty. Students found in their results that there was a common core of beauty criteria held by girls of all ethnic backgrounds that positively correlated with the propensity of those criteria featured in ads or commercials. Students wrote letters and interviewed creative directors at advertising agencies about their knowledge of the influence these ads have on young people.

Cultural Competency

Both the narratives of otherness and the subsequent social justice projects helped students develop cultural competencies, which Howard (1999) suggested are essential to the foundation of a pluralistic and participatory democracy. These competencies are as follows:

1.   Know who we are racially and culturally.
2.   Learn about and value cultures different from our own.
3.   View social reality through the lens of multiple perspectives.
4.   Understand the history and dynamics of dominance.
5.   Nurture in our students and ourselves a passion for justice and the skills for social action. (p. 81)

At the height of social commitment and action, students find themselves ironically in a seemingly apathetic social context. When they are out in the schools, they report that they do not get a sense that seasoned teachers have any social or political views. Teacher lounge talk is rather placid and numbing. Students come back to the university and ask questions like, "Why does it appear that so many teachers are complacent about the state's current chokehold over public education?" "Why has there not been a strong voice of dissent over the narrowing of textbook selections, the profusion of scripted teaching, the encroachment of standardized testing and the erosion of teacher participation and decision-making?" "Where does apathy come from?"

BYSTANDERISM

Why are there so many spectators and so few actors engaged in social justice work in the schools? Psychologists first used the term *bystander apathy* in the early 1960s (*Gale Encyclopedia*, 2001). Bystanderism is the response of people who observe something and do not get involved. Understanding bystanderism is a useful conceptual tool in critical pedagogy. It may also show how the action dimension of critical pedagogy gets obscured. I write this piece to shed light for others as well as for my own edification to name and understand more deeply why some people act and others don't; why sometimes I act and sometimes I don't. When we expect our students to change the world, the tools that they need to acquire must include promising alternatives as well as the identification of likely barriers. In thinking of social justice, the questions that regularly plague the work are, "What are the forces, both internal and external that keep us all from acting?" And ultimately, "If we do nothing, will we have changed the world?"

Learned Bystander Apathy

Learned apathy comes from our political and personal histories. War prisoners and perceived enemies of the state have been socially conditioned for apathy and indifference. Years of socialized indifference under a Communist regime, coupled with fatalistic Chinese philosophies, have significantly encoded political apathy in Chinese people up to the present day (Yung, 1995). Buddhist selflessness, humility, Communism, deference to elders, and the language of silence are social conditions ripe for apathy in political activity. Not only are there Eastern winds that influence my apathy but Western ones also exist. My history is reduced in the California social studies textbooks to railroads, laundries, and the Chinese Exclusion Act. The important work of my great grandparents as herbalists, accountants, and merchants can only be found in alternative courses like Asian Studies at the collegiate level. There are few places for me to learn about my own history. I know more about how African Americans have come to this country than I do about Asian Americans. My historical invisibility fuels apathy.

When those who have the power to name and to socially construct reality choose not to see you or hear you, whether you are dark-skinned, old, disabled, female, or speak with a different accent or dialect than theirs, when someone with the authority of a teacher, say, describes the world and you're not in it, there is a moment of psychic disequilibrium, as if you looked into a mirror and saw nothing (Rich, 1986, p. 199).

Similarly, in the United States, brown minority groups report that they too are taught to not take risks, "don't get involved," and "don't ask questions" in certain circumstances so as to not to bring unwarranted attention to or arouse undue suspicion on their immigration status. The historically embedded fear of being lynched or castrated still causes some African-American mothers to teach their young children to keep their distance when passing white folks (Gaunty-Porter, personal communication, 2003) for fear that any behavior could be misinterpreted. When a mother admonishes her child and says, "Don't act your color" (Matsuda, 1996), she is aware of the different standards from which her child is judged and therefore cautions her child to not act in a way that may invite critical scrutiny by others. Many minority groups have been taught to mind their own business. Because people of color have learned to stay out of white folks' business, Sleeter (2001) said they may not respond as a white person does in a moral situation. Furthermore, Sleeter added, people of color have learned to ascertain the social worth of the messenger before making a commitment to a warranted action. Canvassing the social and political landscapes is a necessary survival skill.

During the Holocaust, ordinary people learned to be extraordinary bystanders. Bystanders were the human beings who were "conspicuous not by their absence, but by their silence" (Barnett, 1999, p. xiii). "Auschwitz is what happens when good people choose to do nothing" (p. xiv). So few people complained or protested because they were led to believe they had nothing to fear if they simply conformed to their new circumstances (Barnett, 1999). On January 12, 2003, National Public Radio news reported that 304 homeless Russians died of neglect in the winter of 2002. Human rights groups responded to this situation, on a poster, "Indifference is murder."

Unfortunately, many incidents of apathy have been reported. "Lack of action when witnessing a crisis is not an isolated event" (Gershaw, 1999, para. 3). In our own backyard, on May 25, 1997, in a Las Vegas casino, Jeremy Strohmeyer molested and murdered 7-year-old Sherrice Iverson. His friend David Cash watched. Cash did not try to stop Strohmeyer or call the police. More than 30 years ago, New Yorker Kitty Genovese was murdered in an attack that lasted 45 minutes and was witnessed by 38 of her neighbors. An AIDS poster seen in Los Angeles in 2004 summed it up, "Apathy is Lethal."

Inner cities have been characterized by the media for their urban jadedness, for uncaring, apathetic city dwellers. Visitors to New York are instructed by tour guides not to look up at the skyscrapers and not to stop for any sidewalk disturbance. They are told that someone who is ostensibly sick on the sidewalk could easily be a ruse to distract pedestrians, making them easy pickpocket targets. Tourists are instructed to walk callously past seemingly homeless, needy people. They are conditioned to accept the unpleasant and seemingly unchangeable realities.

Could it be that bystanders merely failed to see the importance of an issue at hand? Is it possible that bystanders do not grasp the gravity of a particular phenomenon? Can an event be so disorienting that bystanders become confused at its significance? Perhaps bystanders see the problem as someone else's and not theirs? This failure to see the connection with the self is replete in stories about public apathy. John Balzar (2003), a columnist for the *Los Angeles Times,* cites the work on cognitive dissonance of Joel Cooper, a professor of psychology at Princeton University who suggests that denial or the act of resisting evidence of uncomfortable new knowledge is natural for the human being because "to acknowledge it could call into question one's very purpose in society" (p. B13). That is, to admit one has witnessed an unjust situation means that one is compelled to respond with some moral action. Therefore, homeostasis is best achieved if we look the other way, if we cover our eyes and ignore the disruptive phenomenon, thus eliminating psychological dissonance. We learn to take the path of least resistance by ignoring. This allows us to disassociate ourselves with things like homelessness or even war. "People adjust to their political circumstances. Most people are far more preoccupied with maintaining the normal rhythms of their lives than with the wish to become involved" (Barnett, 1999, p. xv).

Forces of Conformity

Schools

We have been socialized to conform in our schools. Students are trained to follow rules and be obedient. We believe compliance is necessary to listen, learn, and maintain order. We reward obedience and punish disobedience. To speak out or speak against typically gets one sent to the principal's office for discipline, thus affirming silence.

The infrequency of speaking up in schools is best exemplified by the fish lesson taught by S. J. Childs (2002), a high school social studies and English teacher. Childs opens the lesson by warning high school students that if they speak out of turn, they will get a referral to the principal's office. The teacher proceeds to scoop two live fish out of a fishbowl onto her desk. No one says a word but just stares in disbelief. The fish are clearly struggling for their lives and there is silence. A couple of students mutter under their breaths, "She's killing the fish." After almost 3 minutes, one student, abandoning sanctions, takes a risk and shouts, "Save the fish!"

The teacher uses this lesson, with reservations about animal experimentation, to teach students about conformity and the cost of keeping quiet when witnessing an injustice. Although she struggles with the moral treatment of the fish, she reasons that this is a small cost to teach human beings empathy and activism. She wants her students to seriously explore why some people speak up and others do not. One student explained that he assumed that the teacher was in charge and therefore, he trusted her decision. Others confessed they didn't want to get into trouble. After weighing the options, only one student felt it was worthwhile to speak up. The others didn't bother. This scenario may give us some insights into the high percentage of 18-year-old voter apathy or adults who believe they can't fight city hall.

Culture of Niceness

Nestled in the schools is the teachers' lounge; home of the copier, coffee-stained mugs, and daily problem solving. It is both a social hub and a problem-solving ward. This is where teachers identify daily crises, craft solutions, and exchange resources with the speed and deftness of emergency room procedures. School gossip, last-minute administrative directives, and commiseration over mandates are expressed here. Typically in elementary schools although not exclusively, lounge activity is embraced by a "culture of niceness." There is an unwritten lounge ethos that prevails that prevents anyone from being too critical or "too negative." People are expected to be "nice," which means they should not make waves. This is not a place for teachers to critically engage or thoughtfully reflect on problems. Our teacher interns tell us that when they bring serious issues like racism into the lounge, their concerns are often reduced to meaningless verbal assuaging. These events, report the interns, prompt teacher complacency and brain drain.

The culture of niceness permeates the classrooms as well. "If you can't say anything nice, don't say anything at all" is a familiar American adage deeply rooted in our notions of civility and politeness. "Classroom talk should be civil, polite and respectful (Berlak & Sekani, 2001 p. 108). "Talk should be rational and dispassionate" (Boler, 1999, p. 63). Students and teachers should not express negative feelings in schools (Berlak & Sekani, 2001; Boler, 1999; Obidah & Teel, 2001). The social protocol of politeness often will mask the search for truth (Agyris, 1990). Herein lies the soil from which bystanderism is grown as honesty and concerns are masked by politeness.

Outsiders to the school who are either unfamiliar with the culture of niceness or who have developed resistance strategies can cause a cultural meltdown as evident by the story told by Sekani (Berlak & Sekani, 2001). Sekani recalled a time in her childhood when her mother complained to the principal about a racist teacher. When the principal offered to move Sekani to another class, her mother's reply was, "Why? She's going to have to deal with asses all her life. She might as well learn all about them now" (p. 23). Audre Lorde (1984) captured the sentiment of how compromised communications under the auspices of niceness can invalidate human beings when she said, "I cannot hide my anger to spare your guilt. . . . For to do so insults and trivializes all our efforts" (p. 130).

Pluralistic Ignorance

> Where all think alike, no one thinks very much.
> —Walter Lippmann (cited in Cialdini, 1993, p. 114)

One way to determine what is the right thing to do is to find out what other people think is correct. Cialdini (1993) maintained that people look for social proof when they are unsure of themselves or in situations of uncertainty and ambiguity. This is how people socially construct what constitutes correct behavior. Social proof can benefit individuals but Cialdini warned that it can also contribute to pluralistic ignorance. Pluralistic ignorance is defined as a herd mentality of mindless compliance. It allows individuals to be mindless and to operate on automatic pilot. "Since 95 percent of the people are imitators and only 5 percent initiators, people are persuaded more by the actions of others than by any proof we can offer" (Cavett, cited in Cialdini, 1993, p. 118). Cialdini's theory provides insight into a Rhode Island nightclub fire where 91 people died because they chose to escape through the door they came in rather than try the other fire exits. Or it may explain the mob mentality of 135 teenagers who broke into their friend's home to loot and destroy his house without every one of them stopping to think what they were doing was wrong (ABC News, 2003).

Finally, conformity is self-sustaining and self-preserving. Groups believe there is safety in numbers and they teach their members not to go astray. Like the crab in the bucket phenomenon, when one tries to climb up the wall of the bucket to escape, the others are quick to pull it down. Groups find ways to maintain conformity and group membership. During the Holocaust, social or authoritarian power was perceived to be so great that it neutralized individual ethics. Holocaust survivors reported that in their attempts to conform, they lost the personal freedom to act with decency (Barnett, 1999).

Fear of Social Alienation

Fear also immobilizes individuals from acting. The continuum of fear runs the gamut from physical threat to social alienation. Some fear is also rooted in biblical quotes. "*Let he who is without sin cast the first stone,*" prompts my colleague to self-reflect, "If I speak up against an injustice, will someone then expose my weaknesses in the future?" (Cardinal, personal communication, 2003). Members of diverse minority groups also report a reluctance to speak up because of cultural prohibitions. To bring attention to one's self by speaking up would violate the virtue of humility. Many Latinas in our teacher preparation program report a double cross to bear with culture and gender acting as barriers to their self-advocacy. C. Wright Mills, a sociologist, wrote an essay titled "Out of Apathy," which suggested that apathy was engineered by elites that benefited from the silent condition of the helpless (Hayden & Flacks, 2002). This condition left the status quo unchallenged.

In the classroom, students are often paralyzed by anticipated social criticism. Unsure of themselves, they hesitate to engage fully in the classroom because they fear humiliation and rejection. One can stay safe by being uncommitted and unengaged. This is understandable. What are perplexing, however, are those times in class when someone says something that should evoke moral outrage and no one says anything. The silence awakens a childhood fear in me as I, the teacher, try to interpret the silence. Is the emptiness felt in my soul, man's inhumanity to man? Do I fear that I am alone in a world that doesn't care?

Skill Building

In a report by the American Education Research Association's (AERA) Consensus Panel on Teacher Education, Etta Hollins (2003), whose role was to examine teacher education programs in their ability to address underserved communities, concluded that these programs offered candidates strong foundational understandings of social justice and constructivism but did not provide comprehensive strategies for candidates to work with underserved populations. In the area of critical pedagogy, what this finding suggests is that although teacher educators are proficient at raising awareness and evoking commitment to certain ideals of equity, justice, and democracy, there is work to do in advancing the necessary classroom strategies to enact these principles.

In fact, many programs produce candidates who are proficient at problem prosing but are short on the actual implementation of strategies in their own classrooms. There are many reasons for this inactivity. Some candidates in our program report that they are faced with institutional barriers that block their ability to operationalize critical pedagogy in their classrooms. Others state that they cannot find ways to integrate new reconceptualizations into old schemas. Still other candidates are frustrated, and more seriously, some are complacent and paralyzed by politics.

During these serious times of standards-based curriculum, test-driven accountability, and state-mandated expectations, it is time for teacher educators who work under the banner of social justice to critically evaluate their programs for the omission of concrete classroom strategies. How does theory get translated into practice? They must ask themselves, "How should we define the competencies that teachers and aspiring teachers need to have effectively address a social justice? What are the skills and abilities that teachers need, to identify, critically examine, and act on issues of equity?"

Critical pedagogy is both the epistemological and instructional arm of critical theory. Students of critical pedagogy acquire skills and become proficient in naming, problem posing, critiquing, creating alternatives, and developing action plans. This work takes place in a dialectical learning context that is supported by norms of risk taking, collegiality, and honest communication. Dynamic student-centered strategies can result from new and emerging social and political literacy. Critical pedagogy should equip candidates with a wide repertoire of alternatives while awakening human consciousness.

Freire's (1995) theory of conscientization involves raising consciousness through developing awareness, questioning one's self, and committment to action. Without action, critical consciousness is incomplete. New insights must be coupled with acts of change. Change does not necessarily have to be large-scale reform but rather it can be achieved by altering daily decisions in our classrooms based on new understandings.

Cialdini (1997) suggested it is not because people are uncaring or insensitive, but rather that they are unsure of what to do, which prevents them from acting. In fact, our current curriculum does not help us distinguish between standing for something and standing up to something. Standing up to be counted is easy, until challenged. Standing up to some authority means one must be prepared to counter opposition while maintaining one's own moral ground. When we examine our current political context, we find that the recent emphasis on standards-driven instruction has temporarily displaced our mission to develop students into thoughtful, engaged participants of democracy. Disillusioned students (SooHoo, 2002) and teachers (Ohanian, 1999) indicate that test-driven accountability has dumb downed the curriculum to learned conformity, passivity, and apathy. These conditions prevent them from seeing the need to focus on moral capacity building.

Students need reflective facilitators of knowledge and forums of democratic dialogue in order to participate on a moral playing field. Opportunities to critically examine conflict and assess the political and social terrain of any given situation should be abundant and accessible. Teachers must offer activities that teach students to name, codify, critique, conceptualize alternatives, and take action. It is in these experiences that students learn to articulate a moral position and develop the courage to stand up for equity, justice, and democracy.

Taking Responsibility

He who passively accepts evil is as much involved in it as he who helps to perpetrate it.
—Martin Luther King (1958, p. 51)

It is not that we educators don't know what needs to be accomplished in our public school classrooms, there is, however, a question about whether we are willing to make some changes (Parker, 1997). Apart from our social and ideological conditioning, do we have the will to change? In certain cases, could we resist the instinct to resort to safe conformity and take action to do what is morally right and just? What courage would it take to put one's self in danger as a means to benefit a whole community? Parker challenged us by suggesting that it is not a question of knowledge, but it is a question of will. She claims it is not that we don't know what to do, but rather, will we do it. Will we commit and act in the name of social justice to dismantle the dynamics of racism, sexism, classism, and the likes?

If we are indeed serious about taking some action, we could start by questioning apathy. There is a euphemistic notion that links bystanderism to innocence; to be an innocent bystander means to be blameless or a mutual victim of a situation. Bystanders can plead ignorance and escape responsibility behind the banner of innocence. However, when we think of the Holocaust, we are deeply troubled by human inhumanity, not only because of genocide but also because of bystanderism. In this context, one's silence is condemning. By doing nothing, we have changed the world. Furthermore, post-Holocaust awareness studies put forward a moral standard: Should one choose to do nothing, one is as complicit of the deed as the perpetrator. Bystanders are held to the same accountability as perpetrators, inferring that one's silence grants permission to the misdeed. "Bystanders are confronted by a wide range of behavioral options, and they bear some responsibility for what happens" (Barnett, 1999, p. 7). Laws have been drafted to make people more responsible for crimes that they witness (Gershaw, 1999), which means that bystanders can no longer hide behind the cloak of blamelessness or innocence; instead they are forced to see their apathy as an ugly manifestation of humankind.

It seems fitting, in this current era of accountability, that we renew our commitments to social justice work. A fresh use of the concept of standards was applied to the social justice work of 10 special interest groups of the AERA (Andrzejewski et al., 2003). They produced draft standards for the safety and respect of (a) gay, lesbian, bisexual, and transgender students; (b) Hispanic students; and (c) Asian-Pacific Islanders. They also drafted standards within interest areas of (a) peace education, (b) global child advocacy (c) ecology (d) social and economic self-determination of teachers, (e) knowledge & skills for democratic citizenship and (f) ethical impact in education. Robert Crafton, (2003) from the National Association of Multicultural Education, summed up their work:

> In general, these standards recognize, at the most general level, the need
> (1) to provide students with an understanding of human rights; (2) to

foster in the student an appreciation of democratic culture; (3) to develop in the student a sense of obligation to protect the rights of all people, and (4) to provide the student with the tools to do so. (p. 3)

Margot Stern Strom (1998), executive director of a multicultural project named "Facing History and Ourselves," reminded that the intellectual direction of our work can be also be achieved merely through our daily conversations, discussions and debates. "Democracy is shaped by ordinary people and the choices they make about themselves and others" (p. 1). "Although the choices may not seem important at the time, little by little, they define an individual, create a community, and ultimately forge a nation" (p. v).

Individually, we can resolve to find ways that are personally and socially compatible with our own consciousness to take steps to pierce the culture of niceness and resist the forces of conformity. We can face our fears, knowing that for every act of courage, there is a personal risk and moreover, visibility. An example of negative consequences resulting from visibility would be when minority groups, who are typically silenced by the majority, speak up and espouse group solidarity. Expressions of group pride can get interpreted as "playing the race card," "flaunting one's sexuality," or "using one's language to exclude others." Pride for something that others are not, can cause disequilibrium for others. Additionally, taking action, speaking up, and political participation are interpreted by some minority groups as "acting white," thus arousing social condemnation and subsequently paralyzing individuals to act.

One strategy available to people who may be unsure of taking an action is to consult with others for clarity, collaboration, and moral support. We sort out our confusion and establish strategies of activism by joining collectively to interrupt the pattern of socially conditioned bystanderism. Democracy is a collaborative struggle whereby we work with others to bring our communities and ourselves up to our ideals. By working within a democratic context, we find opportunities to discover threads that bind us together in the human community (Barnett, 1999) and explore the concept of mutuality. We learn how one's self is connected to the community. If one member of the community is unsafe, all are unsafe because any day the social and political context could change and the new target could be you. Therefore, to do nothing, affirms the continuation of the present social order. "When you don't act, you act" (Kusner, 2002 p. 18). Bystander behavior poses no serious challenge to the existing power structures and offers no critique of the dominant narrative of marginalization. Therefore, to survive, one needs allies, not bystanders.

In closing, teacher educators and teachers have a responsibility to facilitate action as well as awareness. We must conduct an inventory of our programs to ascertain the emphasis we have placed on classroom outcomes and the coupling of theory and practice. We need to calm the voices of our critics who claim our foundation classes yield few classroom applications by routinely conducting research. Marilyn Cochoran-Smith, president-elect of AERA, appealed to multicultural educators at the 2003 annual conference to show and make public how teachers' knowledge base is evident in classrooms. Although our productivity cannot be measured by standardized tests, we are accountable to the higher standard of democracy. Presently, we find ourselves choked by state and federal mandates. Rather than letting this state of affairs undermine our work or deplete our moral energy, we need to act in ways that are consistent with our vision of the world. If we forsake action and theorize on the sidelines, we may realize that we have changed the world by doing nothing.

In conclusion, it is hoped that teachers will come to understand that by not stopping unquestioned schoolyard tyranny of dehumanization, we are complicit with the hegemony that maintains the status quo and inequitable power relationships. By not acting, we allow others to take away our alternatives, our choices, and our responsibilities. Our charge is to become aware of othering and otherness and then do something about it.

So What Are You Going to Do About It?
By Suzanne SooHoo

I wrote this poem after the Columbine tragedy. The title words haunt me when I am searching for moral clarity.

You told me to go out to the schoolyard and make friends
Kids teased me about my glasses and locked me in the dark bathroom
When they let me out, my face and my pants were wet,

And my tormentors said, "So What Are You Going to Do About It?"

You told me to be good, follow the rules and never speak unless called on,
I always raised my hand and waited my turn
But it was the outspoken, articulate, risk taking kid that became valedictorian.

And the teacher said, "So What Are You Going to Do About It?"

You said work hard and go to every practice
I dribbled that ball until my fingers were numb
But you recruited a new player, someone taller and faster
And the coach said, "So What Are You Going to Do About It?"

They said they wanted me to attend their college
They needed diversity on their campus
But they didn't tell me I would be lonely and have no homeboys to kick it
    with

And college admissions said, "So What Are You Going to Do About It?"

Find a girl, get married, have a baby
It happened so fast
Never got a chance to figure out if life would be better with Joe

And my parents said, "So What Are You Going to Do About It?"

Make money, live in the suburbs, away from those "others"
I don't know who I am anymore or where I came from.

And society said, "So What Are You Going to Do About It?"

References

14-year-old girl shoots classmate at school. (2001, March 8). *Los Angeles Times*, p. A18.

ABC News (2003, May 28). Television broadcast. United States.

Agyris, C. (1990). *Overcoming organizational defenses: Facilitating organizational learning*. Boston: Allyn Bacon.

Aiello, B. (1976, April 25). Up from the basement: A teacher's story. *New York Times*, p. 14.

Amos, O.E., & Landers, M.F. (1984). Special education and multicultural education. *Theory into Practice, 23*, 145.

Andrzejewski, J., Baltodano, M., Mitchell, J., Palmer, J.D., Polakow, V., Smith, R.M., Owen, V., Stomfay-Stitz, A., Torres-Velaquez, D., & Walsh, C.S. (2003). *Developing standards for social justice education*. Paper presented at the annual conference of the American Educational Research Association, Chicago, IL.

Anzaldua, G. (1988). *Borderlands: The new metiza=La frontera*. San Francisco: Spinsters/Aunt Lute.

Aronowitz, S. (1998). Introduction. In P. Freire (Ed.), *Pedagogy of freedom* (pp. 1-19). Lanham, MD: Rowman & Littlefield.

Bakhtin, M. (1981). Discourse in the novel (C. Emerson & M. Holquist, Trans.). In M. Holquist (Ed.), *The dialogic imagination* (pp. 259-422). Austin: University of Texas Press.

Balzar, J. (2003, Jan. 8). A scientific name for teflon politics; 'Cognitive dissonance' explains how we can let so many tings slide. *Los Angeles Times*, p. B13

Banks, J. (1993). Multicultural education: Characteristics and goals. In J. Banks & C. Banks (Eds.), *Multicultural education: Issues and perspectives* (pp. 3-30). Boston: Allyn and Bacon.

Banks, J.A., & McGee Banks, C.A. (2003). *Multicultural education: Issues and perspectives* (4th ed.). New York: Wiley.

Barbules, N.C., & Rice, S. (1991). Dialogue across differences: Continuing the conversation. *Harvard Educational Review, 61*(4), 393-416.

Barnett, V. (1999). *Bystanders: Conscience and complicity during the Holocaust.* Westport, CT: Greenwood.

Behind the tragedy, the despair of an outcast. (2001, March 7). *Los Angeles Times*, p. B1.

Bell, L. (2001). Invisible College workshop at the American Education Research Association, New Orleans, LA.

Berlak, A., & Sekani, M. (2001). *Taking it personally.* Philadelphia: Temple University Press.

Berube, A., & Berube, F. (1997) Sunset Trailer Park. In M. Wray & A. Newitz (Eds.), *White trash* (pp. 15-39). New York: Routledge.

Boler, M. (1999). *Feeling power: Emotions and education.* New York: Routledge.

Briggs, J., & Peat, D. (1999). *Seven life lesson of chaos.* New York: HarperCollins Publishers.

Brownfield, P. (2001, March 14). Made bullying a TV trademark. *Los Angeles Times*, p. B6.

Bruner, J. (1986). *Actual minds, possible worlds.* Cambridge, MA: Harvard University Press.

Bruner, D. (1994). *Inquiry and reflection.* Albany: State University of New York Press.

Bulkin, E. (1996). Tippin' the furniture. In B. Thompson & S. Tyagi (Eds.), *Names we call home: Autobiography on racial identity* (pp. 215-230). New York: Routledge.

Bully rule may steal principals' allowance. (2001, March 14). *Los Angeles Times*, p. B3.

Cai, M., & Sims Bishop, R. (1994). Multicultural literature for children: Towards a clarification of the concept. In A. Dyson & C. Genishi (Eds.), *The need for story: Cultural diversity in classroom and community* (pp. 57-71). Urbana, IL: National Council of Teachers of English.

Casey, K. 1995. The new narrative research in education. In M. W. Apple (Ed.), *Review of research in education* (Vol. 21, pp. 211-254). Washington, DC: American Educational Research Association.

Chang Bloch, J. (1997, June 10). *Rise of the Asian woman.* Keynote address. Paper presented at the World Affairs Council, Irvine, CA.

Childs, S. J. (2000/2001, Winter) The story of Rachel and Sadie. *Rethinking Schools*, *15*(2), 16-17.

Chomsky, N. (1997). *Media control: The spectacular achievement of propaganda.* New York: Seven Stories Press.

Chow, E. N. L. (1989). The feminist movement: Where are all the Asian American women? In Asian Women United of California (Ed.), *Making waves: An anthology of writings by and about Asian American women* (pp. 362-377). Boston: Beacon Press.

Chu, J. (1980). *Asian American women workshop.* Los Angeles: UCLA.

Chu, J. (1989). Asian Pacific American women in mainstream politics. In Asian Women United of California (Ed.), *Making waves: An anthology of writings by and about Asian American women* (pp. 405-422). Boston: Beacon Press.

Chung Sai Yat Po (CSYP) Chinese newspaper, June 10, 1903.

Cialdini, R. (1993). *Influence: The psychology of persuasion.* New York: Quill Books.

Cisnernos, S. (1991). *Woman hollering creek.* New York: Vintage Contemporaries.

Clark, K.B., & Clark, M.P. (1947). Racial identification and preferences in Negro children. In T. Newcomb & E.L. Hartley (Eds.), *Readings in social psychology* (pp. 551-560). New York: Holt.

Cochran-Smith, M. (2003). *Diversity, accountability, and equity: Findings and insights from the second edition of the Handbook of Research on Multicultural Education.* Paper presented at the annual conference of the American Educational Research Association, Chicago, IL.

Connelly, M., & Clandinin, D. (1990). Stories of experience and narrative inquiry. *Educational Researcher, 19*(5), 2-14.

Connerly, W. (2003, July 14). Connerly's trivial pursuit. *Los Angeles Times*, p. B10.

Crafton, R. (2003). *Social justice and environmental standard.* Paper presented at the annual conference of the American Educational Research Association, Chicago, IL.

Darder, A. (1991). *Culture and power in the classroom.* New York: Bergin and Garvey.

Darder, A. (2002). *Reinventing Paulo Freire.* Boulder, CO: Westview Press.

Dawson, K. (2001, March 7). School shooting and teen taunting [Letters to the editor]. *Los Angeles Times*, p. B8.

Douglas, M. (1966). *Purity and danger.* New York: Praeger.

Delpit, L. (1988.) The silenced dialogue: Power and pedagogy in educating other people's children. *Harvard Education Review, 58*(3), 302-320.

Dewey, J. (1934). *Art as experience.* New York: Minton Balch and Co.

Dewey, J. (1980). Nationalizing education. In J.A. Boydston (Ed.), *John Dewey: The middle works* (Vol. 10, pp. 202-210). Carbondale: Southern Illinois University Press.

Doetkott, R. (2000). *Riding the teeter-totter of education.* Annual Aims of Education Address. Orange, CA: Chapman University.

Douglas, M. (1966). *Purity and danger.* New York: Praeger.

Du Bois, W.E.B. (1989). *Souls of black folk.* Chicago: A.C. McClurg. (Original work published 1903)

Duarte, E.M. (1998). Expanding the borders of liberal democracy: Multicultural education and the struggle for cultural identity. *Multicultural Education, 6*(1), 2-13.

Dyson, A., & Genishi, C. (1994). Introduction. In A. Dyson & C. Genishi (Eds.), *The need for story: Cultural diversity in classroom and community* (pp. 1-10). Urbana, IL: National Council of Teachers of English.

Eck, D. (2001). *The new religious America.* San Francisco: Harper San Francisco.

Eddy, R. (1996). Introduction. In R. Eddy (Ed.), *Reflections on multiculturalism* (pp. 1-14). Yarmouth, ME: Intercultural Press.

Edgerton, R. (1976). *Deviance: A cross-cultural perspective.* Menlo Park: CA: Cumings Press.

Eisner, E. (2002). What can education learn from the arts about the practice of education. *Journal of Curriculum and Supervision, 18*(1), 4-16.

Eisner, E. (2003). *Education and the arts.* A keynote speech presented at Chapman University, Orange, CA.

Elbow, P. (1986). *Embracing contraries: Explorations in teaching and learning.* Oxford: Oxford University Press.

Ellingwood, K. (2001, March 7). Santee school shootings. *Los Angeles Times*, p. A1.

Ellingwood, K. (2001, March 8). Santee school shootings. *Los Angeles Times*: Suspect Charged with Murder; Students Return to School Shooting, p. A17.

Ellison, R. (1972). *Invisible man*. New York: Vintage Books.

Ellsworth, E. (1989) Why doesn't this feel empowering? Working through the repressive myths of critical pedagogy. *Harvard Educational Review, 59*(3), 297-324.

Ellsworth, E. (1992). Why doesn't this feel empowering? Working through the repressive myths of critical pedagogy. In C. Luke & J Gore (Eds.), *Feminisms and critical pedagogy* (pp. 90-119). New York: Routledge.

Ensler, E. (2000). *Vagina monologues*. New York: Vallard.

Fine, M. (1989). Silencing and nurturing voice in an improbable context: Urban adolescents in public school. In H.A. Giroux & P. Mclaren (Eds.), *Critical pedagogy, the state, and cultural struggle*. Albany: SUNY Press.

Fine, M. (1997). Witnessing whiteness. In L. Weiss, M. Fine, L. Powell, & M. Wong (Eds.), *Off white: Theorizing whiteness* (pp. 56-65). New York: Routledge.

Fischman, D. (1996). Getting it: Multiculturalism and the politics of understanding. In R. Eddy (Ed.), *Reflections on multiculturalism* (pp. 17-46) Yarmouth, ME: Intercultural Press.

Fordham, S. (1996). *Blackened out: Dilemmas of race, identity and success at capital high*. Chicago: University of Chicago Press.

Foucault, M. (1977). *Language, counter-memory, practice* (D. Bouchard, Trans.). Ithaca, NY: Cornell University Press.

Frederickson, J. (1996). *Reclaiming our voices* (An occasional paper series). Ontario, CABE.

Freire, P. (1995). *Pedagogy of the oppressed*. New York: Continuum.

Fu, V. (1999). Preface. In V. Fu & A. Stremmel (Eds.), *Affirming diversity through democratic conversations* (pp. vii-x). Upper Saddle River, NJ: Merrill.

Fu, V. (1999). Stories of we the people: An invitation to join in the conversation on diversity in a democracy. In V. Fu & A. Stremmel (Eds.), *Affirming diversity through democratic conversations* (pp. 3-13). Upper Saddle River, NJ: Merrill.

Fu, V., & Stremmel, A. (Eds.). (1999). *Affirming diversity through democratic conversations*. Upper Saddle River, NJ: Merrill.

Gale Encyclopedia of Psychology (2001). Bystander effect. www.findarticles.com.

Gay, G. (1995, June). Why aren't we getting along? *Holistic Education Review, 8*(2), 30-39.

Gershaw, D. (1999, February 28). *Reducing bystander apathy*. Retrieved from: http://www3.azwestern.edu/psy/dgershaw/lol/bystanderapathy.html

Giroux, H. (1986). Radical pedagogy and the politics of student voice. *Interchange, 17*, 48-69.

Giroux, H. (1993). *Border crossings: Cultural workers and the politics of education*. New York: Routledge.

Giroux, H. (2001). Introduction. In H. Giroux & K. Myrsiades (Eds.), *Beyond the corporate university: Culture and pedagogy in the new millennium* (pp. 1-12). New York: Rowman & Littlefield.

Goffman, E. (1963). *Stigma: Notes on the management of spoiled identity*. Englewood Cliffs, NJ: Prentice-Hall.

Golden, M. (1995). Introduction. In M. Golden & S. Richards Shreve (Eds.), *Skin deep: Black women and white women write about race* (pp. 1-6). New York: Doubleday.

Grant, C., & Sleeter, C. (1998). *Turning on learning: Five approaches for multicultural teaching plans for race, class, gender, and disability*. Upper Saddle River, NJ: Merrill.

Greene, M. (1988). *The dialectic of freedom*. New York: Teachers College Press.

Greene, M. (1994). Multiculturalism, community and the arts. In A. Dyson & C. Genishi (Eds.), *The need for story: Cultural diversity in classroom and community* (pp. 11-27). Urbana, IL: National Council of Teachers of English.

Greene, M. (1995). *Releasing the imagination*. San Francisco: Jossey-Bass.

Groce, N. (1985). *Everyone here spoke sign language*. Cambridge, MA: Harvard University Press.

Guinier, L. (2002) Race, testing and the miner's canary. In L. Christensen & S. Karp (Eds.), *Rethinking school reform: Views from the classroom* (pp. 225-230). Rethinking Schools, Ltd.

Guiterrez, R. (1994). Ethnic studies. In D. T. Goldberg (Ed.), *Multiculturalism: A critical reader* (pp. 157-167). Oxford, UK: Blackwell.

Hahn, C. (2003). *Social studies: Keeping the beast at bay*. Paper presented at the annual conference of the American Educational Research Association, Chicago, IL.

Halprin, S. (1995). *Look at my ugly face: Myths and musings on beauty and other perilous obsessions with women's appearance*. New York: Viking.

Hamilton, C. (1991). *Apartheid in an American city: The case of the black community in Los Angeles*. Van Nuys, CA: Labor Community Strategy Center.

Hanson, C. (Ed.). (1989). *Re-reading the short story*. New York: St. Martin's Press.

Harjo, J. (1977a). Perhaps the world ends here. In J. Harjo, G. Bird, P. Blanco, B. Cuthand, & V. Martinez (Eds.), *Reinventing the enemy's language: Contemporary native women's writings of North America* (pp. 556-558). New York: Norton.

Harjo, J. (1977b). Warrior road. In J. Harjo, G. Bird, P. Blanco, B. Cuthand, & V. Martinez (Eds.), *Reinventing the enemy's language: Contemporary native women's writings of North America* (pp. 55-61). New York: Norton.

Harjo, J., & Bird, G. (Eds.). (1997). *Reinventing the enemy's language: Contemporary native women's writings of North America*. New York: Norton.

Hartigan, J. (1997). Name calling: Objectifying "poor whites" and "white trash" in Detroit. In M. Wray & A. Newitz (Eds.), *White trash* (pp. 41-56). New York: Routledge.

Hayden, T., & Flacks, D. (2002). The Port Huron Statement at 40. *The Nation, 5*(12), 18-21.

High school hasn't changed—except for the gun. (2001, March 9). *Los Angeles Times*, p. E1.

Hill, M. (1997). Can whiteness speak? In M. Wray & A. Newitz (Eds.), *White trash* (pp. 155-173). New York: Routledge.

Hogan, L. (1997). Skin. In In J. Harjo, G. Bird, P. Blanco, B. Cuthand, & V. Martinez (Eds.), *Reinventing the enemy's language: Contemporary native women's writings of North America* (pp. 331-333). New York: Norton.

Hollins, E. (2003). *The AERA Consensus Panel on Teacher Education: A closer look*. Paper presented at the American Educational Research Association, Chicago, IL.

'Hoods as in 'burbs, kids find ways to lash out. (2001, March 28). *Los Angeles Times*, p. B9.

hooks, b. (1990). *Yearning: Race, gender and cultural politics.* Boston, MA: South End Press.

hooks, b. (1994). *Teaching to transgress.* New York: Routledge.

hooks, b. (1999). *Remembered rapture.* New York: Henry Holt.

Howard, G. (1999). *We can't teach what we don't know: White teachers, multiracial schools.* New York: Teachers College Press.

Kanpol, B. (1994). *Critical pedagogy.* Westport, CT: Bergin & Garvey.

Kanpol, B. (1995). *Critical multiculturalism.* Westport, CT: Bergin & Garvey.

Kanpol, B. (1998). *Talking back and breaking bread.* Cresskill, NJ: Hampton Press.

Kanpol, B. (2000). *Cynical reason and joyful possibilities: Critical narrative based leadership in teacher education* (unpublished manuscript).

Kanpol, B., & McLaren, P. (Eds.). (1995). *Critical multiculturalism: Uncommon voices in a common struggle.* Westport, CT: Bergin & Garvey.

Kaye/Kantrowits, M. (1996). Jews in the U.S.: The rising costs of whiteness. In B. Thompson & S. Tyagi (Eds.), *Names we call home* (pp. 121-137). New York: Routledge.

Keeley, M. (1978). A social justice approach to organizational evaluation. *Administrative Science Quarterly, 23*(2), 272-292.

Kimball, S., & Garrison, J. (1999). Hermeneutic listening in multicultural conversations. In V. Fu & A. Stremmel (Eds.), *Affirming diversity through democratic conversations* (pp. 15-27). Upper Saddle River, NJ: Merrill.

King, M.L. (1958). *Stride towards freedom: The Montgomery story.* New York: Harper.

King, M.L. (1967). *Where do we go from here: Chaos or community.* New York: Harper & Row.

Kingsolver, B. (2000). *Prodigal summer.* New York: Harper-Collins Publishers.

Kivel, P. (1996). *Uprooting racism: How white people can work for social justice.* Gabriola Island, BC: New Society Publishers.

Kozol, J. (1991). *Savage inequalities.* New York: Crown.

Kozol, J. (1994). The new untouchables. In J. Kretovics & E. Nussel (Eds.), *Transforming urban education* (pp. 75-78). Boston: Allyn and Bacon.

Kusner, T. (2002, July 1). A word to graduates: Organize! *The Nation,* p. 18.

Ladson-Billings, G. (1994). *The dream keepers: Successful teachers of African American children.* San Francisco, CA: Jossey-Bass Publishers.

Lai, T. (1992). Asian American women: Not for sale. In M.L. Andersen & P.H. Collins (Eds.), *Race, class and gender: An anthology* (pp. 163-171). Belmont, CA: Wadsworth.

Lampley, O.F. (1993, April). The wig and I. *Mirabella Magazine,* pp. 144.

Langer, S. K. (1976). *Philosophy in a new key: A study in the symbolism of reason, rite, and art* (3rd ed.). Cambridge, MA: Harvard University Press.

Lather, P. (1989). Postmodernism and the politics of enlightenment. *Educational Foundations, 3*(3), 7-28.

Lawrence-Lightfoot, S. (1994). *I've known rivers, lives of loss and liberation.* Reading, MA: Addison-Wesley.

Lee, S. (1996). *Unraveling the "model majority" stereotype.* New York: Teachers College Press.

Li, H.-I. (2001). Silences and silencing silences. *Philosophy of Education Yearbook 2001, 157-165.*

Lorde, A. (1979). Comments at the personal and the political panel, Second Sex Conference. Reproduced in C. Moraga & G. Anzaldua (1981). *This bridge called my back.* New York: Kitchen Table Women of Color Press.

Lorde, A. (1991). The master's tools will never dismantle the master's house. In C. Moraga & G. Anzaldua (Eds.), *This bridge called my back: Writings by radical women of color* (pp. 98-101). New York: Kitchen Table.

Lorde, A. (1984). *Sister outsider.* Freedom, CA: Crossing Press

Matsuda, M. (1996). *Where is your body? And other essays on race, gender and the law.* Boston: Beacon Press.

McIntosh, P. (1988). *White privilege and male privilege. A personal account of coming to see correspondences through work in women's studies.* Wellesley, MA: Wellesley College Center for Research on Women.

McLaren, P. (2003). *Life in schools: An introduction to critical pedagogy in the foundations of education* (4th ed.). Boston: Allyn and Bacon.

Meyer. L (1995). *Barrio buddies: Learning through letters about kids, cultures, communities, and self-confrontation.* California Perspectives.

Miller, R. (1999). *Motives for writing.* Mountain View, CA: Mayfield.

Moll, L.C. (Ed.). (1990). *Vygotsky and education: Instructional implications and applications of sociohistorical psychology.* Cambridge, MA: Cambridge University Press.

Moore, B. (1999, June 7). News, trends, gossip and stuff to do: The best lesbian and gay reading. *Los Angeles Times,* p. 2.

Moore, M. (2001). *Stupid white men.* New York: HarperCollins Publishers.

Mouffe, C. (1988). Radical democracy: Modern or postmodern? In A. Ross (Ed.), *Universal abandon? The politics of postmodernism* (pp. 31-45). Minneapolis: University of Minnesota Press.

National Crime Prevention Council. (2003, January 15). *Bullying, not terrorist attack, biggest threat seen by U.S. teens.* Retrieved September 11, 2005, from http://www.jointogether.org/gv/news/alerts/reader/0,2061, 556109,00.html

Newitz, A., & Wray, M. (1997). Introduction. In A. Newirtz & M. Wray (Eds.), *White trash: Race and class in America* (pp. 1-12). New York: Routledge.

Ng, F. (1987). The sojourner, return migration, and immigration history. In Chinese Historical Society of America (Ed.), *Chinese America: History and perspectives* (pp. 53-71). Author.

Nieto, S. (1992). *Affirming diversity.* New York: Longman.

Obidah, J., & Teel, K. (2001). *Because of the kids.* New York: Teachers College Press.

Ohanian, S. (1999). *One size fits few: The folly of educational standards.* Portsmouth, NH: Heinemann.

Palmer, P., & Livsey, R. (1999). *The courage to teach.* San Francisco, CA: Jossey-Bass.

Parker, G. (1997). *Trespassing: My sojourn in the halls of privilege.* New York: Houghton Mifflin.

Pinar, B. (1993). Notes on understanding curriculum as a racial text. In C. McCarthy & W. Crichlow (Eds.), *Race, identity, and representation in education* (pp. 60-70). New York: Routledge.

Purpel, D. (1995). Eyewitness to higher education: Confession and indictment. *Taboo, 1,* 185-202.

Ragaza, A. (1999, February 8). I don't count as diversity. *Newsweek*, p. 15.

Ramirez, M., & Castaneda, A. (1974). *Cultural democracy: Bicognitive development and education*. New York: Academic Press.

Remen, R. (1996). *Kitchen table wisdom*. New York: Riverhead Books.

Reynolds, C. (1994). Doing women's studies: Possibility and challenges in democratic praxis. In J.M. Novak (Ed.), *Democratic teacher education: Programs, processes, problems, and prospects* (pp. 57-62). Albany: SUNY Press.

Reza, H.G. (2001, March 9). Santee school shootings. *Los Angeles Times*, p. A24.

Powers, R. 2002. A presentation made at the Global Education Associates Partners Conference, New York City, NY.

Rich, A. (1986). Invisibility in academe. In A. Rich (Ed.), *Blood, bread, and poetry: Selected prose 1979-1985* (pp. 198-201). New York: Norton.

Roghenberg, P. (1992). *Race, class and gender in the United States*. New York: St. Martin's Press.

Ropers-Huilman, B. (1997, June 20-22). *Advocacy education: Intersections as the other in teaching/research*. Paper presented at The First Annual Qualitative Methodology Conference, University of Southern California, Los Angeles.

Sacks, O. (1996). *The island of the colorblind*. New York: Vintage Books.

Scheurich, J. (1993a). A difficult, confusing, painful problem that requires many voices, many perspectives. *Educational Researcher, 22*(8), 14-16.

Scheurich, J. (1993b). Toward a white discourse on white racism. *Educational Researcher, 22*(8), 5-10.

Scheurich, J., & Young, M. (1998). Rejoinder: In the United States of America, in both our souls and our sciences, we are avoiding white racism. *Educational Researcher, 27*(9), 27-32.

Shapiro, S., & Purpel, D. (Eds.). (1993). *Critical social issues in American education*. New York: Longman.

Shevin, M. (1997). On being a communication ally. *Facilitated Communication Digest, 7*(4), 2-14.

Shipler, D. (1997). *A country of strangers: Blacks and whites in America*. New York: Knopf.

Shirvani, H. (2001). *In search of values: A contextual framework*. Paper distributed to Chapman University faculty.

Shor, I. (1987). *Freire for the classroom: A sourcebook for liberatory teaching*. Portsmouth, NH: Heinemann.

Simmons, R. (2002) *Odd girl out*. New York: Harcourt.

Simon, R. (2000). The touch of the past: The pedagogical significance of a transactional sphere of public memory. In P. Pericles Trifonas (Ed.), *Revolutionary pedagogies* (pp. 61-82). New York: Routledge Falmer.

Sleeter, C. (1993). How white teachers construct race. In C. McCarthy & W. Crichlow (Eds.), *Race, identity, and representation in education* (pp. 157-171). New York: Routledge.

Sleeter, C. (1996a). Advancing a white discourse: A response to Scheurich. *Educational Researcher, 22*(8), 13-15.

Sleeter, C. (1996b). *Multicultural education as social activism*. Albany: SUNY Press.

Sleeter, C. (2001). *Culture, power and difference*. New York: Teachers College Press.

Sleeter, C., & Grant, C. (1999). *Making choices for multicultural education.* Upper Saddle River, NJ: Prentice Hall.

Smith, L. (1999). *Decolonizing methodologies: Research and indigenous peoples.* London: Zed Books.

SooHoo, S. (2002). *A middle school student's perspective of standardized testing.* Paper presented at the Paulo Freire Democratic Project Conference. Chapman University, Orange, CA.

SooHoo, S. (2003). Woman warrior liberating the oppressed and the oppressor: Cultural relevancy through narrative. In J.J. Romo, P.S. Bradfield-Kreider, & R.A. Serrano (Eds.), *Reclaiming democracy: Educators' journeys towards transformative teaching* (pp. 258-279). Upper Saddle River, NJ: Prentice-Hall.

SooHoo, S. (2004). Crossing cultural borders into the inner city. In Chapman University Consortium of Social Justice Educators (Ed.), *Essays on urban education: Critical consciousness, collaboration and the self* (pp. 163-180). Cresskill, NJ: Hampton Press.

SooHoo, S., & Wilson, T. (2004). Thinking through collaboration, change, justice and aesthetics. In Chapman University Consortium of Social Justice Educators (Ed.), *Essays on urban education: Critical consciousness, collaboration and the self* (pp. 7-33). Cresskill, NJ: Hampton Press.

Stanfield, J.H. (1985). The ethnocentric basis of social science knowledge production. In E. Gordon (Ed.), *Review of research in education* (Vol. 12, pp. 387-415). Washington, DC: American Educational Research Association.

Stanfield, J. H. (1992). Ethnic modeling in qualitative research. In N.K. Denzin & Y.S. Lincoln (Eds.), *Handbook of qualitative research* (pp. 175-188). Newbury Park, CA: Sage.

Steffey, S., & Hood, W. (Eds.). (1994). *If this is social studies, why isn't it boring?* York, ME: Stenhouse Publishers.

Stern Strom, M. (1998). *A guide to choosing to participate.* Brookline, MA: Facing History and Ourselves National Foundation.

Swindler Boutte, G. (2002). *Resounding voices: School experiences of people from diverse ethnic backgrounds.* Boston: Allyn & Bacon.

Taliaferro, D. (1997). *The boundaries of my blackness: An autobiographical mapping of constructions and deconstructions of blackness.* Unpublished manuscript.

Tatum, B. (1997). *Why are all the Black kids sitting together in the cafeteria.* New York: Basic Books.

Thompson, B. (1996). Time traveling and border crossing. In B. Thompson & S. Tyagi (Eds.), *Names we call home* (pp. 93-109). New York: Routledge.

Tilove, J. (1995, December 29). A color left out of the multicultural rainbow. *San Francisco Examiner,* pp. A1, A20.

Triggers of violence still elusive. (2001, March 7). *Los Angeles Times,* p. A 1.

Tyson, C. (1998). A response to "Coloring Epistemologies: Are our qualitative research epistemologies racially biased?" *Educational Researcher, 27*(9), 21-22.

Valentine, C. (1971). Deficit, difference, and bicultural models of Afro-American behavior. *Harvard Educational Review, 41,* 137-157.

Villenas, S. (1996). The colonizer/colonized Chicana ethnographer: Identity, marginalization and co-optation in the field. *Harvard Educational Review, 66*(4), 711-731.

Villenas, S. (1998). *What's diversity got to do with qualitative research?* Paper presented at the annual meeting of the American Educational Research Association, San Diego, CA.

Vygotsky, L.S. (1978). *Mind in society.* Cambridge, MA: Harvard University Press.

Walker, A. (1995). The revenge of Hannah Kemhuff. In M. Golden & S. Richards Shreve (Eds.), *Skin deep: Black women and white women write about race* (pp. 189-207). New York: Doubleday.

Waish, C. (1989). *Pedagogy and the struggle for voice.* New York: Bergin and Garvey.

Walsh, C. (Ed.). (1991). *Literacy as praxis: Culture, language, and pedagogy.* Norwood, NJ: Ablex.

Watts, A. (1995). What is stopping us from celebrating differences? *Holistic Education Review, 8*(1), 45.

Welch, S. (1985). *Communities of resistance and solidarity: A feminist theology of liberation.* Maryknoll, NY: Orbis.

Welch, S. (1989). *A feminist ethic of risk.* New York: Fortress Press.

West, C. (1993). *Race matters.* Boston: Beacon.

Wheatley, M. (1999). *Leadership and the new science.* San Francisco: Berrett-Koehler Publishers

Wolcott, H.J. (2001, March 28). Teen pleads guilty in shooting death. *Los Angeles Times,* p. B4.

Wolf, N. (1995). The racism of well-meaning white people. In M. Golden & S. Richards Shreve (Eds.), *Skin deep: Black women and white women write about race* (pp. 37-46). New York: Doubleday.

Wong, J. S. (1950). *Fifth Chinese daughter* (1st ed.). New York: Harper.

Yeo, F. (1995). The conflict of difference in an inner-city school: Experiencing border crossings in the ghetto. In B. Kanpol & P. McLaren (Eds.), *Critical multiculturalism: Uncommon voices in a common struggle.* Westport, CT: Bergin & Garvey.

Yeo, F. (1997). *Inner-city schools, multiculturalism and teacher education.* New York: Garland.

Ybarra, M. J. (2002, June 10). In one color, He sees many shades. *Los Angeles Times,* p. E1.

Yeskel, F., & Leondar-Wright, B. (1997). Classsism curriculum design. In M. Adams, L. Bell, & P. Griffin (Eds.), *Teaching for diversity and social justice: A sourcebook for teachers and trainers.* New York: Routledge.

Yung, J. (1995). *Unbound feet.* Berkeley: University of California Press.

Author Index

211

Subject Index

Printed in the United States
47570LVS00002B/73-120

9 781572 736467